T0391918

Through the Grapevine

Chicago Studies in American Politics

A series edited by Susan Herbst, Lawrence R. Jacobs, Adam J. Berinsky, and Frances Lee; Benjamin I. Page, editor emeritus

ALSO IN THE SERIES:

America's New Racial Battle Lines: Protect versus Repair
by Rogers M. Smith and Desmond King

Partisan Hostility and American Democracy
by James N. Druckman, Samara Klar, Yanna Krupnikov, Matthew Levendusky, and John Barry Ryan

Respect and Loathing in American Democracy: Polarization, Moralization, and the Undermining of Equality
by Jeff Spinner-Halev and Elizabeth Theiss-Morse

Countermobilization: Policy Feedback and Backlash in a Polarized Age
by Eric M. Patashnik

Race, Rights, and Rifles: The Origins of the NRA and Contemporary Gun Culture
by Alexandra Filindra

Accountability in State Legislatures
by Steven Rogers

Our Common Bonds: Using What Americans Share to Help Bridge the Partisan Divide
by Matthew Levendusky

Dynamic Democracy: Public Opinion, Elections, and Policymaking in the American States
by Devin Caughey and Christopher Warshaw

Persuasion in Parallel: How Information Changes Minds about Politics
by Alexander Coppock

Radical American Partisanship: Mapping Violent Hostility, Its Causes, and the Consequences for Democracy
by Nathan P. Kalmoe and Lilliana Mason

The Obligation Mosaic: Race and Social Norms in US Political Participation
by Allison P. Anoll

Additional series titles follow index.

Through the Grapevine

Socially Transmitted Information and Distorted Democracy

TAYLOR N. CARLSON

The University of Chicago Press
Chicago and London

The University of Chicago Press, Chicago 60637
The University of Chicago Press, Ltd., London

Published 2024
Printed in the United States of America

33 32 31 30 29 28 27 26 25 24   1 2 3 4 5

ISBN-13: 978-0-226-83415-3 (cloth)
ISBN-13: 978-0-226-83417-7 (paper)
ISBN-13: 978-0-226-83416-0 (e-book)
DOI: https://doi.org/10.7208/chicago/9780226834160.001.0001

Library of Congress Cataloging-in-Publication Data

Names: Carlson, Taylor N., author.
Title: Through the grapevine : socially transmitted information and distorted democracy / Taylor N. Carlson.
Other titles: Chicago studies in American politics.
Description: Chicago : The University of Chicago Press, 2024. | Series: Chicago studies in American politics | Includes bibliographical references and index.
Identifiers: LCCN 2023046438 | ISBN 9780226834153 (cloth) | ISBN 9780226834177 (paperback) | ISBN 9780226834160 (ebook)
Subjects: LCSH: Politics in social media—United States. | Social networks—Political aspects—United States. | Online social networks—Political aspects—United States. | Political psychology—United States. | Misinformation—Social aspects—United States. | Misinformation—Political aspects—United States. | Democracy—United States.
Classification: LCC PN4565.P65 C37 2024 | DDC 302.302850973—dc23/eng/20231031
LC record available at https://lccn.loc.gov/2023046438

♾ This paper meets the requirements of ANSI/NISO Z39.48-1992 (Permanence of Paper).

Contents

1

How Political Conversations Change the Information Environment

> The man who never looks into a newspaper is better informed than he who reads them; inasmuch as he who knows nothing is nearer to the truth than he whose mind is filled with falsehoods & errors.

> The FAKE NEWS media (failing @nytimes, @NBCNews, @ABC, @CBS, @CNN) is not my enemy, it is the enemy of the American People!

The news media is regularly under attack, as shown by the two quotations above. Although they make a similar point, questioning the credibility, accuracy, and honesty of news outlets, they were penned by two very different people in two very different times. In 1807, Thomas Jefferson wrote the first passage in a letter to John Norvell, an aspiring newspaper publisher. Over two hundred years later, in 2017, Donald Trump wrote the second one, calling five of the nation's largest media outlets the enemy of the American people, to millions of followers on Twitter. Despite the two-century gap between these statements and the immense changes our media environment has undergone, concerns about misinformation and political bias in the media have been part of American democracy since its onset.

While concerns about misinformation and media bias have regularly lingered throughout American history, there is a heightened sense of urgency to address these problems now. By some accounts, American democracy is hanging by a thread. Thousands of voters joined elected officials in denying (in 2020) and protesting (in 2016) presidential election outcomes. Allegations of voter fraud and foreign interference in elections continue to spur fear and distrust, with groups on both sides of the aisle calling attention to election security (Thompson 2023). Americans are hesitant to help or engage with neighbors who disagree politically, especially when they are angry (Webster, Connors, and Sinclair 2022). Trust in media is at record lows, with only 34 percent of Americans trusting the media to report the news "fully, accurately, and fairly" (Brenan 2022). Americans of all political stripes believe and spread misinformation, initiated and repeated by politicians, media elites, and friends and family (Jerit and Zhao 2020).

Despite these challenges, American democracy is not entirely broken. With the highest turnout rate in the twenty-first century, the 2020 presidential election brought to the polls over two-thirds of American adults (US Census Bureau). Americans also consumed more news in 2020 than they had in years, likely as a result of the COVID-19 pandemic (Molay and Essling 2020). Although trust in government and trust in media are low, Americans have engaged more with politics and the news. More to the point, key government actions still unfolded. While it may not have been easy and not everyone was happy with the outcomes, elections occurred, Supreme Court justices were confirmed, and laws were passed, with some considering the 117th Congress the most functional and productive in decades (e.g., Leonhardt 2022).

This mix of signals about the strength of American democracy can be puzzling, with the grim realities getting more attention. A common thread driving both the light and dark interpretations of American democracy is *information*, which can structure what people believe to be true, what to trust, and whether to act. The information people are exposed to and believe can shape many of their political choices in ways that can foster both the challenges and the opportunities in American politics today. Indeed, since the nation's founding, politicians have pointed to an informed citizenry as the key to a successful democracy. Today—in 2023—this should be a simple task. Dozens of television channels and radio stations, hundreds of podcasts and newspapers, and thousands of news websites are widely available. But the onslaught of information available today, largely as a function of the internet, has not always yielded the democratic benefits scholars once thought it would.

The mass media is only relevant if people consume it. Many Americans are simply not interested in consuming the news directly. Yet recent evidence suggests that most Americans maintain a modest level of understanding of the basic goings-on in the country (Angelucci and Prat 2021). How? Lingering in the background of hundreds of years of development of our media ecosystem has been an information source as old as time itself: interpersonal communication. Conversations. Gossip. Church. Craft guilds. Barbershops. Watercooler talk. Phone calls. Chat rooms. AOL Instant Messenger. Facebook. Twitter. TikTok. For as long as humans have been able to communicate socially, information has passed from one person to another.

In his best-selling book, *Sapiens*, Yuval Noah Harari argues that the communication skills our species developed nearly seventy millennia ago paved the way for gossip, which not only helped build social cooperation essential for our survival, but provided a key way in which information could be shared. This *socially transmitted information*—information communicated by others in online and face-to-face conversations—affects how people make their way through daily life. People rely on communication with others for essential information. Considering what a typical person *today* needs to know to get by, Harari (2014, 49) writes, "You need to know a lot about your own tiny field of expertise, but for the vast majority of life's necessities you rely blindly on the help of other experts, whose own knowledge is also limited to a tiny field of expertise."

Interpersonal communication skills have proven essential for human survival as a species. They not only help people make it through the day, but they also help people learn about their broader communities and those who govern them. Even with the growth of the mass media, in the many forms it has taken over time, conversations have been a staple in the information environment. But the social spread of information has not come without its consequences. Some of these consequences are rooted in mundane social lives, but others have aggregated to affect the broader sociopolitical environment.

For example, the 1967 race riots in Detroit were thought to have been initiated in part by rumors that the police were training white suburban residents to launch an armed invasion of Black neighborhoods. These rumors, largely spread by word of mouth, were so concerning that the mayor set up a Rumor Control Center (Knopf 1975). More recently, news about the 2018 US elections spread through conversations among a caravan of migrants. One migrant, Avel Antonio Mejia, said in an interview with the *Washington Post*, "There was a rumor going around that Donald Trump had supposedly lost, but I don't know if it's true. I do know that there was an election. . . . Many times other people pass on news by word of mouth, but we don't know if it's true or false" (Sieff and Averbuch 2018). In this particular case, Donald Trump was not even on the ballot.

The growth of social media has opened the door for increased exposure to socially transmitted information online. Informational exchanges on social media are certainly not immune to the distorting effects of word of mouth. On September 10, 2018, President Trump tweeted inaccurate information about the state of the economy: "The GDP Rate (4.2%) is higher than the Unemployment Rate (3.9%) for the first time in over 100 years!"[1] As many journalists quickly pointed out, the tweet contained an extra zero: the GDP rate was higher than the unemployment rate for the first time in *10* years, not 100 (McGraw 2018). Although journalists tried to quickly correct the information, the tweet reached thousands of people, and comments and retweets by everyday Twitter users were marked by substantial enthusiasm about the state of the economy, thinking about the hundred-year record.

Stories like these are not unique to the United States. Many countries around the world have been concerned about the spread of political misinformation on social media, particularly in the context of elections and protest. Scholars and journalists alike have pointed to WhatsApp, a direct instant messaging app owned by Meta, as a conduit for the spread of distorted and inaccurate information during recent elections in Brazil (Avelar 2019). WhatsApp is wildly popular in Brazil, with over 120 million users (Periera et al. 2022). While the app allows users to communicate with one another, the unregulated informational exchanges could have enabled the spread of thousands of messages containing false, misleading, or biased information during the 2018 election. In fact, some journalists suggest that the distorted content spread interpersonally over WhatsApp could have skewed the election outcome by misinforming and biasing voters (Avelar 2019). Even more striking is the fact that many countries without reliable or widespread access to the internet or related technology rely on word of mouth for spreading political information out of necessity. This naturally creates opportunities for the development and spread of false, as well as biased, information. If this tattered information spreads, it could in turn affect what people think about political issues and what they do about it, both of which are important features that can determine the fate of democratic functioning.

Several of these examples describe situations in which people amplified the spread of information that was initially false. However, it is not difficult to imagine scenarios in which even initially accurate, objective information can become inaccurate and biased as it spreads socially. For example, in 2020, *USA Today* tweeted, "The United States, the only country to record anywhere near 1 million cases of the coronavirus, has reached another somber milestone,"[2] alongside a graphic of COVID-19-related deaths. Replies to this tweet by everyday users quickly changed the narrative, calling the coronavirus a hoax or downplaying the severity of the situation. As one person replied, "Um . . . US has the worlds third largest population behind China, who's #s are not to be trusted, and India . . . who have only tested 3mil people . . . out of 1.3 BILLION . . . the US has tested 15mil out of 330mil . . . that took me 5 min to research & reshape. maybe I should be a journist [*sic*]? Btw . . . 1mil positives are less than ⅓ of 1 percent of the US population." *USA Today* (presumably) tweeted accurate information, but the socially transmitted information in the replies changed the story to paint a different picture.

Echoing the importance of socially transmitted information in the context of the global pandemic, Dr. Rhea Boyd emphasized the influence face-to-face conversations had in shaping COVID-19 vaccine hesitancy. In an interview with *The Atlantic* (Yong 2021), she said, "But I think we're too limited in our thinking about who is a trusted messenger. People use informal communication chains: They have side conversations with the grocery-store clerk, or their niece and nephew. People will believe anecdotal health-care information that their family member suggests over the credible info that a health-care professional is giving."

These two examples show that socially transmitted information—both online and face-to-face—can differ meaningfully from that communicated by health care providers and the mainstream media. Yet some people rely on their peers.

Despite the abundance of information available from news sources today, many individuals learn about politics from conversations like those in these examples. About 65 percent of Americans report learning about politics via word of mouth, according to a 2014 American Press Institute survey. The World Values Survey reports that in 2017, 38.6 percent of Americans use word of mouth for information on a *daily* basis, a striking percentage that is still markedly lower than that of other countries, such as Nigeria and Vietnam where over 60 percent of respondents use word of mouth for political information daily. Nationally representative survey data from the American Social Survey (TASS) suggests that in 2020, approximately one-third of Americans reported that they bump into the news or hear about it from other people rather than actively seek it out. If large segments of the public use conversations to learn about politics, but those conversations can quickly change the narrative, as illustrated in the examples above, how much are people actually learning? Are there patterns in how information becomes distorted through social transmission? How does this convenient but distorted information affect political attitudes and behavior?

In this book, I argue that learning about politics through the proverbial grapevine fuels *distorted democracy*. Distorted democracy is marked by an underinformed, polarized, but engaged public, driven by changes to the information environment created by members of the public. As people discuss what they read in the news, the information exchanged in conversations becomes distorted: it becomes sparse, cloaked in partisan bias, less accurate, and more mobilizing relative to the information initially communicated by the news. This means that when individuals primarily learn about politics from others instead of the news, they are likely to be exposed to distorted information that can affect their decision making. Specifically, individuals could learn less, believe more misinformation, and develop more polarized policy preferences, but engage more in politics.

I focus my attention on *information*, capturing how it changes through social transmission and how these changes can affect political learning, attitudes, and engagement. As exemplified in the opening anecdotes, the stakes for American democracy are high. While these may be isolated, rare, but powerful instances, they share some social roots. However, previous scholarship has suggested that there are many benefits of certain types of socially transmitted information, such as increased tolerance for the other side (e.g., Mutz 2006; Rossiter 2020; Levendusky and Stecula 2022) and learning (e.g., Lupia and McCubbins 1998; Downs 1957).

Throughout this book, I carefully consider the normative implications of socially transmitted information. Socially transmitted information can distort democracy from what some might consider ideal, but it does not necessarily render it entirely dysfunctional. Socially transmitted information can reshape the way people think about American democracy. Like an abstract expressionist painting, it is still recognizable, but we have to look carefully. The institutions are still there, and, on average, they work. Yet, on closer inspection, some components might not be as sharp as they could be. I demonstrate in this book that socially transmitted information causes people to be underinformed, polarized, but engaged. But the extent to which these outcomes are necessarily bad for democratic functioning requires closer examination.

A Theory of Distorted Democracy

Distorted democracy manifests when there is an underinformed, polarized, but engaged public. This combination of characteristics might sound surprising. Indeed, one of the classic tenets of American political behavior is that the American public is generally ill informed and disengaged (e.g., Delli Carpini and Keeter 1996). Yet I argue that socially transmitted information can foster a situation in which a large group of Americans are ill informed but politically engaged.

Let me start by outlining what I mean by each component of distorted democracy. By *underinformed*, I am referring broadly to both a lack of accurate knowledge about politics, government, or current events (i.e., an uninformed public) and beliefs in inaccurate, false information about politics, government, or current events (i.e., a misinformed public). Previous studies have carefully drawn a distinction between the uninformed and the misinformed (e.g., Kuklinski et al. 2000), and I do so in chapter 5, but the umbrella term "underinformed" refers to both uninformed and misinformed individuals.

Next, by *polarized*, I am referring to a polarized public in terms of extreme policy preferences and whether those preferences are consistently sorted into political parties. While there is substantial debate in the literature over the extent to which the public is polarized and becoming more extreme, a distorted democracy is marked by one in which this active group of voters has extreme policy preferences *and* those preferences are predictably sorted along partisan lines. Empirically, I examine the extent to which socially transmitted information can polarize attitudes, meaning that it pushes people to the extremes and that they are more sorted.

Finally, by *engaged*, I am referring broadly to political engagement. One could argue that an underinformed, polarized public is irrelevant if it is not politically active. As such, distorted democracy comes closest to crossing the line to dysfunctionality when this group of underinformed, polarized people also becomes politically engaged. My key focus with political engagement as it relates to distorted democracy is that socially transmitted political information can cause individuals to become more engaged.

How do we get to distorted democracy? I argue that socially transmitted information fans the flames that can produce the underinformed, polarized, yet engaged public that characterize a distorted democracy. As people discuss what they read in the news, the actual information exchanged in conversations becomes distorted: it becomes sparse, more biased, less accurate, and more mobilizing. This means that when individuals primarily learn about politics from others instead of the news, they are likely to be exposed to distorted information that can impair their decision making. Specifically, individuals learn less, update their beliefs in polarizing directions, and are more likely to believe misinformation. What is more, the changes in content as information flows through the grapevine can be mobilizing, leading to a world in which a large segment of the public is politically engaged based on distorted information.

Socially transmitted information fuels distorted democracy through a two-step process. First, some individuals consume the news directly. This group of people, the *actively informed*, seek out news from professional news outlets. They tend to be more politically engaged and stronger partisans, but these are not requirements for being actively informed. The actively informed then share information about the news with their peers who do not seek out news directly from media outlets; these people are the *casually informed*. The casually informed tend to be less interested in politics and weaker partisans, but these characteristics are not prerequisites. Some readers might recognize this process as the "two-step flow" (Lazarsfeld, Berelson, and Gaudet 1944; Katz 1957; Katz and Lazarsfeld 1955). Indeed, at this point, my theory is exactly what was outlined decades ago by scholars belonging to the Columbia School of political behavior but with a slightly different conceptualization of the key actors involved.

What the original portrayal of the two-step flow missed is a critical examination of what exactly flows. We, as a field, came to understand the power that opinion leaders (a subset of the actively informed) had to shape their peers' attitudes, candidate preferences, and political engagement. But we did not really understand why. Implicitly, we assumed it was because of information being shared and social pressure. But I show that there is more to the story.

The actively informed do not pass on precisely what they heard, read, or saw on the news. They package it in a way that reflects their cognitive and partisan biases. Indeed, individuals with strong partisan identities are likely to consume (e.g., Arceneaux and Johnson 2013; Levendusky 2009) and interpret (e.g., Lodge and Taber 2013) information in a way that is biased in favor of their partisan stripes. This means that when the actively informed communicate to others what they read in the news, it is presented through the lens of their own political preferences. For example, in some of my previous work, I found that the amount of information available shrinks dramatically as it flows from the media to person to person (Carlson 2018). Moreover, partisans tend to selectively transmit information that favors their party (Carlson 2019) and highlight the self-serving behavior of political elites (Bøggild, Aarøe, and Petersen 2021). The actively informed distort the information they read in the news.

By considering the ways in which information changes as it flows from the media to person to person, we can think more critically about the potential consequences of relying on socially transmitted information. When the casually informed choose to learn about politics from others instead of reading the news directly, they expose themselves to distorted information. To the extent that information shapes political decision making, they are then basing their decisions on warped information. In much the same way that partisan media bias and fake news can affect political learning and decisions, distorted information from peers can reduce learning, polarize attitudes, and increase misinformation.

Beyond the informational consequences that shape how individuals come to understand and think about politics, I argue, socially transmitted information can have a mobilizing effect absent from information in the media. As individuals transmit information to their peers, they inject mobilizing calls to action. Rather than simply restate facts from the news article, individuals encourage their peers to *do* something with that new information. They encourage their peers to do more research, vote, protest, donate, and take all sorts of political actions. These literal calls to action in the content of the messages paired with the mobilizing effects of social pressure to engage in politics (e.g., Bond et al. 2012; Sinclair 2012; Gerber, Green, and Larimer 2008), lead individuals relying on their peers for information to be more likely to engage in politics.

What's New? Contributions to the Field

My argument might sound simple, telling you something you already know from lived experience. In some ways, this is true. The core of my argument is very relatable. Many people have shared or heard about the news from others, and it is relatively simple to imagine the ways in which this could go awry. Yet the vast majority of social science scholarship on political learning and attitudes has focused on the media. Some of this research has been paradigm shifting: it has enabled an understanding of the effects of priming in the news on presidential evaluations in laboratory experiments (Iyengar and Kinder 1987), the polarizing effects of partisan media (Levendusky 2009), Americans' preferences for entertainment over news (Arceneaux and Johnson 2013; Kim 2023), the impact of local newspaper closures on polarization and learning (Hayes and Lawless 2015; Darr, Hitt, and Dunaway 2018), and the presence (or absence) of partisan echo chambers online (Guess 2021; Barberá 2020). The media plays an important role in political behavior and has received the lion's share of attention in political communication research.

Separately, researchers have explored the impact of social networks on political behavior. Pioneering research from the Columbia School identified the significant impact our peers can have on political attitudes and participation. This work has been extended greatly with new methodological insights, allowing for stronger causal inferences. Seminal research by scholars such as Bob Huckfeldt, Betsy Sinclair, and Diana Mutz presents compelling evidence that close social ties can influence people to engage in politics and to be persuaded to share similar political preferences. Beyond observational and survey data, some scholars use innovative experiments to capture the less rosy impact that socially transmitted information can have on political behavior (e.g., Ahn, Huckfeldt, and Ryan 2014; Connors, Pietryka, and Ryan 2022).

The bottom line is that there are currently two impressive bodies of research—one focused on the media and one focused on social networks—that have remained isolated from each other. In part, this is the result of empirical limitations rather than lack of interest or theoretical oversight. Major surveys in the social sciences, such as the American National Elections Study (ANES), the General Social Survey (GSS), and the Cooperative Congressional Elections Study (CCES), rarely include socially transmitted information as a response option to questions about where people learn about politics. For example, one standard ANES question is, "From which of the following sources have you heard anything about the presidential campaign?" Respondents can mark all that apply from the following choices: television news programs (morning or evening), newspapers, television talk shows, public affairs or news analysis programs, internet sites, chat rooms, blogs, or radio news or talk shows. There is no opportunity for respondents to report that they learn via word of mouth; the "chat rooms" option is the closest conceptually to socially transmitted information in one specific context. Elsewhere in the survey, on political participation batteries, respondents are usually able to report how often they discuss politics, but this does not mean that they have learned about political events such as a presidential campaign from these discussions, nor does it mean that they actively choose to become informed about the news this way.

My critique of the literature would be misguided if socially transmitted information was not a dominant way in which people learned about politics. But an analysis of World Values Survey data suggests just that. Learning about politics from conversations is more common than learning about politics from newspapers in all but three countries examined in the World Values Survey. Focusing only on the media as an information source means that we have overlooked the source from which millions of people across the world obtain news. Similarly, by not accounting for the ways in which information travels from the media into our political conversations, political discussion and social network scholars have essentially missed analyzing the first step in the sequence of events that lead to the political behavior outcomes they observe.

Socially transmitted information plays an important role in the information environment. It was there before there was mass media, and I suspect it will remain even as the media environment shifts (see, e.g., Standage 2013). Socially transmitted information arguably plays an even more important role today with the growth of social media than it did twenty years ago. Today, millions of people log on to Facebook, Twitter, and Instagram and are (intentionally or unintentionally) exposed to socially transmitted information about the news. Even during a global pandemic that prevented face-to-face interactions, people were exposed to socially transmitted information online.

In this book, I aim to convince you that socially transmitted information matters and needs to be considered in conversation with research on the media and, more directly, in research on political discussion. The book unites these two fields of research in a way that sets the agenda for future political communication research. Research on media effects needs to consider what happens *after* someone is exposed to some form of media. Research on political discussion needs to consider what happens *before* a conversation ensues.

More specifically, my theory challenges seminal research in the field that suggests interpersonal political communication can adequately substitute for direct news consumption (Lupia and McCubbins 1998; Berelson et al. 1954). I join scholars who question the ability of the American public to be self-educating (Ahn, Huckfeldt, and Ryan 2014), but I do so using new methodological approaches and a broader theoretical framework that emphasizes the ways in which information changes as a result of social transmission. While socially transmitted information can sometimes yield benefits for the casually informed, it can also facilitate troubling downsides, such as increased belief in misinformation.

This book pushes back on research that points to news elites and politicians as the key sources of misinformation and polarization. Instead of this top-down explanation for two of the biggest challenges in American politics today, I demonstrate that people play an important—yet previously understudied—supporting role. First, I demonstrate that people who believe misinformation are more likely to have been exposed to the relevant false information socially. Above and beyond people retweeting or sharing fake news stories on social media, word of mouth is a common channel by which individuals are exposed to—and come to believe—misinformation. Moreover, some false information actually arises when individuals (inadvertently) distort information in conversation instead of simply repeating false information they read in the news. In order to correct misinformation going forward, we need to more carefully consider the impact of social transmission.

Second, I demonstrate that even if individuals initially consume nonpartisan information from moderate sources, as many online news consumers do (Guess 2021), that information can quickly become partisan and inaccurate through social transmission. Building on work demonstrating that individuals can develop polarized attitudes by simply talking to someone else who consumed *partisan* media (Druckman, Levendusky, and McLain 2018), I show that similar patterns occur even in the absence of partisan media. While debates continue over the existence and impact of partisan media bias, my work shows that everyday people can still create biased information through conversation regardless of whether the news is communicated in a biased way.

Altogether, the book brings together media and social network analysis to provide fresh insights about political communication. Despite the potential for socially transmitted information to improve democratic functioning through educating and mobilizing others, it could also further sour the information environment, leading to polarization and misinformation. Moreover, people are often exposed to this biased information without even knowing it. I opened this chapter by listing some of the major threats American democracy is currently facing. Throughout this book, I demonstrate that at least some of these threats have social roots.

So What? Broader Implications

Beyond the ominous connotation of the term, why is distorted democracy something we should care about? Why is it a problem if people are underinformed, polarized, but engaged? Despite all the attention to an "unenlightened" public being troublesome for democracy, the real point to consider is political engagement. When people are mobilized to political action through socially transmitted information, they are likely to do so while being less informed (or possibly misinformed) and having more extreme preferences. A politically active *and* misinformed public can threaten democratic functioning (Hochschild and Einstein 2015). A politically active and extreme public can also create challenges for representation (Hall 2015) and promote political violence (Mason and Kalmoe 2022).

While socially transmitted information could have had the power to create this trifecta for distorted democracy throughout history, we are seeing traces of this outcome now. Why? One reason is that the problems caused by an active and misinformed public might be especially likely during an era of what Eitan Hersh (2020) calls political hobbyism. According to Hersh, many Americans today view politics as a spectator sport. They consume the news for its entertainment value rather than to become enlightened voters seeking to improve daily life through policy. Political hobbyists are thus drawn to the most salacious news that emphasizes conflict, partisan identity, and other social cleavages. Political hobbyists might also be the actively informed people responsible for informing their peers about politics. This means that the casually informed—those who bump into the news and hear about it from other people—are likely to be exposed to a stronger dose of socially transmitted information at its worst: polarized, extreme, mobilizing, and (perhaps) drawn from questionable news sources. Explaining the growth of political hobbyism and why it is part of our political culture now is work best left to other researchers, but it could partially explain why socially transmitted information is (potentially) much more troubling now than it might have been previously.

Another reason that socially transmitted information has the *potential* to be so damaging to American politics now is because of the rise of social media. Over the past two decades, the internet has dominated the information environment. With this change has come the ability for individuals to access millions of stories published by professional news outlets, in addition to even more content published by everyday users like themselves. The sheer volume of socially transmitted information available online is overwhelming. While face-to-face conversations are still a common way in which individuals learn about politics, the rise of social media has greatly increased individuals' exposure to socially transmitted information about politics. Despite significant research on social media, politics, and misinformation, there is still much to learn about how social media affects what (mis)information people see and believe (Nyhan 2020).

We are at a critical moment in American politics. People are turning away from mainstream media at the same time that they are bombarded with socially transmitted information online. Growing portions of the public question the very electoral institutions and values that hold democracy together. If we are to understand the threats to American democracy, we need to understand how people engage with information beyond what is communicated in the news. That means we need to understand other sources of information that people use to make sense of the political world. We need to understand how socially transmitted information fits into the current information environment and how it might help or hinder democratic functioning.

Overview of the Book

To develop and test the theory of distorted democracy, this book is organized in two theoretical and four empirical chapters, as described below. The concluding chapter summarizes the core findings while drawing out their key implications for future research on political communication.

In chapter 2, I outline the core theory advanced in this book. I argue that relying on socially transmitted information to learn about politics drives distorted democracy, which arises when segments of the public are underinformed, polarized, but engaged. I argue that because individuals are subject to cognitive and partisan biases that affect their ability to process, recall, and transmit information, they distort information they consume in the news as they discuss it with their peers. This means that when individuals primarily learn about politics from others instead of from the news, they are likely to be exposed to distorted information that can affect their decision making while mobilizing them to take action. In developing this theory, I draw on extensive previous literature and make a broader point about how studying the content of socially transmitted information uncovers previously hidden dynamics in the two-step flow.

In chapter 3, I provide the context for interpreting results presented in this book. Building on the theoretical framework outlined in chapter 2, I conceptually and empirically characterize the key actors in the two-step flow, with my renewed emphasis on information: the actively and casually informed. I carefully trace previous theoretical conceptualizations of similar actors, such as "opinion leaders," and note what they miss by not giving enough attention to where these key actors are getting information. I distinguish between the actively informed and opinion leaders, in the traditional sense, and I introduce my measurement strategies. I use nationally representative survey data to analyze differences between the actively and casually informed, demonstrating that the actively informed are stronger partisans than the casually informed, but they are otherwise demographically similar. I then conceptualize socially transmitted information and how we can measure what it looks like when it flows from the actively to the casually informed. I critically evaluate previous research in this area, noting where their theoretical and empirical approaches fail to sufficiently account for information distortion and then introduce my solution to the empirical limitations: telephone game experiments.

Chapter 4 is the first empirical chapter of the book. I use a variety of methods to analyze results from eight telephone game experiments to illustrate how information changes as individuals transmit information about news articles they read. I first show that social transmission causes information to become sparse, more biased in favor of the preferences of the actively informed, less accurate, and more mobilizing relative to the original news articles on which the socially transmitted information is based. I supplement the results from experiments with an observational analysis of Twitter data to highlight that the patterns uncovered in the experiments are similar to patterns in socially transmitted information communicated on Twitter. Focusing specifically on a case study of the Capitol insurrection on January 6, 2021, I analyze replies to tweets and quote tweets originally posted by news outlets. This chapter reveals that some information distortions are rare overall, but they are more common in socially transmitted information than in information communicated by the news.

In chapters 5 through 7, I shift my inquiry from describing the ways in which information changes to showing the political consequences of these distortions. That is, I begin to focus on the *consequences* of relying on our peers for information, given that chapter 4 showed that socially transmitted information is sparse, more biased, less accurate, and more mobilizing than information from the news. Each chapter is dedicated to one of the three arms of distorted democracy: underinformed, polarized, and engaged.

Chapter 5 focuses on how socially transmitted information affects the first component of distorted democracy: to what extent are the casually informed *underinformed*? Using experimental designs introduced in some of my previous work (Carlson 2019), I find that individuals who receive information from another person learn less than they would from a news article. While socially transmitted information appears to damage our ability to learn about politics, it turns out that some types of people can adequately summarize the news. When people who know more about politics share information with copartisans, they can inform just as well as a news article. While conversations can *sometimes* help people learn objective facts, they also facilitate belief in misinformation. Across three nationally representative surveys and twelve unique false statements, I find that the casually informed are typically equally likely to be misinformed as the actively informed. However, where there are differences between the groups, it is the casually informed who are more likely to be misinformed. Further, misinformed people were more likely to recall learning from social sources than were correctly informed people. Results from two experiments suggest further that socially transmitted information can cause people to be misinformed, both in a social media context and more broadly.

In chapter 6, I explore the second feature of distorted democracy: polarization. I examine the extent to which exposure to socially transmitted information causes people to have more extreme policy preferences that are more sorted along partisan lines. I use two experiments in which I randomly assign participants to read a news article, another person's summary of that news article, or nothing at all, and measure within-subject change in policy preferences. I find that on both highly salient, polarized issues, such as immigration, and less salient but still polarized issues, like environmental policy, socially transmitted information from copartisans causes individuals to develop more sorted policy preferences. For less salient issues, exposure to socially transmitted information from copartisans also causes individuals to adopt more extreme preferences. Together, these results suggest that socially transmitted information—even when it is based on initially nonpartisan media—can indeed contribute to attitude polarization among the American public, but I find no evidence that information source affects affective polarization, that is, the extent of animosity between Democrats and Republicans.

Chapter 7 examines the final component of distorted democracy: engagement. A core part of the theory I advance in this book is that socially transmitted information is *mobilizing*. If the casually informed are not politically engaged, then it might be less relevant that they are underinformed and polarized. I therefore examine the extent to which exposure to socially transmitted information, compared to news articles or no information at all, leads to increased political engagement. Across two experiments, I find that exposure to socially transmitted information from a copartisan led individuals to be more likely to report that they would be more likely to engage in politics by contacting their legislator about the issue at hand, donating to relevant interest groups, or signing up to receive emails from relevant interest groups. I complement the experiments with an analysis of nationally representative survey data, showing that the more people relied on socially transmitted information leading up to the 2022 election, the more likely they were to contact a legislator about election integrity concerns and attend a protest. Finally, I discuss several real-world examples of instances of political engagement partially driven by socially transmitted information. The results in this chapter suggest that socially transmitted information, even without the contours of actual social interactions or the relationships inherent in social networks, can have a mobilizing effect. These results have important implications for considering the role that socially transmitted information plays in political mobilization—for better (i.e., voting) and for worse (i.e., political violence).

Chapter 8 returns to the opening motivation for this book. I discuss my core findings and my contributions, both theoretical and empirical, to our understanding of political communication. The implications from the research presented in this book and the future work that it inspires extend far beyond variation in learning from an objective news article or someone's summary of that article. This work leads us to reconsider the ways in which we are able to find valuable information with which to make informed political decisions. Moreover, I discuss both optimistic and pessimistic interpretations of the empirical results presented throughout the book in an effort to unpack whether socially transmitted information causes democracy to be so distorted that it becomes dysfunctional. If we are to understand the informational landscape in which we live today, we must consider the human component.

2

Distorted Democracy

"Megan. It is grandpa. I read an article that other countries are using data from a website called TikTok to use it against America. Do you have a TikTok? [Please] be careful. Love, gpa." Despite this sweet warning from her grandfather, Megan did use TikTok, and she had her social media moment in 2021 when she went viral for sharing fun videos that featured text messages like this that her grandfather sent her (Moore 2021). We do not know anything about the article Megan's concerned grandfather read, but we can imagine that it probably looked different from his message. His message is short and does not provide details about the ways in which other countries were using data against America. In trying to inform his granddaughter about the news, this concerned grandfather could have changed the narrative.

Conversations like this happen a lot. What used to be restricted to the watercooler at work or to the dinner table at home now occurs around the clock via text message and social media. It is such conversations—in which people share the news with others—that I argue merit deeper study in political communication. In what ways could Megan's grandfather have changed the content of the information he shared with her from the original article that he read? In what ways did the information he shared affect Megan's attitudes and behavior?

Existing social science scholarship does not currently provide good answers to these questions. Decades of research have focused on understanding how people learn about politics and why it matters, but the vast majority of research on information and politics focuses on either media effects or network effects. Research on media effects examines how *exposure to mass media* affects how much and what people know about politics; research on network effects examines how *discussion with peers* affects how much and what people know about politics. Previous research has largely not considered how media and social networks contribute jointly to the information environment and subsequent political attitudes. Work that does examine both media and network effects often sees them in competition rather than in concert, working together to create new challenges or opportunities for people to participate in politics. These literatures by and large ignore what comes *in between* the media and social networks: socially transmitted information.

People might only learn about politics by reading, watching, or listening to the news. But the moment they share with others what they have learned, they create *socially transmitted information*. This information is communicated by another person and packaged in their own words, online or face-to-face. Many people around the world rely on this secondhand socially transmitted information to learn about politics. For example, the most recent World Values Survey suggests that 38.3 percent of respondents across fifty-one countries report learning about the news via word of mouth on a *daily* basis, with only 4.1 percent of respondents reporting that they never learn about the news in this way.

Although the importance of socially transmitted information in politics has been largely overlooked in our scholarship, it has a central place in early theorizing about American politics. Some seminal theories in political science suggest that turning to peers could actually be a useful information shortcut. The idea is that individuals facing high information costs could forgo sifting through the news and instead turn to better-informed members of their social networks who share their preferences to cut information costs and acquire just enough information to vote in line with their interests (e.g., Downs 1957). This view of using more knowledgeable, like-minded social connections as an information shortcut is akin to the two-step flow theory of communication (Lazarsfeld, Berelson, and Gaudet [1944] 2021; Katz 1957; Katz and Lazarsfeld 1955).

The two-step flow theory suggests that information flows from the mass media to a group of politically interested, engaged, and motivated people ("opinion leaders") to others who are less interested and engaged in politics. In one view of this model, individuals are rational, utility-maximizing agents who seek to minimize the costs of finding information on their own by asking informed members of their social networks instead of seeking the information from the media themselves (Downs 1957; Katz and Lazarsfeld 1955; Zaller 1992). While the model has not been without criticism, its elegance and somewhat provocative nature have sparked decades of research.

Broadly, I think the two-step flow nicely captures how individuals learn about politics. Especially with the growth of access to information on social media, individuals can easily be exposed to information about politics secondhand, filtered by their social networks. My theory rests on the idea that the two-step flow is an accurate depiction of information diffusion.

But, past and current conceptualizations and measurements of the two-step flow are incomplete. They have not sufficiently accounted for the ways in which information changes as it flows from the media to person to person. If people are going to bestow on their peers the power to be their primary information source about politics, scholars need to study the content that they produce with the same scrutiny that they would give to the media. By examining how information changes as it travels through the two-step flow, we can more fully understand how this process affects political attitudes and behavior.

In this chapter, I introduce a theory of distorted democracy, which focuses on understanding how information changes as it flows from the media to the actively informed (those who directly consume the news) to the casually informed (those who primarily rely on socially transmitted information from the actively informed) and how these changes affect key components of participatory democracy: (mis)information, attitudes, and engagement. Specifically, I argue that information becomes sparse, biased, less accurate, and more mobilizing through social transmission. As a result, the casually informed could become underinformed, polarized, and engaged.

The theory of distorted democracy focuses on the content of socially transmitted information and its consequences for American political behavior. Because socially transmitted information is exchanged both online and face-to-face, the broad contours of my argument should extend to both spaces. However, these are two fundamentally different ways of communicating, and several scholars have thoughtfully explained some of the differences (Mallen, Day, and Green 2003; Stromer-Galley, Bryant, and Bimber 2020; Min 2007; Barnidge 2017; Baek, Wojcieszak, and Delli Carpini 2012). Throughout this book, I speculate about variation in the effects of socially transmitted information that is communicated online and face-to-face, but this is not a theory about face-to-face conversations, nor is it a theory about social media; it is about socially transmitted information, which appears in both contexts.

At first glance, this unique combination of an ill-informed and polarized but engaged public might seem troubling, fostering some salient events that have challenged American democracy. However, I argue that socially transmitted information produces *distorted* democracy, not dysfunctional democracy. While threatening political events like the January 6 insurrection and "pizzagate" are troubling and could very well be rooted in socially transmitted information, they are rare. On average, most casually informed people navigate politics without storming pizza restaurants or the Capitol, and the normative implications of my theory are mixed. But importantly, my core theoretical contribution is to demonstrate that we are missing something big by not including information distortion in other theoretical frameworks, such as the two-step flow, media effects research, and social networks research. That we can arrive at two very different views of American politics by better accounting for socially transmitted information suggests that it is central to future research.

I proceed as follows. First, I interrogate the two-step flow and the seventy-some years of research it has sparked, highlighting where I think it falls short. Specifically, I focus on conjectures that *information* is flowing from media to opinion leaders to others that lack measurement of the information itself. Second, I introduce my theory of distorted democracy, articulating how adding information back into the two-step flow in a more rigorous way leads to unique sets of consequences for how the casually informed engage in politics. In so doing, I explain why I expect information to change as it flows from the media to social networks and the central role that the key actors—the actively and the casually informed—play in the process. I conclude by addressing some key questions about the scope of the theory, such as the role of the internet in this process.

Reexamining the Two-Step Flow

The two-step flow hypothesis emerged as a happy accident. Paul F. Lazarsfeld, Bernard Berelson, and Hazel Gaudet, authors of the landmark study published in *The People's Choice* ([1944] 2021), did not set out to test this expectation but developed it in passing as they analyzed their data. The authors' proposition, that ideas flow from the media to opinion leaders to everyone else, was provocative at the time, when researchers were otherwise focused on understanding the extent to which the mass media manipulated American voters. The idea of the two-step flow suggested that voters were more competent and less susceptible to manipulation by mass media than previously thought. Reflecting on the two-step flow hypothesis, Katz (1957, 61) wrote, "It was a healthy sign, they [Lazarsfeld, Berelson, and Gaudet] felt, that people were still most successfully persuaded by give-and-take with other people and that the influence of the mass media was less automatic and less potent than had been assumed." While the two-step flow set the agenda for decades of research in communication, political science, and sociology, Katz (1957, 62) noted that "of all the ideas in *The People's Choice*, however, the two-step flow hypothesis is probably the one that was least well documented by empirical data."

Intrigued by the concept, many scholars sought to remedy the empirical limitations in *The People's Choice*. For example, Katz (1957) reviews four studies that improve on methodological challenges in the book. His critiques focus on the inability to draw on real network dyads or the relationships between specific opinion leaders and followers, which future studies sought to address using creative snowball sampling techniques and revised survey questions. Years later, Weimann (1982, 765) highlighted five theoretical and methodological critiques of the two-step flow, many of which had been raised by other researchers over time. For example, he noted that the two-step flow as originally conceived ignores evidence of a direct, one-step flow; ignores the possibility that influence occurs at other stages of the diffusion process; ignores the notion that opinion leadership might be more of a continuum than a strict dichotomy between leaders and followers; and ignores the idea that opinions may be shared horizontally among opinion leaders rather than given from opinion leader to follower.

These theoretical and methodological critiques largely focus on the network structure between opinion leaders and followers and the direction in which ideas flow. Many of these critiques have been largely resolved with new innovations in survey methodology, such as using name generators to measure social networks and snowball sampling to measure the preferences of as many people within a network as possible (e.g., Huckfeldt and Sprague 1995). While critiques about network positioning and measurement are important for understanding social influence, they overlook what actually occurs in the conversations. As Sokhey and Djupe (2011, 57) note, "We know very little about what political discussion looks like in networks, including what is discussed; the content of political discussion and disagreement. . . . These unexplored concerns affect the effectiveness of communication, whether discussion is influential, and how political discussion contributes to particular choice situations; additionally, they play a central role in answering such questions as: Can networks help people make 'good' decisions?"

If the two-step flow is supposed to be about *communication* and how *information* flows between people, it is curious that the empirical tests of the theory and the conclusions we take from them are silent about the key concept: information.

INFORMATION, INFLUENCE, AND THE TWO-STEP FLOW

In introducing the two-step flow, Lazarsfeld, Berelson, and Gaudet noted that ideas flowed from mass media to opinion leaders to everyone else. Early responses to the two-step flow tried to unpack what they meant by "ideas." For example, Robinson (1976) highlighted that there should be a distinction between the flow of *information* and the flow of *influence*, both of which could reasonably be captured by the vague term "ideas." That is, the two-step flow might not make people more aware of certain events via information being passed along, but people could be influenced to adopt certain attitudes about those events. From this perspective, information probably has more of a one-step flow contributing to awareness, but influence might have a two-step flow. Indeed, Troldahl (1966, 611) argued that "at least for learning effects, there is a *one*-step flow of communication, direct from the mass media to members of the social system. A review of the Lazarsfeld-group research revealed no findings that contradict this conclusion. Most of their data pertaining to learning factors involved general media habits rather than the learning of particular pieces of information" (emphasis in original).

Despite this distinction between information and influence and the call to understand how particular pieces of information are learned, few studies fully engaged with the concept of information, focusing instead on influence (i.e., changing others' preferences or knowledge). Those that focused on learning typically examined whether people were aware of major current events, such as the assassination of John F. Kennedy. Some studies found that people initially heard about events from opinion leaders but then confirmed their awareness by watching the news (Deutschmann and Danielson 1960; Troldahl 1966). Although measuring awareness of major events is a nice way to measure what information people had, we still do not know what exactly they were told either by an opinion leader or in news broadcasts. The Kennedy case is particularly interesting to consider because of the conspiracy theories that arose. Did opinion leaders tell others that Kennedy had been assassinated, as well as their take on who did it? Did they speculate that he was actually still alive? Did they elaborate on what this means for governance? Without investigating the content of the information communicated socially, we are left knowing that some people became *aware* of Kennedy's death, but we know little about the story they were told.

Even studies that claimed to examine the content of information flows did so by examining whether people were aware of various news stories and whether they learned about the events from other people or from the mass media (e.g., Deutschmann and Danielson 1960). While these studies nicely account for whether awareness of specific pieces of information spread interpersonally or from the media, they do little to tease out what the information looked like and how it was interpreted when it reached the respondent. Thinking about the ways in which information can be stretched and altered through social transmission might help explain mixed evidence surrounding the flow of information vis-à-vis the flow of influence.

Moreover, it is not clear that information and influence are mutually exclusive. Opinion leaders can simultaneously communicate facts and opinion, leading to both learning and influence. Communicating opinion could be interpreted as fact and lead to learning, just as communicating facts could in turn lead to attitude change. Although prominent social network scholars argue that "Political conversations need not be informative to have an effect" (Sinclair 2012, 2), *information* ought to be at the center of our understanding of the two-step flow. Huckfeldt, Johnson, and Sprague (2004, 207) argue that "democratic electorates are composed of individually interdependent citizens who depend on one another for political information and guidance, and political communication and persuasion are thus central to citizenship and democratic politics." Moreover, despite critiques that the two-step flow might be more likely to capture the flow of opinion than the flow of information, Mutz (2006, 143) argues that in "American political life, expertise and factoids are elevated over opinion and passion as what is seen as the appropriate currency for political communication." Taken together, although social influence through conversation *can* occur without information, communicating information is valued more than communicating opinion, and these conversations are essential for democratic functioning.

IMPROVEMENTS IN MEASUREMENT

The theoretical limitations of understanding the role information played in the two-step flow may have been driven in part by methodological challenges. Some researchers were bothered by the lack of emphasis on socially transmitted information in early work on social networks and sought to address this with new tools. The pioneering work by Bob Huckfeldt, John Sprague, and Paul Beck, among others, used advanced interdisciplinary techniques to measure social networks, their composition, and the extent to which political preferences were shared within them. Like much of the work before them, they primarily analyzed the characteristics of the information senders and receivers, but they acknowledged the important role that socially transmitted information could play in shaping political behavior.[1]

Present in much of the work in this tradition is the assumption that information communicated conversationally drives people to update their attitudes or decisions to participate in politics. In some of the work, researchers theorize extensively about how information can be distorted. For example, in one paper, Huckfeldt and colleagues motivate their inquiry as follows:

> A great deal of political discussion and communication is likely to be imbedded in ambiguity and uncertainty. And the uncertainty of ambiguous communication gives rise to distortions based on the characteristics of the person sending the message, the characteristics of the person receiving the message, and the various environments and settings within which the message is interpreted.
>
> In this paper we are concerned with the clarity of political signals transmitted through political conversation and the accuracy with which those signals are perceived. The potential for distorted communication arises due to individual and environmental effects operating at several nested and overlapping levels. (1998, 997)

This sounds similar to the point I have been making in this book. The authors acknowledge—even argue—that information can be distorted and that these distortions might affect how recipients of socially transmitted information internalize it and use it to form their attitudes. The theoretical emphasis is on point, but their empirical examination falls short of actually measuring distortion, at least in the way I conceptualize it. In this paper, the authors consider information distorted if it results in receivers misperceiving the senders' candidate preferences. For example, Huckfeldt and colleagues write:

> We shift our focus in this section to a direct analysis of distortion and the sources of distortion in political communication. The criterion variable is whether or not individuals correctly perceive the political preferences of their discussants. . . . This variable provides us with a direct measure of perceptual accuracy, where incorrect perception indicates that distortion has rendered communication ineffective. (1998, 1012)

The authors have measured accuracy in perceiving their discussants' preferences, and they have done so very well, using innovative name generators that mapped political discussion networks. However, information distortion is simply assumed to be the mechanism through which (in)accuracy occurs. They note several reasons that some people might communicate their candidate preferences more clearly than others; for example, some people might intentionally obfuscate their preferences to avoid social discomfort, and others might be so passionate about their preferred candidate that they are eager to unambiguously support them. While I do not doubt the authors' theory, they have not analyzed distortion directly. They have perhaps measured a consequence of distortion, but the distortion itself is left unmeasured.

This is but one paper in a larger body of work that has in many ways set the agenda for how we think about social networks and political behavior. But it is a prime example of many papers in this tradition that claim socially transmitted information is likely to be distorted but do not measure it. This work also inadequately accounts for the relationship *between* media and opinion leaders and the rest of one's network. In fact, much of the work in this tradition places media and social networks in competition for influence (e.g., Beck et al. 2002) instead of considering how the two information sources work together. This literature has provided invaluable insights about the relationship between political discussion and political preferences, but it has done so without satisfactorily measuring information distortion.

Building on this tradition to allow for cleaner measures of socially transmitted information and causal identification, lab experiments emerged. These experiments largely follow methods employed in behavioral economics (see Connors, Pietryka, and Ryan 2022). While no two studies are exactly the same, they try to mirror real-world communication. They allow for real-time interactions between people while randomizing characteristics of interest in a controlled setting. Researchers can directly manipulate access to information and observe what individuals do with that information. For example, those who have information might (intentionally or unintentionally) share misleading information with others. The information participants obtain may or may not help them vote for the candidate whose preferences are closest to their own, and they may or may not show evidence of learning.

This approach is an important way to shed light on the causal effects of interpersonal communication on political preferences. By stripping away the complexities of language in real conversations, researchers can precisely measure whether people transmit biased or inaccurate information to others. They can also tightly control and randomize who is an opinion leader, who has expertise, and how costly information is, allowing for clean causal identification on these important independent variables that are otherwise difficult to isolate in the real world. That said, experiments of this sort can only push the field so far, especially when it comes to understanding information distortion. The abstract conversational settings intentionally gloss over the nuances of language in interpersonal communication. For example, there is little room for participants to inject opinion, express certainty, or add the emotional contours of human language that make political discussion—and socially transmitted information—so interesting and perhaps so important.

SUMMARY: WHAT HAVE WE BEEN MISSING?

Although the two-step flow came to the field inadvertently, it sparked over seventy years of research. However, as this scholarship has unfolded, research on media effects and research on social networks have grown increasingly siloed, even though the initial theory emphasized the interplay between the two. As a result, there are three major theoretical and methodological gaps in our understanding of the two-step flow.

1. Information is largely overlooked in two-step flow research, focusing instead on the features of the discuss*ants*, with little attention to the content of the discuss*ion* and how it changes through the two-step flow.
2. Information and influence are not mutually exclusive. We cannot understand influence without understanding the information that is exchanged conversationally.
3. Previous approaches to measuring information distortion are incomplete. Name generators assume but do not measure distortion. Lab experiments provide precise measurement but do not sufficiently capture the nuances of language in communication.

I seek to address these gaps by developing a new theory of political communication that unites research on media effects with research on social networks and puts *information* at the center of the two-step flow. By focusing on how the content of information changes as it travels through the two-step flow and by introducing new research designs aimed to better capture this process, I address many of the limitations above. I return to the seminal work in communication that emphasizes the importance of the sender, the receiver, and the *message* in understanding communication (Hovland 1954). This is how I examine the two-step flow in a new way. I bring information back into the story and develop a theory to explain (1) how information changes as the actively informed summarize the news for their peers; and (2) how this distorted information affects political behavior among the casually informed. In so doing, I arrive at a nuanced theory of distorted democracy, in which the consequences of the two-step flow for political behavior—and American democracy more broadly—are complex.

A Theory of Distorted Democracy

Distorted democracy occurs when changes to the information environment created by the public lead people to become underinformed and polarized but engaged. First, an event happens in the world and the media reports on that event. Those who are sufficiently interested in the news consume that news directly, whether by reading about the event online, hearing about it on the radio, or watching a TV news broadcast. I call these news consumers the *actively informed*. Some of the actively informed then go on to share what they learned in conversations with others. These conversations sometimes happen organically in "small talk" and sometimes when the actively informed try to directly inform or persuade other people who do not seek news directly, the *casually informed.*

These conversations, importantly, *change* the information that was initially communicated by the media. The conversations cause the information to become sparse, more biased, less accurate, and more mobilizing relative to the information communicated by the media. The casually informed have thus been exposed to a tattered version of the originally communicated information, which could in turn affect (1) their factual beliefs, resulting in being underinformed; (2) their preferences, resulting in polarization; and (3) their likelihood of participating, or being engaged. All three outcomes have been investigated in previous research on the two-step flow, social networks, and political discussion. But the role socially transmitted information plays in shaping these outcomes has not received as much attention.

Distorted democracy is the end game of a series of changes to the information environment brought on by conversations about politics. Sometimes democracy can be distorted in a way that leads to an optimistic, high-functioning view of American politics. But sometimes it can be distorted in a way that questions whether people should ever discuss politics at all. The broader point is that socially transmitted information matters. Just as we have spent decades trying to understand the effects of news content on political behavior, we need to also investigate the effects of socially transmitted content on political behavior.

Ultimately, I argue that by focusing only on the features of the people exchanging information, we have overlooked the process through which the two-step flow could contribute to some of the biggest problems in American politics today. Armed with a broader theoretical framework about the ways in which information changes as a result of social transmission and new tools to examine these changes, I join scholars who suggest that social information transmission is a *political* process that will not always lead to positive outcomes.

HOW SOCIAL TRANSMISSION DISTORTS INFORMATION

There are several reasons that the quality and content of information transmitted socially is different from information transmitted directly by the media. As I detail below and elaborate in chapter 4, I expect information to become more sparse, more biased, less accurate, and more mobilizing through social transmission. These are not the only four ways in which information can change as a result of social transmission, but they are a starting point within a broad framework for considering information distortion.

Sparse

At a basic level, the simple process of summarizing information naturally means that some information is going to be omitted. Humans are subject to limitations in memory and cognitive capacity, which can restrict the amount of information that can be transmitted to others. When people read, watch, or listen to political information in the news, they are unlikely to recall every detail (Findahl and Höijer 1985; Neuman 1976). If the actively informed are only able to recall a subset of the information to which they are exposed, they cannot transmit all of the information to their peers. Consistent with previous research, I expect that socially transmitted information is sparse relative to information communicated by the media (Carlson 2018; Moussaïd, Brighton, and Gaissmaier 2015).

More Biased

It is not surprising that information gets lost through social transmission, and this expectation is likely to persist in nonpolitical information flows too. Assuming that some information gets lost in transmission, it is important to understand the information that remains and how it differs from the information the news media initially tried to convey. This is where the *political* context matters. I argue that socially transmitted information becomes biased in favor of the actively informed person's preferences. Both through gatekeeping and presentation bias, the actively informed (intentionally and unintentionally) transmit biased information to their casually informed peers.

Individuals interpret the news in a way that largely confirms their preexisting beliefs (Lodge and Taber 2013; Kunda 1990). The actively informed might be especially susceptible to selective interpretation because they are stronger partisans who might, in turn, view the world through a stronger partisan perceptual screen (Campbell et al. 1960). These biases affect the information that they report in political conversations.

The desire to transmit information that supports one's own beliefs can come in (at least) two forms. First, the actively informed have control over the specific pieces of information they choose to transmit to others. Just as media outlets serve as gatekeepers (Shoemaker 1991; Soroka 2012), so too can the actively informed serve as "citizen-gatekeepers" (Kraft et al. 2020). If their motivation is driven by self-presentation motivations, individuals might select positive rather than negative content from a news article to transmit to others (Kraft et al. 2020). If their motivation is accuracy (e.g., Pietryka 2016), individuals might select as many details as possible to share with others, in the hope of truly informing them. But if driven by partisan motivations—or other cognitive biases related to the way in which partisans consume the news—individuals might pass on only the details that make their party look good.

Given that partisan motivations tend to drive much political behavior in American politics, especially among strong partisans like the actively informed, my theory is primarily premised on partisan motivations driving information distortion through the two-step flow. As strongly partisan actively informed people use their gatekeeping function, they shield their casually informed peers from information that makes their party look bad, presenting them with a biased subset of information on which to base their political attitudes.

Second, the actively informed can twist the way in which information is presented to the casually informed. In addition to selecting only certain facts to transmit to others, the actively informed can change the way they describe those facts in an effort to make the information appear as though it favors their political preferences. This can happen by trivializing bad information about one's party, exaggerating good information about one's party, misrepresenting facts, and adding editorial comments that contextualize the information in a biased manner. The actively informed can thus add presentation bias to the information they share with the casually informed. This can occur unintentionally, driven by how the actively informed interpret information in the first place, or intentionally, as they try to strategically repackage information in a way that they think will persuade their peers.

Less Accurate

Because of a combination of partisan bias, simple human error, and resource constraints, socially transmitted information is likely to be less accurate than information communicated by the media. Partisan biases in information processing could lead individuals to (strategically or inadvertently) pass along information that is not accurate if it supports their views. A less nefarious explanation is that sometimes humans just make mistakes. But these simple mistakes can be problematic if they are passed along to others as if they are accurate. Although the actively informed could certainly be capable of verifying facts before sharing them with others, especially before posting them online, this could be unlikely to occur. And once someone shares something, they might not feel motivated to double check the information and correct it if it turned out to be false. After all, no one likes to be wrong.

All of this together suggests that socially transmitted information might be less accurate than information communicated by the media. Previous research has shown that in abstract settings individuals will transmit biased, inaccurate information to their peers (Ahn, Huckfeldt, and Ryan 2014), but these effects are likely driven by partisan rather than accuracy or prosocial motivations (Connors, Pietryka, and Ryan 2022). However, these findings were uncovered using highly controlled lab experiments in which the information exchanged was limited and numeric. This allows for precise measurement of accuracy and bias, but it leaves out the nuance of how people transmit information from the news in their own words.

More Mobilizing

There is at least some evidence from previous research that socially transmitted information is sparse, biased, and less accurate relative to the original information on which it is based. But a distinguishing feature of distorted democracy is that socially transmitted information can lead people to become more engaged in politics. This is because socially transmitted information has mobilizing content that was absent in information from the news media. Notably absent in previous research on information transmission is the ability of the actively informed to *add* content that was not previously there. This additional content could indeed contribute to the biased and inaccurate content described previously, but it could also be mobilizing. Socially transmitted information could be mobilizing as a result of both cognitive biases and motivated distortions.

On the cognitive bias side, people have a general tendency to prefer action over inaction (Patt and Zeckhauser 2000). This action bias could lead people to highlight the importance of taking action, in addition to simply relaying information. People also tend to communicate information with emotionally charged language that could trigger emotions likely to spark political action, such as anger and enthusiasm (Valentino et al. 2011; Phoenix 2019). On the motivated distortion side, the actively informed could intentionally try to mobilize others to engage in politics, particularly in ways that support their preferences. The actively informed are stronger partisans who are more engaged in politics, as I demonstrate in chapter 3, which could make them especially likely to want others to participate politically too. Those who are deeply involved in politics generally want to see others participate (Krupnikov and Ryan 2022). In contrast, news outlets rarely directly encourage individuals to take political action and tend to focus more on reporting the news, leaving the decision to act on that information up to the reader or viewer. The actively informed have no professional norms stopping them from proselytizing, which means that socially transmitted information should be more likely to contain mobilizing calls to action than information communicated directly by news outlets.

In summary, there are many reasons we should expect information to change as the actively informed communicate with the casually informed. In chapter 4, I provide more theoretical background to describe the specific ways in which information can change through social transmission. After further developing the theory, I also provide evidence for these informational changes. But for now, the key point is that the actively informed can *change* the content of information they share with their peers, leaving the casually informed with a subset of information that is likely sparse and biased, at least relative to the original information from the news.

In this book, I do not distinguish between intentional, motivated information distortion and unintentional distortion as a result of cognitive biases. This distinction is certainly important, particularly for considering the implications of the theory. For example, if most distortion is occurring intentionally, that suggests a different set of tools to address the problem than if the distortion is mostly a consequence of cognitive biases. Moreover, other work points to the importance of motivations in understanding interpersonal political communication (Connors, Pietryka, and Ryan 2022). Distinguishing between these two types of distortion would require a different research design than I employ throughout the book. I therefore acknowledge this limitation and encourage future work to rigorously investigate the differences between intentional and unintentional information distortion.

HOW SOCIALLY TRANSMITTED INFORMATION LEADS TO DISTORTED DEMOCRACY

Demonstrating the ways in which information changes as it flows from the media to person to person is an important contribution in and of itself, but the next question is, So what? How does the distorted information affect political behavior? Recall that my underlying theory is that information transmitted socially to the casually informed affects their knowledge, preferences, and participation. I take each of these outcomes in turn, explaining why the information distortions described in the previous section make these outcomes more likely.

Underinformed

The first component of distorted democracy is that socially transmitted information can affect what people know about politics. This can refer to both a *lack* of information about politics and current events and *misinformation* about politics and current events. What role does the two-step flow play in shaping how much the casually informed can learn about politics and whether they are misinformed?

On the one hand, we might expect individuals to learn the same amount from socially transmitted information and from the media. If the actively informed are appropriately summarizing information and packaging it in a way that is more accessible than the longer, more detailed information provided by the media, then individuals might learn the same amount, regardless of the information source. That is, the actively informed could be operating in the idealized two-step flow in which they are communicating unbiased, trustworthy, concise information that allows the recipients of that information to become better informed. Moreover, socially transmitted information might operate similarly to soft news by increasing political knowledge to an otherwise inattentive audience, or the casually informed (e.g., Baum 2002, 2003).

On the other hand, if the socially transmitted information leaves out crucial details or is inaccurate or biased, individuals might learn less accurate information from other people than they would have learned from the media. Given the mechanisms outlined previously, this seems likely. The actively informed could fall short of facilitating the idealized two-step flow.

In addition to affecting the ability to learn facts and subsequent preferences, relying on our peers for information might also exacerbate beliefs in misinformation, political rumors, and conspiracy theories. Conversations can contribute to misinformation in (at least) two ways. First, the actively informed can spread political rumors and misinformation that they learn from the media. Flynn, Nyhan, and Reifler (2017, 141) suggest that media coverage "shapes the flow of false claims to the public both directly in its coverage and indirectly via its influence on elite behavior." This means that the actively informed can be exposed to rumors, false claims, and misinformation as they regularly engage with the media. What Flynn, Nyhan, and Reifler miss, however, is that the process does not stop there. The actively informed can then go on to tell their friends about the rumors, much like nonpolitical rumors can spread by word of mouth.

There is also the possibility that the actively informed take initially accurate information from the media and distort the content that they present to their peers. In chapter 4, I show that about 4.8 percent of the socially transmitted information based on accurate news articles contained at least one factual inaccuracy. In any case, individuals who rely on the actively informed for information could be more likely to be exposed to misinformation than they would be absent exposure to any information and absent exposure to accurate media. Individuals are certainly exposed to misinformation from the news. But the reality is that the news is not the only way in which individuals can learn about and come to believe political rumors and conspiracy theories.

Polarized

The second component of distorted democracy is that distorted socially transmitted information can affect political preferences, leading to polarization. I just argued that information from peers and information from the media could lead to differential learning and misinformation, so it seems natural to expect the information to also affect subjective preferences, which in turn could affect broader societal-level outcomes, such as polarization.

When it comes to attitudinal polarization, it is important to consider how individuals use information to update their preferences (or not). If people use information to update their preferences, exposure to distinct information should result in different preferences.[2] At first glance, this seems intuitive, and it is consistent with recent evidence that, on average, people update their preferences in the direction of information (Coppock 2022). This recent evidence stands in contrast to previous work suggesting that the relationship between information and preferences is not so simple. Some scholars question whether learning facts can affect preferences at all (Kuklinski et al. 2000). There is also mounting evidence that individuals sometimes fail to update their preferences to align with the facts, even when they believe those facts (e.g., Gaines et al. 2007; Nyhan et al. 2020). While the extent to which learning objective facts affects preferences is inconclusive, it is important to consider how the presentation of facts by peers and the media might lead individuals to update their preferences differently.

The social networks literature confidently suggests that there is a strong degree of social influence in preference development. Individuals can persuade members of their social networks (Huckfeldt and Sprague 1995; Huckfeldt, Johnson, and Sprague 2004). Of particular importance to this project, Druckman, Levendusky, and McLain (2018) show that political conversations can actually have a greater impact on attitudes than media exposure. They find that individuals who were not exposed to any partisan media but discussed politics with people who watched a partisan news clip had more extreme attitudes than those who just watched the partisan news clip but did not have a conversation about it. This suggests that the two-step flow can be powerful in amplifying attitude polarization.

I argue that socially transmitted information can affect attitudes, even when it is based on nonpartisan media sources. Earlier in this chapter, I explained why we should expect opinion leaders to transmit biased information to their peers. The biases contained in socially transmitted information can have the effect of amplifying the bias in partisan media or even transforming nonpartisan media into partisan information. The latter point is crucial, especially if those receiving the information do not recognize the bias. If individuals turn to a peer for information and know that that person generally consumes nonpartisan media, they might trust that the information communicated in their conversations is objective. But in reality that information is likely to be tainted by the preferences of the actively informed person.

Ultimately, I expect the bias contained in socially transmitted information to have an effect on preferences similar to the bias contained in partisan media. If people update their preferences in the direction of the information they receive (Coppock 2022), then people could be nudged in one direction or the other from socially transmitted information, just as they could from information from partisan media. However, given some of the challenges in identifying the partisan bias of peers relative to media sources, the casually informed might have a harder time properly discounting the information from their peers and could be more susceptible to persuasion by learning from their peers than from a news outlet.

Engaged

The third component of distorted democracy is that socially transmitted information drives more political engagement than does information from the media. Social networks influence a variety of political behaviors (Huckfeldt, Mendez, and Osborn 2004; Bond et al. 2012; Sinclair 2012; Mutz 2002). There is compelling evidence that more social mobilization strategies, such as face-to-face canvassing, social pressure mailers, and social reminders to vote on Facebook, are effective tools to increase voter turnout (Gerber, Green, and Larimer 2008; Gerber and Green 2000; Bond et al. 2012). While these studies do not exclusively point to information as the mechanism driving the effects, there is reason to think that it is a relevant part of the story.

As information gets distorted as it flows from the media to person to person, individuals are likely to add information that could be mobilizing. For instance, the actively informed could transmit information they obtained from the news but then add comments about the importance of voting or personal opinions about getting involved in politics that would not be contained in information directly from the media (see ch. 4). Because the actively informed are more politically engaged, they should be more likely to encourage their peers to become active in politics as well—something that professional journalists might be less likely to do.

In addition, the social delivery of the information might signal social acceptance of participation, which could make the recipient more likely to want to participate. Even if the information is not about political participation specifically, the social contact about politics could trigger a desire to participate that would be absent from information supplied by the media. The broad idea with engagement is that socially transmitted information creates social pressure to participate by including a direct invitation or a nudge.

Conclusion

In this chapter, I presented my theory of distorted democracy, which brings information back into the two-step flow. In reviewing previous scholarship inspired by the two-step flow, I identified three key limitations in our understanding and sought to address them with my new approach. I explained how my theory builds on the two-step flow by examining the *content* of information exchanged between the actively and casually informed. I outlined the process through which information diffuses and how it is likely to change, becoming sparse, more biased, less accurate, and more mobilizing, compared to the original information from the news.

Finally, I explained how each of these changes to the informational content can contribute to the three criteria that characterize a distorted democracy by affecting what the casually informed know, what they think, and what they do about politics. A pessimistic outcome of the two-step flow is an electorate that is underinformed and polarized but engaged as a result of exposure to socially transmitted information. In contrast, an optimistic view suggests that the casually informed instead become more knowledgeable than they would be if they acquired no information at all, develop more ideologically consistent attitudes, and are more likely to engage in politics.

New theories come with questions of scope conditions and generalizability. One of the biggest questions about the theory of distorted democracy is whether it is about information exchanged in face-to-face conversations or on social media. As I stated at the start of the chapter, the general thrust of my theory applies to both contexts. There are surely differences in how information becomes distorted in online and face-to-face contexts, but the broad patterns I theorize here and test in chapter 4 are likely to hold. That said, there are three key differences between online and face-to-face communication that I want to highlight for consideration and future research.

First, social media has dramatically changed the scale at which people can be exposed to socially transmitted information. With around 3.8 billion people per month actively using social media platforms in the Meta family in 2023, the reach of socially transmitted information on social media is extraordinary. This means that the actively informed have the potential to influence the political behavior of large numbers of people. This scale alone may not change the ways in which socially transmitted information differs from information communicated by the news, but the exposure to socially transmitted information can be far greater than is possible in face-to-face communication.

Second, social media has changed the types of people from whom we receive information about politics. In face-to-face conversations, people primarily discuss politics with people they know personally, especially those within their household (Huckfeldt and Sprague 1995; see also ch. 3). While people certainly do discuss politics with people they know personally online, there is an increased opportunity to see socially transmitted information from strangers. This is an important difference between interpersonal political communication online and offline. On the one hand, social influence is strongest between close social ties (e.g., Sinclair 2012), which could suggest that socially transmitted information would have a greater impact on behavior in face-to-face contexts that are more likely to occur between close social ties. On the other hand, it could be harder to properly discount socially transmitted information from strangers on social media. Although people can infer people's political leanings on social media (Settle 2018), it could be harder to do for strangers than for people within one's immediate network. This means that on social media, people are exposed to socially transmitted information from people they may not know well enough to gauge whether they are sharing information that is biased or inaccurate. This could exacerbate some of the consequences of socially transmitted information. This problem is not exclusive to social media, but it is arguably more pronounced in this context than in face-to-face interactions. As millions of people scroll through their social media feeds, they are exposed to countless social messages, but they sometimes have limited information about the author of each post. This challenges our ability to properly locate like-minded, knowledgeable informants, which Lupia and McCubbins (1998) identified as crucial. Moreover, it emphasizes the importance of considering the content of information above and beyond the features of the people involved in the exchange.

Third, social media may exaggerate the echo chambers we otherwise observe in daily life. Political discussion networks are generally politically homogeneous, even if there is more disagreement than expected (Mutz 2006; Carlson, Abrajano, and García Bedolla 2020a; Carlson and Settle 2022; Minozzi et al. 2020; Huckfeldt, Johnson, and Sprague 2004). As Barberá (2020) importantly notes, the conventional wisdom that social media creates echo chambers in which people are only exposed to others similar to themselves is not cleanly supported by empirical evidence, which presents a more nuanced view. Although social media can connect like-minded people and put them in echo chambers, there is also extensive exposure to cross-cutting information, particularly from weaker social ties (Barberá 2015; Barberá et al. 2015). As I detail in chapters 5 through 7, shared partisanship between the actively and the casually informed shapes the impact of socially transmitted information on behavior. Specifically, it is socially transmitted information from *copartisans* that leads the casually informed to learn more than they would from the news, have more extreme and sorted policy preferences, and be more likely to participate in politics. To the extent that social media can increase exposure to socially transmitted information from copartisans by enabling people to create echo chambers, social media could be a context in which socially transmitted information has a larger impact. This might be particularly important for political extremists who might have limited access to like-minded people in a face-to-face context but can use social media to reach beyond geographic boundaries to connect to like-minded people.

Ultimately, overlooking the content of the information exchanged between people is a glaring omission in previous research in and of itself, but it is particularly relevant in our new media environment that increases individuals' exposure to socially transmitted information, even from strangers. By reconsidering the role of information in the two-step flow, we can also reevaluate how Americans learn about politics, form their attitudes, and decide to engage. Those who rely on socially transmitted information—the casually informed—could be more likely to be misinformed and adopt more extreme preferences and engage in politics. Whether these outcomes of the two-step flow are normatively good or bad for American democracy depends on one's stance on whether being informed (and not being misinformed) is necessary for rational voting behavior, whether attitudinal polarization is good or bad for representation and American politics more broadly, and whether more participation is always good. I leave the answers to these normative questions to others. I do not take a position on whether these outcomes distort democracy to the point of dysfunction or whether they help democracy function better. Instead, I close each empirical chapter with a consideration of how the evidence stacks up on each side.

3

Conceptual and Empirical Measurement

In chapter 2, I introduced a theory about the role socially transmitted information can play in distorting American democracy. I argued that we need to bring information back into the two-step flow, directly examining how it changes as it flows from the media to the actively informed to the casually informed. Doing so illuminates ways in which socially transmitted information can change the narrative media outlets intended, creating a sparse, biased, less accurate, and mobilizing information environment for the casually informed.

In order to analyze my theory, I need to accomplish two empirical tasks. First, I need to identify and characterize the casually and actively informed, the key players in the two-step flow. Second, I need to measure what information looks like when it flows from the actively to the casually informed. In this chapter, I explain my approaches to accomplishing these two tasks, noting their strengths and weaknesses.

Rethinking Opinion Leaders

My theory of distorted democracy suggests that information changes as it flows from the media to the actively informed to the casually informed, and these changes to the information environment can cause the casually informed to become misinformed and polarized, but engaged. My theory is a revitalization of the two-step flow, with a stronger emphasis on information. Although my theory follows the general framework of the two-step flow (i.e., information flows from the mass media to one group of people to others), I consider slightly different groups of people as the key actors.

OPINION LEADERS AND THE TWO-STEP FLOW

The two-step flow is typically conceptualized as information (or "ideas") flowing from opinion leaders to followers. As the concept of an opinion leader matured through additional research on the two-step flow, Katz and Lazarsfeld (1955) more formally defined what opinion leadership means. Though their definition was not exclusive to politics, they defined opinion leadership as "casually exercised, sometimes unwitting and unbeknown, within the smallest groupings of friends, family members, and neighbors. It is not leadership on the high level of Churchill, nor of a local politico; it is the almost invisible, certainly inconspicuous form of leadership at the person-to-person level of ordinary, intimate, informal, everyday contact" (138).

This definition of opinion leadership has structured conceptualizations of the two-step flow since. Although some work would consider political elites, such as politicians and pundits, as opinion leaders too (e.g., Zaller 1992), most of the work on interpersonal networks that refers to opinion leaders focuses on more intimate connections. Katz (1957) suggests that distinguishing an opinion leader from a follower involves three criteria: who one is, what one knows, and whom one knows. This means that opinion leaders have unique personality traits and values that make them suitable for leadership, that they are viewed as more knowledgeable or competent on a given topic than are followers, and that they are centrally located in their social networks.

Decades of research on opinion leadership generally continued to follow this emphasis on personal traits, expertise, and network positioning. Weimann and colleagues (2007) summarize the key qualities of opinion leaders, relative to followers, that have been identified by researchers over time: they are (1) in every social level, (2) in all demographic groups, (3) more socially involved and more centrally located within their networks, (4) considered experts by their peers, (5) more exposed to mass media; (6) more involved in the topic of interest (politics in this case); (7) experts in one area but not others; (8) involved in more personal communication; and (9) aware that they are an information source for others. Most of these attributes are not associated directly with information or the media. Rather, they focus on the position of opinion leaders within their networks and their perceived credibility on the topics over which they have influence. Opinion leaders have therefore been conceptualized in a way that puts information on the back burner in a theory that should place it front and center.

OPINION LEADERS AS A SUBGROUP OF THE ACTIVELY INFORMED

The classic definition of opinion leadership, including the qualities summarized by Weimann and colleagues, does not clarify the role of information. But my argument rests on its central importance in the two-step flow. I therefore conceptualize the players in the two-step flow more broadly. The actively informed get most of their information directly from the mass media, whereas the casually informed get most of their information from the actively informed. Opinion leaders are essentially a subgroup of the actively informed: all opinion leaders are actively informed, but not all the actively informed are opinion leaders. To unpack this further, I discuss two key distinctions between the actively informed and opinion leaders to illustrate the importance of broadening the description of the people who transmit information from the mass media to their peers.

First, the individual characteristics of opinion leaders and their relationships with followers are less important to understanding the actively and casually informed. As summarized by Weimann and colleagues, opinion leaders have a number of characteristics, most of which do not necessarily have to do with where they learn about politics. For example, opinion leaders are to be viewed as experts by their peers, centrally located within their networks, and well aware that they are information sources to others. These characteristics are not necessarily tied to where they acquire information. These features are therefore less central when trying to understand the role that *information* plays in the two-step flow. In my broader conceptualization of the two-step flow, the actively informed *could* have these characteristics, but they are not required to. My focus is less on the context in which influence occurs, and instead rests more heavily on the ways in which people engage with information. The key feature that distinguishes those at the second step of the two-step flow from those who come next is how they generally access information about politics. All of the other characteristics outlined by Weimann and colleagues that define opinion leaders are not requirements to be actively informed.

Second, unlike many conceptualizations of opinion leaders, being actively informed is not necessarily a static personality trait. While some may have a general tendency to be actively or casually informed, this is not necessarily a fixed "type" of person. Rather, some people may be casually informed in one domain (e.g., immigration policy), but actively informed in another (e.g., elections). This is similar to the concept of issue publics, wherein people may be deeply invested in some issues, but not others (Converse 1964). People within an issue public tend to have stable preferences and considerable knowledge in the political domains they care about, but have less awareness or preference stability in other domains (e.g., Krosnick 1990). People within an issue public are likely to be actively informed in that domain, but they might be casually informed in other domains in which they are less invested.

In addition to being actively or casually informed across issue domains, people may change their information consumption over time with ebbs and flows in current events. Just as people tune into and out of the news in response to major events like wars or negative partisan coverage (Kim and Kim 2021), people might shift between being casually and actively informed in response. In fact, in other collaborative work, my colleague and I use nationally representative panel data to show that Trump supporters were more likely to opt out of media consumption (being actively informed) and into socially transmitted information (being casually informed) immediately after the 2020 election (Pedersen and Carlson 2022).

To understand the consequences of the two-step flow, it is important to more carefully consider the information to which people are exposed. Distinguishing between the actively and casually informed based on where they typically learn about politics (the news media or other people) shifts the focus back to information. In so doing, we can more thoughtfully analyze how information changes through the two-step flow, how the casually and actively informed are exposed to different information environments, and why it matters. Addressing these questions is more difficult when the focus of the two-step flow is on the relationships between opinion leaders and followers and their unique characteristics, rather than the information to which they are exposed.

MEASUREMENT STRATEGIES

Just as conceptualizing opinion leadership has been challenging over time, so too has been measuring the concept. In this section, I briefly review some past approaches to empirically identifying opinion leaders to introduce my measurement strategies for identifying the actively and casually informed.

Lazarsfeld, Berelson, and Gaudet ([1944] 2021) stumbled upon the two-step flow by measuring "opinion leaders" by asking survey respondents to report whether other people ask them for advice. Specifically, opinion leaders were identified as answering "yes" to two questions: "Have you recently tried to convince anyone of your political ideas?" and "Has anyone recently asked you for your advice on a political question?" Although opinion leaders were found to be more interested in politics and have more exposure to the media, this was a *correlate*, rather than a key defining feature of what an opinion leader is. By this measurement, opinion leaders could, theoretically, not pay any attention to the news at all but simply communicate their political opinions to others in conversation.

Since then, researchers have critiqued the original measurement of an opinion leader, seeking to focus more on network position, perceived competence, and personality traits of the opinion leaders (e.g., Weimann et al. 2007; Katz 1957; Weimann 1982). For example, researchers have asked people to self-report whether they are influential in their communities (e.g., King and Summers 1970), to identify influential members of their communities, considering people listed more than once to be influential (e.g., Weimann 1982), engaged in ethnographic research to directly observe who is influential, and personality measures. Each measure brings its advantages and disadvantages, considering time, resources, and validity. One commonly used measure that has gone through fairly extensive validation is the Personality Strength (PS) Scale (Noelle-Neumann 1983). The ten-item scale captures leadership characteristics that correlate with other measures of opinion leadership.

Although the PS Scale has been widely used, it has some important conceptual limitations. The scale items capture many general leadership qualities, such as "I like to assume responsibility," "I often notice that I serve as a role model for others," "I am good at getting what I want," "I usually rely on being successful in everything I do," and "I like to take the lead when a group does things together." However, these qualities do not speak to whether the person has any expertise on the topic at hand, one of the distinguishing characteristics suggested by Katz (1957), nor do they capture how the person engages with information. A few items are more closely related: "I often give others advice and suggestions" and "I enjoy convincing others of my opinions." But these too do not require that the person be informed or that the person became informed by the news. These characteristics capture the extent to which the person might (try to) influence others' decisions but not necessarily as a result of information they share.

Although the actively informed are different from opinion leaders, reviewing how opinion leaders have been measured in previous work is useful for developing an appropriate measure for being actively and casually informed. The previous measurement strategies, perhaps including the PS Scale, might very well correlate with the construct of being actively informed. But, the measure should more closely match the construct and the previously used measures of opinion leadership do not sufficiently focus on information consumption preferences.

To properly measure whether someone is actively or casually informed, we need to consider the sources from which they receive information. Because people can shift between being actively and casually informed across domains and over time, I want to capture their *general* tendency, acknowledging that it will not capture how a person engages with information on every topic at every moment in time. Moreover, because people tend to overreport their news consumption (Prior 2009), the question needs to provide for a softer description of what it means to acquire information socially.

My preferred question wording is the one routinely employed by the National Opinion Research Center (NORC) at the University of Chicago and widely used by the American Press Institute (API). Respondents are asked: "Choose the statement that best describes you, even if it is not exactly right. In general, . . ." Respondents then choose between "I bump into news and information as I do other things or hear about it from others" and "I actively seek out news and information." Those who report actively seeking out news and information are considered actively informed, whereas those who report bumping into news and information as they do other things are considered casually informed. This question nicely captures the key distinction between the actively and casually informed in a way that is different from the distinctions between opinion leaders and followers. The focus is on *information* and how they generally access it.

Like any measure, this one is not perfect either. It relies on self-reported information, parts of it are open to interpretation about what it means to "bump into news," hearing about the news from others is an option but not the only option for the casually informed, and it does not account for networks in any meaningful way. Throughout this book, I use additional measurement strategies to distinguish between the casually and actively informed, largely dependent on which questions were available in the surveys that I use. For example, in a 2016 survey, I asked respondents to report whether they get most or all of their information directly from other people (casually informed) or whether they get most or all of their information directly from news outlets (actively informed). In another survey fielded in 2017, I asked participants to report what percentage of their information about politics, candidates, and elections came from a variety of sources, including "conversations with other people (online or face to face)." These measures still keep information front and center, but they do not focus as much on intent and are likely more subject to social desirability bias in overreporting reliance on news sources.

Across several surveys, each offering slightly different measurements of being casually or actively informed, one thing remains clear: many Americans are casually informed. As of March 2020, data from a national probability sample collected by NORC at the University of Chicago suggests that 33 percent of Americans bump into the news as they do other things or hear about it from others. This is consistent with results from the American Press Institute's surveys in 2016 and 2018 using the same question and sampling frame, suggesting that 36 and 37 percent of Americans, respectively, bumped into the news. Although very few rely *entirely* on socially transmitted information (only 7 percent of respondents to the 2016 Cooperative Campaign Analysis Project [CCAP], a nationally representative survey fielded by YouGov, reported that they get *all* of their information directly from other people), these results make it clear that socially transmitted information is an important part of how Americans learn about politics, but we currently know little about what socially transmitted information looks like and why it matters.

Understanding the Actively and Casually Informed

Although I have challenged previous work that exclusively focuses on the characteristics of the people exchanging information, I do not deny the importance of these characteristics. In this section, I describe the features of the casually informed and—where relevant—how they differ from the actively informed. I primarily focus this section on the casually informed because they have received less attention by researchers. In so doing, I answer two questions: (1) Who becomes casually informed? and (2) How do people become casually informed?

WHO BECOMES CASUALLY INFORMED?

Examining the characteristics of the casually and actively informed is important for understanding how social information transmission contributes to distorted democracy. The features of the actively informed help us understand how and why they distort information from the news, allowing us to develop expectations about how socially transmitted information differs from information communicated by the media. The features of the casually informed help explain why this distorted information could matter for their political behavior.

To examine the characteristics that distinguish the casually from the actively informed, I use data from the March 2020 iteration of TASS and two surveys from the API in 2016 and 2018, all of which had the same question wording for measuring the casually informed, had the same covariates avail-

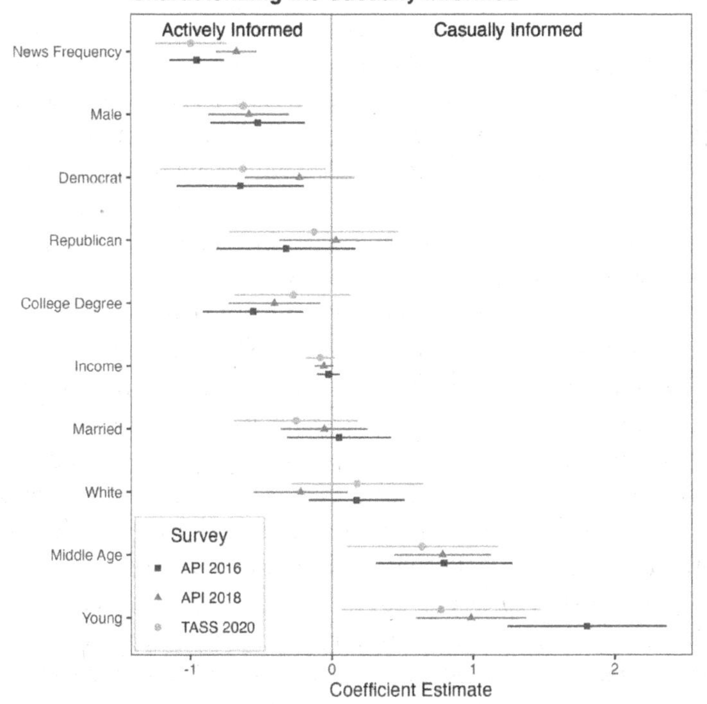

FIGURE 3.1. Characterizing the casually informed. Coefficients from logistic regression models, including survey weights. Horizontal lines represent 95% confidence intervals. Data are from the American Social Survey (TASS 2020) and two surveys conducted by the American Press Institute (API 2016, 2018).

able, and used national probability samples from NORC at the University of Chicago. I consider the casually informed those who report that they generally bump into the news as they do other things or hear about it from other people. I conducted a weighted logistic regression model for each of the three surveys, using common demographic characteristics as covariates. The coefficient estimates are plotted in figure 3.1, with positive values indicating that the characteristic was associated with being casually informed and negative values indicating that the characteristic was associated with being actively informed.

Across three surveys, some key patterns stand out. Most intuitively, people who consume the news less frequently were more likely to be casually informed. This result is almost tautological, but important to demonstrate empirically. This provides more confidence in the measure for being casually and actively informed, indicating that information is indeed likely flowing between the actively informed who consume a lot of news directly and the casually informed who do not.

Generally speaking, the casually and actively informed are more demographically similar than they are different. This is important because it indicates that my theory of distorted democracy is not necessarily restricted to certain demographic groups. Moreover, given that social networks are largely composed of people who are similar to one another, this suggests that social networks can likely include both actively and casually informed people in them, just as research on opinion leadership shows that opinion leaders and followers exist in all social groups (e.g., Katz and Lazarsfeld 1955; Lazarsfeld, Berelson, and Gaudet [1944] 2021).

That said, two demographic groups stand out. First, women are more likely to be casually informed than are men. While some of this may be due to gender differences in survey reporting (e.g., men may be more willing than women to overreport their active news-search behavior), if it is an accurate reflection of the informational landscape, this has important implications for how we think about gender and political participation. Previous work has shown that women tend to avoid political discussions more than men (Carlson, Abrajano, and García Bedolla 2020b; Carlson and Settle 2022; Djupe, McClurg, and Sokhey 2018), that women do not speak up as much in conversations (Karpowitz and Mendelberg 2014), and that women are more likely than men to rely on but be led astray by biased socially transmitted information (Krupnikov et al. 2020). All of these features, paired with the evidence presented here that women are more likely to be casually informed, raise an important issue for thinking about what information women are exposed to, compared to men, and how that might affect their subsequent political engagement and downstream representation.

Second, the casually informed are younger than the actively informed. Older Americans are generally more engaged in politics and follow the news more closely than younger Americans, so it is perhaps intuitive that the actively informed are older. However, this could be an important point to consider if older people are also more likely to read "clickbait" headlines (Luca et al. 2022; Munger 2020) and believe misinformation, which could be due in part to variation in digital literacy (Guess and Munger 2023). If older Americans are consuming more clickbait, partisan, and potentially inaccurate information, this could have important implications for understanding the content that the casually informed might ultimately be exposed to.

The political composition between the actively and casually informed is also important. In two of the three surveys, Democrats were slightly more likely to be actively informed than Independents. Republicans were no more likely to be actively or casually informed than Independents. Although Republicans and Democrats are equally likely to be casually informed, the im-

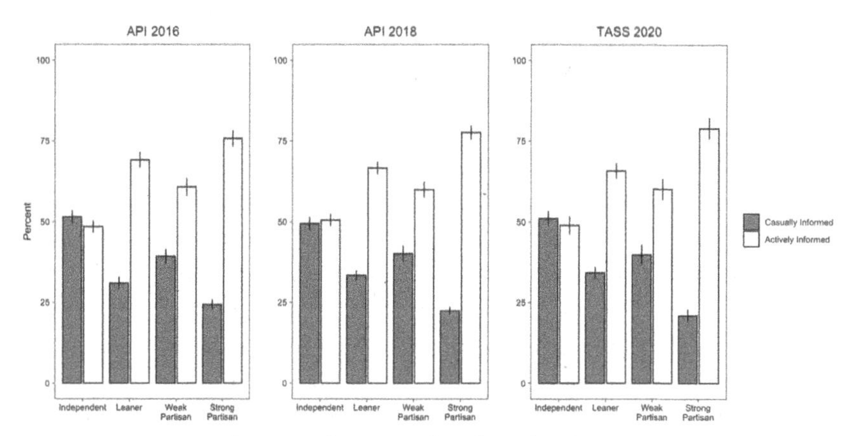

FIGURE 3.2. Percentage of partisans who are casually and actively informed across three surveys. Bars represent the percentage of respondents in each strength of partisanship category who are casually informed (gray) and actively informed (white). Strength of partisanship is measured by folding the seven-point party identification scale so that "strong partisans" include both strong Republicans and strong Democrats, "weak partisans" include weak Republicans and weak Democrats, "leaners" include those who reported they were Independents but leaned toward either the Republican or Democratic Party, and "Independents" are those who reported that they do not lean toward either party. Percentages were calculated using survey weights. Vertical lines represent 95% confidence intervals.

portant criteria to evaluate when it comes to partisanship is *strength* of partisanship. This is important because if the actively informed are stronger partisans, they might be more likely to pass along biased information to the weaker partisans and Independents who make up the casually informed.

Figure 3.2 shows the percentage of respondents who are actively and casually informed by strength of partisanship. Across all three surveys, the same pattern emerges: pure Independents are most likely to be casually informed and strong partisans are least likely to be casually informed. For example, in 2020, 51 percent of Independents were casually informed, compared to only 21 percent of strong partisans. In contrast, about 49 percent of Independents were actively informed, whereas 79 percent of strong partisans were actively informed.

Of course, there are other theoretically meaningful characteristics that could differentiate the casually and the actively informed. For example, political engagement was not available in all three of the surveys analyzed in figure 3.1, but I was able to examine it in other surveys. In a 2022 nationally representative YouGov survey and a 2022 survey of partisans in key primary states, I find that the casually informed engaged in significantly fewer political activities than the actively informed. This is not surprising given that the actively informed are stronger partisans who consume the news directly; however, it could have important implications for thinking about how the actively informed could mobilize the casually informed to take action.

Understanding the types of people who are casually and actively informed is important for understanding how information flows and why it matters. The key results shown in figures 3.1 and 3.2 indicate that information could be flowing from strong partisans (on both the left and the right) who consume a lot of news to Independents or weak partisans (on both the left and the right) who do not consume much news otherwise. Although this analysis does not directly test information flows because I do not incorporate actual network data, the pattern is suggestive that this is a real possibility. Information flowing from stronger partisans to weaker partisans or Independents is a key feature that structures many of the downstream consequences of socially transmitted information.

HOW DO PEOPLE BECOME CASUALLY INFORMED?

Finally, we need to understand how someone becomes casually informed. This is important for two reasons. First, this analysis provides context for understanding where and between whom information is transmitted socially. The information environment has changed dramatically since the two-step flow was initially developed. In contrast to the early work on social information transmission, the casually informed can now learn about politics socially online via social media, in addition to face-to-face conversations. But the social contours of these two experiences are remarkably different, so it is important to understand the extent to which the casually informed are primarily exposed to socially transmitted information online or face-to-face.

Second, it is important to understand the relationships between the actively and casually informed and the features of the *networks* in which information is exchanged. Just as scholars examine the specific news sources people consume, I examine the specific types of people the casually informed turn to for their news. While this might be less immediately central to understanding the *content* of the information exchanged, it might shape how that information is interpreted and the extent to which people trust it to be true. Moreover, given the ample research on the effects of the partisan composition of discussion networks on political behavior (e.g., Huckfeldt, Johnson, and Sprague 2004; Mutz 2006; Klofstad, Sokhey, and McClurg 2013; Carlson, Abrajano, and García Bedolla 2020a, 2020b), it is important to understand the extent to which the casually informed are generally connected to others who agree or disagree with them. This distinction could then shape the extent to which we should expect their attitudes to polarize in response to socially transmitted information, for example.

The Casually Informed Bump into the News Socially

To set the stage for *how* individuals become casually informed, I analyzed more data from the American Social Survey (TASS) in 2020. Respondents who were identified as being casually informed were asked a follow-up question about how often they bump into the news in each of the following ways: reading content posted by others on social media; reading content posted by news outlets, politicians, or ads on social media; watching entertainment TV programs; engaging in face-to-face conversations with others, listening to radio programs or podcasts; or reading non-news sections of newspapers or magazines. This was measured on a four-point scale, ranging from almost never (1) to just about always (4).

Figure 3.3 shows the average frequency of bumping into the news from each method. Reading content posted by others on social media was the most commonly used form of bumping into the news, followed by the content posted by news outlets and politicians on social media and face-to-face conversations. The least common methods of bumping into the news were entertainment TV programs and the non-news sections of newspapers. The results indicate that the most social methods were the most common ways in which the casually informed bumped into the news.

To contextualize these results, about 32 percent of the casually informed reported that they bump into the news via face-to-face conversations with

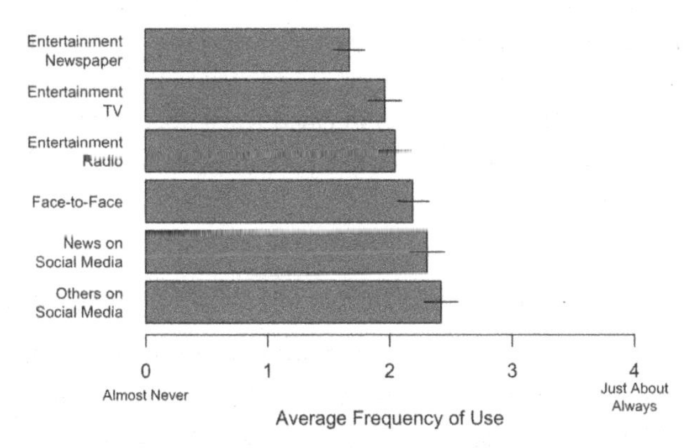

FIGURE 3.3. How the casually informed bump into the news. Average frequency of bumping into the news via each method. Horizontal lines represent 95% confidence intervals. Means and standard errors calculated using survey weights. Data come from TASS 2020.

others most of the time or just about always. In contrast, only 15 percent of the casually informed reported that they bump into the news via the non-news sections of newspapers. This suggests further that being casually informed is more likely to be characterized by social interactions with other people, making it distinct from consuming soft news entertainment. While seminal research on low-information voters suggested that many individuals can become inadvertently informed about politics as they flip to the sports section of the newspaper (Popkin 1991) or by watching soft news programming (Baum 2002; Baum and Jamison 2006), it seems that at least today this is far less common than becoming informed in face-to-face conversations.

Almost all of the casually informed (80 percent) report that they bump into information through others' social media posts at least some of the time. This is important because recent work has demonstrated that inadvertent exposure to news content on social media can increase political knowledge (Bode 2016; Feezell and Ortiz 2021), but it can also facilitate misinformation and overconfidence (Anspach, Jennings, and Arceneaux 2019). What is perhaps even more alarming is that even the content generated by social media users, such as comments on a news article, can contain false, biased information and actually lead people to become misinformed, even if the news article itself contains the factual information (Anspach and Carlson 2020). Moreover, the way in which people engage with political content on social media can foster brooding animosity toward those who think about politics differently (Settle 2018). In fact, Settle (2018) finds that perceptions of how responsibly others consume the news is one of the key drivers of affective polarization on Facebook.

All told, these results indicate that the casually informed largely rely on *social* channels when they bump into the news. This gives more confidence in using this broad measure to capture those who rely on socially transmitted information to learn about politics, as opposed to the strict measure used in the 2016 CCAP. If the casually informed learn about politics from their peers, both online and face-to-face, the next important question is who exactly those peers are.

The Casually Informed Turn to Like-Minded Strong Ties

On the March 2020 iteration of TASS, I also asked the casually informed to report the frequency with which they bumped into information from family members, friends, coworkers, acquaintances, and strangers. The results, presented in figure 3.4, indicate that the casually informed tend to learn about politics most often from those with whom they have stronger social ties. In

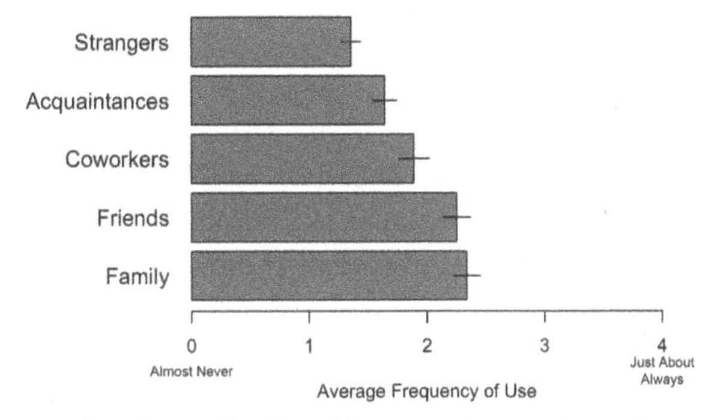

FIGURE 3.4. From whom the casually informed bump into the news. Average frequency of bumping into the news from each type of person. Results reflect weighted means. Horizontal lines represent 95% confidence intervals. Data come from TASS 2020.

fact, there is a nearly linear relationship between strength of tie and frequency of learning about politics from each type of person. For example, about 35 percent of respondents reported that they bump into information from their family most or all of the time, whereas about 5 percent report bumping into information from strangers most or all of the time.

As described in chapter 2, previous research on political discussion networks and the two-step flow indicates that socially transmitted information can be an effective information shortcut when it comes from people who are knowledgeable copartisans. Are the casually informed likely to bump into information from copartisans? To answer this question, I asked respondents to the 2020 iteration of TASS to indicate approximately what percentage of the people with whom they discuss politics face-to-face and on social media are Republicans or Democrats. In the analysis, I recoded these variables so that higher values indicate a greater percentage of copartisan discussants. Because it is difficult to conceptualize copartisans for pure Independents, they are removed from this analysis.

The results suggest that the actively informed are in significantly more homogeneous networks than are the casually informed. Specifically, 65 percent of the face-to-face discussants of the actively informed are copartisans, whereas 59 percent of the discussants of the casually informed are copartisans. This pattern is similar for discussants on social media: the actively informed discuss politics online with about 63 percent copartisans, whereas the casually informed discuss politics online with about 57 percent copartisans. The results here are not dramatically different substantively: both the actively informed and the casually informed discuss politics primarily with copartisans. However, the differences are statistically meaningful and have important implications for the type of information to which the casually informed are exposed. These results suggest that the casually informed are likely exposed to a somewhat greater variety of information, which *can* facilitate increases in political knowledge (Eveland and Hively 2009). However, it can also lead to apathy (Mutz 2006), persuasion (Huckfeldt, Johnson, and Sprague 2004), conformity (Carlson and Settle 2016; Levitan and Verhulst 2016), and voting against one's interest (Ahn, Huckfeldt, and Ryan 2014).

This concludes my descriptive exploration of the key actors in the information diffusion process that facilitates distorted democracy. With a better understanding of *who* the casually informed are and *how* they acquire socially transmitted information, I turn in the next section to explain how I measure the ways in which information changes as it flows from actively to casually informed.

Measuring Information

In the first part of this chapter, I conceptually and empirically described the actively informed and the casually informed. Now I turn to explaining how I measure the most important component of the two-step flow: the information itself. I start by highlighting the challenges in measuring how information changes as it moves through the two-step flow. I then review previous approaches to measuring information and conclude by introducing the approach I use in this book.

CHALLENGES IN MEASURING SOCIALLY TRANSMITTED INFORMATION

Despite incredible advances in political methodology, quantitatively measuring socially transmitted information is difficult. I focus on three major challenges: lack of observational data, threats to causal inference, and unmeasured outcome variables. These are some of the key challenges to measuring socially transmitted information, but this list is not exhaustive.

Lack of Observational Data

First, socially transmitted information often flows through people's everyday conversations, but there is no accessible data repository that stores the content of these conversations. It could be possible to create such a dataset by recruiting participants to consent to have their Google Home or Amazon Echo recordings analyzed or to opt in to using an app that records their conversations. Ethical considerations aside, there would be important generalizability concerns to this approach if the type of person willing to be "bugged" is different from the type of person who is not.

An alternative approach would be to sacrifice more external validity and analyze political discussions that occur in a lab setting. Although many scholars have used lab experiments to study the effects of political discussion on various political outcomes, the conversations themselves are often excluded from the analysis. In some of my previous work with Jaime Settle, we analyzed the content of political discussions that were part of a lab experiment (see Carlson and Settle 2022, ch. 7). These analyses were important for our purposes, but they of course lack the external validity of real conversations between people who are choosing to engage with one another about politics and the specific topics of their choosing. It is definitely possible to design lab experiments in a way that allows researchers to observe socially transmitted information directly. Indeed, video and text chat software has provided new opportunities to study actual conversations (e.g., Rossiter 2020; West 2022), but the samples are often small, and the context is still somewhat artificial.

Analyzing social media data is an important opportunity to evaluate directly observable socially transmitted information. Although people engage with one another differently online and face-to-face, this provides one avenue through which researchers can analyze socially transmitted information in the wild. Aside from missing the face-to-face interactions, social media data are limited to what is made available by social media companies, which can change over time. Obtaining the text of posts from everyday users is possible on some platforms, like Twitter, depending on each user's privacy settings. However, this is currently not possible on Facebook, even using CrowdTangle. Within some limitations, it is possible to directly observe socially transmitted information exchanged on social media platforms, but social media provides only one context in which socially transmitted information is exchanged.

Threats to Causal Inference

The second major challenge to measuring socially transmitted information involves causal identification. Causal identification challenges threaten a researcher's ability to answer two types of questions related to socially transmitted information: Do people distort information differently depending on the person with whom they are communicating? What are the effects of relying on others for information as opposed to the media (or nothing at all)?

For the first question, researchers would not only need to measure the content of the socially transmitted information exchanged, but they would also need to randomize the people with whom the actively informed are communicating. This is, of course, a threat to external validity, but it is something that could be done in a laboratory setting. Yet if researchers wanted to use observational data, such as directly observable socially transmitted information on Twitter, they would lack the ability to say that various features of the relationship between the actively and casually informed Twitter users caused any observed changes in information distortion.

For the second type of question, we need to reevaluate the choices people make in their information consumption. The types of people who opt in to being casually informed are different from the types who opt in to being actively informed. As a result, directly comparing actively and casually informed people leaves much to be desired by way of the causal effect of information exposure. Barring unique exogenous shocks (e.g., internet outages, social distancing brought on by a pandemic limiting face-to-face interactions, news blackouts), it is hard to imagine commonly occurring scenarios in which people would be forced into being actively or casually informed on a topic.

Unmeasured Outcome Variables

The third challenge is that many outcomes of interest are difficult to observe directly. Even if we were able to satisfy the above challenges to analyzing socially transmitted information with observational data, we would need to measure the outcomes of interest, such as political beliefs, preferences, knowledge, and participation. This could be done using aggregate-level survey data or proxies based on web-tracking data, but in general, obtaining individual-level measures would prove to be exceptionally difficult without some form of survey data collection.

Altogether, these challenges point us to the need for some form of researcher intervention in data collection. Researchers can do their best to complement experimental work with the best available observational data to try to balance internal and external validity. This is true in many research agendas and is not unique to studying socially transmitted information. However, it is somewhat unusual that the key quantity of interest, the content of socially transmitted information, is difficult to observe in reality, making experiments a necessary feature of this research agenda.

PREVIOUS APPROACHES TO MEASURING SOCIALLY TRANSMITTED INFORMATION

The reality is that the second step of the two-step flow, when information flows from the actively informed to the casually informed, remains largely undetected. This challenge could be one reason previous work on the two-step flow has not engaged directly with the information itself. As noted in chapter 2, many researchers point to the importance of information but do not measure it or engage with it theoretically in the way that I do by contrasting it with information from the media. In this section, I briefly review some previous approaches to studying socially transmitted information: name generators and lab experiments.

Name Generators

One of the most powerful tools in all of social network analysis is the name generator. In this approach, survey respondents are asked to list people with whom they discuss important matters. Respondents are then asked a number of questions about each person in their network. In an ideal case, researchers are then able to follow up with each person they listed and survey them as well. Name generators have been used to answer countless important questions in the field, but only some of these questions focus specifically on socially transmitted information. As I discussed in chapter 2, some scholars suggest that when a respondent incorrectly guesses their peer's candidate preference, it must be the result of information distortion in their conversations. While this could be true, it does not provide much information about what those distortions looked like. Moreover, the inaccuracy could be driven by uncertainty (Eveland et al. 2019). Ultimately, name generators cannot provide data on what information was actually exchanged in the conversations.

Lab Experiments

Experimental approaches have more carefully engaged with measuring socially transmitted information. Sacrificing the external validity of analyzing the effects of organic conversations within real social networks, lab experiments have made great strides in identifying causal effects of information (for a detailed overview of this methodology, see Connors, Pietryka, and Ryan 2022). As described in more detail in chapter 2, these studies typically allow participants to communicate with each other via networked computers. Who has information, how much information "costs," and the alleged accuracy of that information can be manipulated as part of the study, but participants can often exchange information with each other. The context is abstract, rarely utilizing real candidates, partisan cues, or communication in words. Instead, the information people share back and forth typically consists of numbers that represent policy positions.

This experimental approach has the unique advantage of capturing the information people are willing to share with each other in conversation. The abstract nature of the information makes it easy to measure important characteristics like bias and accuracy. If Candidate A was actually at position 3, but one participant told another that Candidate A was at position 7, that participant provided inaccurate information (3 is not equal to 7), and it was biased by 4 points. This provides clean, precise measurement and allows researchers a peek into the information that is actually exchanged.

But this is not how people communicate. While all research designs involve tradeoffs between internal and external validity, one sacrifice in terms of external validity with this approach concerns the construct of interest: information. In reality, political information and the news are complex. The words news outlets, and in turn the actively informed, use to describe what is going on in the political world can structure how people interpret that information and our subsequent attitudes (Cramer Walsh 2006). These lab experiments miss the possibility of framing, priming, misleading but not necessarily inaccurate content, calls to action, injections of opinion, and many other features of real-world information transmission that matter.

TELEPHONE GAME EXPERIMENTS

How do we capture socially transmitted information in a way that allows us to examine it with the same scrutiny with which we examine information from the news media? How do we measure how they differ from each other? My solution to this problem is a telephone game experiment (Carlson 2018, 2019; Aarøe and Petersen 2020). This design is adapted from the serial reproduction task (Bartlett 1932), which is a tool primarily used by psychologists to study topics like the social transmission of gender stereotypes, event knowledge representation, and memory. The concept is simple, as illustrated in figure 3.5. Participants are asked to read a news article and then write a message telling someone else about what they read. This mirrors what the actively informed do when they pass information on to their casually informed peers: they read information directly from a news outlet and then tell others about what they read.

This procedure allows researchers to analyze text generated by participants in the experiment (the messages) and compare it to the original articles they were asked to read. The design is flexible and can accommodate a variety of research questions by varying the original news article participants read, the partisanship of the people sending and receiving information, the specific instructions given to participants (e.g., to inform vs. to persuade), and so forth.

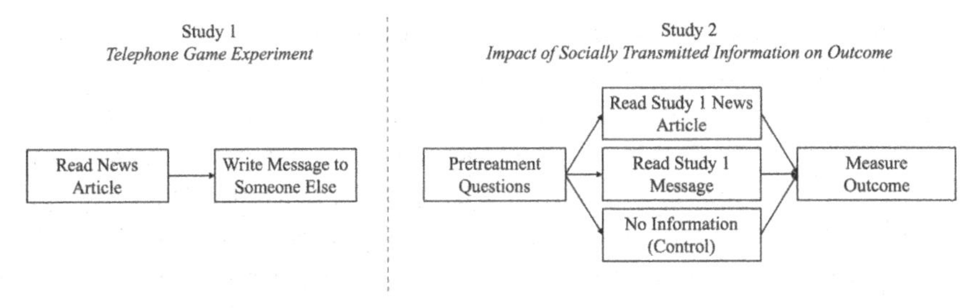

FIGURE 3.5. The telephone game experiment.

The procedure is also flexible analytically. Researchers can analyze the text in any number of ways. In some of my work, for example, I have had research assistants hand-code the messages for different types of information distortions (Carlson 2018; and see Moussaïd, Brighton, and Gaissmaier 2015 for the codebook on types of distortions) and used measures of text similarity to measure information distortion between news coverage and the social messages generated in the experiment (Carlson 2019). Importantly, the messages can be broken down into units of information, or statements that communicate a single idea, that can be further evaluated as (dis)appearing throughout the chain or examined for accuracy, bias, and other features. Other researchers have used similar approaches to examine the extent to which certain types of media frames are more likely to propagate through social networks (Aarøe and Petersen 2020). Others have also used similar designs to hand-code for specific, theoretically driven content, such as references to self-serving behavior of politicians (Bøggild, Aarøe, and Petersen 2021).

The Study 2 portion of a telephone game experiment, shown on the right-hand side of figure 3.5, allows researchers to examine the effects of exposure to social information, compared to information from the media, and no information at all, depending on the counterfactuals of interest. In Study 1, all participants are actively informed, as they have been directly exposed to information from the media (regardless of whether they would do so in the real world); in Study 2, participants are randomly assigned to be actively informed (those assigned to read the Study 1 news article) or casually informed (those assigned to read a message written by a Study 1 participant). In Study 2, participants answer pretreatment questions (demographics, measures of the outcome of interest, etc.), are shown an information treatment (e.g., the full news article, a message about that article from a Study 1 participant, or no information), and then answer additional questions designed to measure the outcome of interest (attitude change, learning, misinformation, engagement, etc.).

Study 2's design is also flexible. Researchers can vary the information participants have about the person who wrote the social message they received and the partisanship of the "dyads" (e.g., a Republican sending information to another Republican, compared to a Republican sending information to a Democrat), and they can measure a wide range of outcomes. With this approach, researchers can estimate the causal effect of the information itself on the outcomes of interest. In the experiments in this book, I analyze within-subject variation in their pretreatment and post-treatment knowledge, preferences, and engagement. Although this allows for granular measurement, it runs the risk of repeated exposure to the same questions in a short period of time. The design is sufficiently flexible to allow for purely between-subjects designs too. Researchers can also examine the extent to which features of the information mediate the causal effect of some other characteristic, such as the partisanship or gender of the actively informed person who wrote the message, the topic, or the original news source.

In this book, I analyze eight unique telephone game experiments I fielded between 2016 and 2021. The experiments vary in news source, topic, instructions, outcomes measured, and pretreatment covariates included. Some studies focus only on the Study 1 portion of the design. In table 3.1, I summarize the experiments that will be analyzed in this book.

Limitations

Although telephone game experiments offer many advantages uniquely suited to testing the two-step flow, they have several limitations. This design is still abstract and washes away many of the features of political discussion that very well could be meaningful in fully capturing information transmission in the two-step flow. I think about these challenges in four broad categories: network dynamics, conversational features, news limitations, and selection concerns.

First, this design, as implemented so far, involves communication between complete strangers. Participants in Study 1 have very limited information about the person to whom they are sending information (e.g., their partisanship, whether they follow the news, or other information the researcher may choose to provide). Participants in Study 2 similarly have limited information about the person from whom they are receiving information. In reality, it is likely that two people communicating with each other about politics know each other personally. They might be able to leverage their relationship with the other person to discount (or upweight) the information that they share. These network characteristics are part of what the original conceptualization

TABLE 3.1. Summary of Telephone Game Experiments

Study 2						
Study Name	*Original News Article*	*Randomization*	*Sample*	*Outcome*	*Randomization*	*Sample*
Economic News Study (2017)	Reuters	Writing to Rep, Dem, or Ind	MTurk	Learning	Information from media or social information from Rep, Dem, or Ind	SSI
Immigration Policy Experiment (2021)	*USA Today*	Writing to Rep, Dem, or Ind	Lucid	Polarization, Engagement	Information from media, social information from Rep or Dem, or no information	Lucid
Environmental Policy Experiment (2021)	*USA Today*	Writing to Rep, Dem, or Ind	Lucid	Polarization, Engagement, Misinformation	Information from media, social information from Rep or Dem, or no information	Lucid
Presidential Candidates Study (2016)	*New York Times*	Writing to Rep, Dem, or Ind	MTurk			
Local Election Study (2016)	California Voter Guide on two local candidates	Writing to Rep, Dem, or Ind	Student Sample			
Racialization Study (2018)	Associated Press article on ISIS trial	Explicit reference to ISIS or not; writing to Rep, Dem, or Ind	CCES			
Topic and Source Replication (2018)	Variety of sources (participants could choose), Gun Control, Tax Policy, Unemployment	Topic (gun control, tax policy, or unemployment); writing to Rep, Dem, or Ind	Lucid			
Partisan Bias Study (2020)	Fox or MSNBC article on Marijuana Legalization	Fox or MSNBC article; forced choice or free choice of news source	MTurk			

of an opinion leader tried to maintain, and I have abstracted from that here in an effort to better understand the role of information.

Second, telephone game experiments involve unidirectional, one-shot communication. These are not conversations in which the casually informed participants can ask follow-up questions to clarify, learn more, or even challenge the actively informed person. In reality, all of these dynamics are possible. Moreover, in-person conversations can carry additional informational cues through variation in vocal pitch, tone, and facial expressions that can in turn affect the casually informed person's behavior. While tone can be captured in text to some degree, text alone is not as powerful as speech (Damann, Knox, and Lucas n.d.). Finally, in some of my previous work with Jaime Settle, we emphasize the importance of the social dynamics of political discussion, highlighting that the content exchanged in political discussions can be obscured by individuals' desire to maintain social relationships (Carlson and Settle 2022). In that work, we do not tackle information exchanged directly, but the emphasis on the social process of political discussion gets lost in a telephone game experiment.

Third, for the actively informed, the news options available are limited. In reality, the actively informed seek news from whatever sources they prefer, on whatever topics they like, and share information with others, perhaps aggregating across sources and topics. While some of my experiments, like the Topic and Source Replication and the Partisan Bias Study, allow participants to choose their information source, the choices they have are still limited to what I present in the study, and they are still only given the option to read one article. Although this can be modified in future work, the limitation is important to keep in mind while reading the results presented in this book.

Finally, another relevant consideration is selection. As I demonstrated in this chapter, people choose whether (and when) to be actively or casually informed, and this choice is correlated with other political characteristics, such as strength of partisanship. In most of the Study 1 experiments, participants are asked to behave as if they were actively informed, regardless of whether they actually were. The actively informed have likely cultivated skills in reading the news, and perhaps in relaying information to others, that the casually informed have not. Asking some casually informed people to behave as if they were actively informed presents an important threat to external validity. On the Study 2 side, I try to isolate the effect of information on various outcomes by randomly assigning some people to be exposed to socially transmitted information or information from the news. As a result, however, I introduce the same selection problem that poses a threat to external validity. The casually informed may have learned how to navigate political life relying on socially transmitted information but may have difficulty navigating a news article, for example. I attempt to address this problem in the Immigration and Environmental Policy Studies, where the Study 1 participants were deliberately recruited to only be people who are actively informed and Study 2 participants were deliberately recruited to only be casually informed. Future work could aim to implement full-fledged Patient Incorporating Choice and Assignment (PICA) designs (de Benedictis-Kessner et al. 2019), though survey firms often struggle to commit to recruiting large enough samples of casually informed participants to make a PICA design tenable.

I want to be fully transparent about the limitations of using telephone game experiments to measure how information changes as it travels through the two-step flow and how this socially transmitted information affects political attitudes and behavior. While I view this approach as a large advancement over past approaches due to its ability to measure more complex forms of information distortion and its attempt to capture otherwise unobserved content (socially transmitted information), it is not perfect. Ideally, researchers would be able to observe conversations between the actively and casually informed directly, with full knowledge of the information to which the actively informed were initially exposed. We would ideally be able to leverage exogenous shocks to the decision to be actively or casually informed, as well as the social relationships themselves, allowing researchers to causally identify the effects of being casually or actively informed on a range of political outcomes, for which we would also conveniently have measures. Of course, most of this is not practical or even possible. But the telephone game experiments help address many possible limitations from previous work, even if they fall short of the ideal. I hope that future work can continue to develop new methods to improve the designs used here, with a continued focus on information.

Conclusion

In this chapter, I built on the theoretical groundwork laid in chapter 2 to identify, characterize, and measure the actively and casually informed. I explained how they differ from opinion leaders, both theoretically and empirically, and I described some of their key characteristics. While these characteristics are not requirements for being casually or actively informed, I showed that the actively informed are more likely to be stronger partisans than the casually informed, but these two groups are otherwise very similar to one another demographically, just as opinion leaders were thought to exist in every social group.

I then explained how I measure the ways in which information changes as it flows from the media to the actively informed to the casually informed.

I noted that this is particularly challenging because observational data on political conversations are largely nonexistent. I described my approach to addressing this challenge—telephone game experiments—but included a thorough discussion of the limitations as well.

In the next chapter, I demonstrate what this analysis of socially transmitted information looks like in action. Examining socially transmitted information generated in the eight experiments described in table 3.1, I test whether information does indeed become sparse, more biased, less accurate, and more mobilizing as it journeys through the two-step flow. I then complement this analysis by examining observational data from Twitter. Together, these analyses show that information can become distorted through social transmission.

4
Distortion

As massive wildfires ravaged the Pacific Northwest in 2020, hundreds of people in the region spent months protesting racial injustice in law enforcement. Although many of the protests were peaceful, some resulted in violent encounters with counter-protesters and law enforcement, riots, looting, vandalism, arson, and even the death of a Donald Trump supporter (Flaccus 2020). In such a tense moment, officials struggled to communicate to the public, which was simultaneously exposed to misleading information on social media. On September 8, 2020, the Portland Police Department tweeted, "To those attending the demonstration tonight: Keep in mind the immediate risk the use of fire poses to community members. Since fire danger is very high right now due to high winds and the current dry climate, fire will spread quickly and could affect many lives." They followed up with a reply: "We ask you to demonstrate peacefully and without the use of fire."[1] It did not take long for this ambiguous plea to be interpreted as a signal that left-wing protesters were responsible for the wildfires (Ovide 2020). The rumors became so pervasive that local law enforcement dedicated time trying to dispel the rumors. For example, the Douglas County Sheriff's Office posted the following on Facebook: "Rumors spread just like wildfire and now our 9-1-1 dispatchers and professional staff are being overrun with requests for information and inquiries on an UNTRUE rumor that 6 Antifa members have been arrested for setting fires in DOUGLAS COUNTY, OREGON."[2]

This example highlights the potentially dire consequences of information distortion. Official law enforcement communications simply asked protesters not to use fire in their demonstrations. But this request was reinterpreted and retransmitted as indicating that the protesters were responsible for the devastating wildfires. What began as a simple plea quickly turned into a rumor that carried a different meaning.

Although this example involves communication on social media, information distortion is not new. As long as people have been able to communicate, they have been able to twist the truth. Many scholars have documented the challenges inherent in information spread via word of mouth. Anthropologists and psychologists have documented the adaptive functions of communication, such as sharing information necessary for survival, while also noting the possibility for exaggerated, inaccurate information to spread (e.g., Brewer 2007).

Especially when people are faced with uncertainty, as they often are with political news, they start to fill in the gaps with their imaginations, which can in turn distort the truth, leading to rumors and gossip (Allport and Postman 1947). The ways in which people fill in the gaps structures how information can be distorted in conversations. They are also predictable and extend beyond gossip to many forms of communication. Due in part to cognitive biases, people have a tendency to pay attention selectively and share details that make themselves look better, make others look worse, and prioritize content that they expect will result in an emotional reaction from the other person (Zuckerman 1979; Bøggild et al. 2021; Heath, Bell, and Sternberg 2001).

Layering these cognitive biases onto the context of political discussion reveals how political information distortion can occur—and why it might matter. People process political information through a partisan lens, interpreting the world through "red-" and "blue-"colored glasses (e.g., Campbell et al. 1960; Green, Palmquist, and Schickler 2002). While everyone shares a general tendency to present themselves well, the type of information that would be privileged as a result of this bias differs between Democrats and Republicans, for example. Democrats and Republicans regularly view the same information differently, in a way that favors their party. For example, evaluating the same economic conditions under the Reagan administration in the 1980s, Republicans were much more positive about how the economy performed than were Democrats (Bartels 2002). The broader idea of biased information processing along partisan lines has been demonstrated time and again in social science research (e.g., Lodge and Hamill 1986; Rahn 1993; Redlawsk 2002; Bullock 2009; Jerit and Barabas 2012; Lodge and Taber 2013; Ditto et al. 2019). If Republicans and Democrats interpret the same information fundamentally differently, should we expect them to transmit the same information to their peers?

Probably not. We should expect people to pass along information that makes them or their fellow partisans look good. Whether this is motivated by an attempt to persuade others directly or is a consequence of cognitive biases in information processing, the social transmission of information from the actively informed to the casually informed is likely to change the narrative that news outlets intended to communicate.

This biased information transmission can happen in many ways. In addition to choosing to pass along only facts that make one's party look good, information can become biased by exaggerating positive information while trivializing negative information about one's party. It could also be the result of sharing *false* information—intentionally or unintentionally—that benefits one's party. Each of these outcomes reflects increased partisan bias but could perhaps have distinct consequences for political behavior.

Some information distortion will fall along partisan lines, with partisan bias increasing as information flows from the media to the actively informed to the casually informed. But other distortions will reflect something less partisan and something more universal about information processing and how we communicate socially. For example, that a lot of information gets lost as it travels from the news to person to person is a product of being human. The bottom line is that the casually informed, who learn about politics via conversations with others who read the news directly, are exposed to distorted information that is more likely to be sparse, biased, less accurate, and more mobilizing, compared to information from the media.

Information distortion from the actively to the casually informed presents the crux of the challenge of why political conversations and the two-step flow produce distorted democracy. As I argued in chapter 2, when the actively informed summarize the news, the information itself changes. In this chapter, after providing more detail on the theoretical foundation of the changes we should expect, I provide empirical evidence of these changes using data from eight telephone game experiments (table 3.1), as well as from observational data from Twitter.

This descriptive chapter provides rich examples of *how* the actively informed can distort information from the news as they pass it along to the casually informed. I show that information distortion happens in the ways we should expect based on a long line of research in other disciplines, from evolutionary, social, and cognitive psychology to marketing to communication. The political nature of how we communicate about the news amplifies some of these previously identified patterns.

Why Does Information Change?

In chapter 2, I explained that information changes as a result of both cognitive biases that lead the actively informed to inadvertently distort information and strategic incentives that motivate people to intentionally change the story. Here my goal is to document some of the ways in which political information changes through social transmission and to identify some of the political consequences of these changes. As a result, I do not focus on disentangling which of these cognitive biases or motivations drive the information distortions observed.

COGNITIVE BIASES

Social scientists have uncovered dozens of cognitive biases and heuristics that affect decision making and behavior. For better and for worse, our brains are structured in a way that encourages shortcuts. While these shortcuts can often help people navigate an otherwise too complex environment, they can sometimes lead people astray. In the political context, scholars have examined the extent to which many cognitive biases affect public opinion and vote choice. Here I highlight the ways in which cognitive biases might facilitate information distortion.

At a basic level, working memory capacity limits the amount of information that people are able to recall and transmit to others. Psychologists have long studied human memory, with a focus on how much people can store in short-term memory. Largely by measuring how many digits or letters people can recall, psychologists have identified "magic" numbers that reflect how many items people can store in short-term memory. Miller (1956) famously argued that people can store 7 (plus or minus 2) items in working memory, while more recent work suggests that if people are not able to "chunk" items together, the magic number is slightly smaller, 4 (plus or minus 1) (Cowan 2001). Regardless of the actual magic number, the general consensus is that people can only store a limited amount of information in short-term memory. This suggests that if someone read a news article and then immediately told a friend about what they read, they would likely only be able to report a few things from that article. The information that ultimately makes its way into long-term memory is also likely to be limited. It is therefore even more important to understand the contours of the information that remains.

Which pieces of information do people pay attention to, remember, and pass along to their peers? How do they present that information? Confirmation bias is perhaps the dominant cognitive bias that explains information processing (Wason 1960), especially in the political context (Taber and Lodge 2006; Lodge and Taber 2013; Redlawsk 2002, 2006). Confirmation bias suggests that people are more likely to seek out information consistent with their beliefs and disregard or distort contradictory information. Moreover, they are likely to interpret ambiguous information as consistent with their beliefs (Charman, Kavetski, and Mueller 2017; Gaines et al. 2007). There are several points in the process of social information transmission at which confirmation bias could lead information to become more biased in favor of the actively informed person's political preferences.

First, the actively informed are likely to select news stories (and topics) that fit their worldview. This could mean choosing partisan news sources that are ideologically consistent (Arceneaux and Johnson 2013; Levendusky 2013) or choosing to pay attention to politics and consume the news *at all* when their party is doing well (Kim and Kim 2021). Related to the latter point, it could also be the case that the actively informed seek out information on topics that they expect to be congenial to their views. If their party is not doing well in the polls, perhaps they avoid election coverage and investigate other topics instead. Second, once a news article is selected, they are likely to pull out the details most supportive of their views, ignoring information that is inconsistent. At this stage, people could engage in leveling (ignoring details that are deemed unimportant) and sharpening (exaggerating details that are deemed important) in a way that continues to promote a narrative consistent with their views (Allport and Postman 1947). This could happen even if the person chose to read a nonpartisan article at the start of the process. Third, the actively informed may selectively interpret the information that remains as favoring their views.

At each stage of the process, confirmation bias can drive the actively informed to understand the news in a way that is consistent with their beliefs, which they pass on to their peers. The process of leveling and sharpening, in particular, can also lead people to *add* politically consistent details that were not present in the news article (e.g., Ganske and Hebl 2001). In part as a consequence of how people seek, interpret, and recall information, social transmission is likely to introduce or amplify political bias from the news. Moreover, confirmation bias can also contribute to information becoming less accurate through social transmission. Even if the original news article is accurate, individuals might interpret information in a way that leads them to twist it to the point of inaccuracy as they pass it along to others. In this scenario, individuals change the facts so much in what they relay to others that it is no longer in keeping with the facts reported in the article.

There are a number of other cognitive biases that can shape how information changes through social transmission. For example, Bøggild, Aarøe, and Petersen (2021) find that people prioritize sharing information about self-interested politicians as a consequence of an evolutionarily adaptive preference for this type of information to facilitate cooperation. Particularly on topics in which group cleavages are salient, in-group biases derived from social identity theory (Tajfel and Turner 1979) and a suspicion of outsiders (Brewer 2007; Pickett and Brewer 2001) can lead people to prioritize information that favors their in-group. Stubbersfield and colleagues (2019) show that moral content is more likely to be socially transmitted, which can have important implications for political contexts. Other biases, such as risk aversion and loss aversion (Tversky and Kahneman 1991, 1992), could further affect how people interpret and frame information and repackage it as they transmit it to others. Aarøe and Petersen (2020) have demonstrated that certain types of frames—those that focus on an individual story—are more likely to be transmitted socially.

In this book, I focus on general patterns in information distortion that are likely to span policy and topic domains in the news. For this reason, the types of information distortion I investigate are more closely aligned with confirmation bias. I am confident that other biases contribute to information distortion in theoretically driven ways, but this is a subject for other research.

MOTIVATED DISTORTION

Socially transmitted information can become distorted as a result of intentional, conscious choices in what information to share with others. Political scientists have considered this possibility from a theoretical standpoint, suggesting that people can intentionally transmit misleading or biased information in an effort to persuade others (Ahn, Huckfeldt, and Ryan 2014). Lupia and McCubbins (1998), in particular, draw on Downs's (1957) framework to highlight that opinion leaders are a reliable information shortcut only if they are more knowledgeable and have the same political preferences as the person receiving the information. Although there is strong theoretical and some empirical evidence for the notion that people can intentionally, strategically transmit biased or false information to others, the precise ways in which that socially transmitted information differs from the original news sources has been underexplored. Moreover, other disciplines have examined this question, shedding light on psychological, rather than political, motivations that can shape social information transmission.

Scholars across the social sciences have conducted extensive research on social information transmission. Each discipline offers a unique perspective, often focusing on different outcomes or topics of communication, but many of the underlying principles remain applicable across fields. Marketing researchers have been particularly prolific in the study of social information transmission, which they typically refer to broadly as word of mouth (WOM).

Primarily driven by a desire to understand how people talk about products and how those conversations can affect sales, scholarship in this area has uncovered important insights about what types of information people share with others.

Rooted in a psychological need to be perceived positively by others, people might selectively transmit information that makes them look good (e.g., Chung and Darke 2006). For example, Berger (2014) suggests that when people are driven by this type of impression management, they are more likely to transmit information that is entertaining (i.e., surprising, funny, extreme), and they might distort information in ways that make it sound more extreme or interesting (Burrus, Kruger, and Jurgens 2006). With regard to transmitting information from the news, this can result in people focusing on the most sensational content, highlighting gaffes, conflict, extreme policy positions, or conspiracy theories. On the positive side, however, Berger (2014) also notes that impression management can motivate people to share useful information because it makes them appear knowledgeable and cooperative. It is possible that if people are motivated to be viewed in this way, they might transmit information that would be most useful to others, which can reduce bias in some cases.

Both political science and marketing scholars have considered whether motivations to persuade others shape the information they transmit. If the actively informed are motivated by persuasion, they might transmit information that makes their preferred outcome look ideal. This is likely observationally equivalent to information transmission being driven by confirmation bias. Marketing researchers highlight another way in which persuasion motivations can change information through social transmission. Berger (2014) argues that persuasion motivations can lead people to share emotionally polarizing or otherwise arousing content. The idea is that this can spark action in the recipients. The goal of the person transmitting the information, then, is to foster arousing, mobilizing emotions, such as anger or excitement, because that in turn could lead them to act (Davidson 1993). These insights from marketing research add an important element to how we might expect information from the news to change through social transmission. When driven to persuade others, the actively informed might select the details that strategically advantage their preferences, but they might also deliver that information in a way that tries to mobilize action, both through emotional valence and direct calls to action.

WHAT TO EXPECT

There are many reasons we should expect information to change as it flows from the media to the actively informed to the casually informed. This can happen as a result of cognitive biases or deliberate motivations, or some combination of the two. As I articulated in chapter 2, I expect that socially transmitted information will be sparse, more biased, less accurate, and more mobilizing than the original information from the media. There are many cognitive biases and strategic motivations that could produce these outcomes. My discussion in this chapter is not exhaustive. There are certainly other cognitive and motivational explanations for socially transmitted information to become sparse, biased, less accurate, and mobilizing and result in other distortions. I focus on broad patterns that should characterize information transmission about a wide range of political news topics. Future research could develop narrower expectations for other types of information distortion, such as communicating group stereotypes, positive or negative tone, or using different types of frames (e.g., Aarøe and Petersen 2020), where other cognitive biases or motivations could be relevant.

In the remainder of this chapter, I present quantitative evidence that social information transmission results in sparse, biased, less accurate, and more mobilizing content relative to the news. While these information distortions might not seem normatively ideal in principle, it is possible that the casually informed are not always made worse off after exposure to socially transmitted information (see chs. 5–7).

Evidence of Information Distortion

Having laid the groundwork for what types of information distortion I expect to observe, I now present evidence of these changes. I examine information distortion using eight experimental studies using research designs outlined in some of my previous work (Carlson 2018, 2019) and explained in more detail in chapter 3. The idea behind these telephone game experiments is that individuals are asked to play the role of the actively informed. Participants read an assigned news article and are then asked to write a message telling someone else about the article they just read. As summarized in table 3.1, each study varies in terms of topic, original news article, randomization, and sample. Because of the limitations in this design, I conclude this chapter with an analysis of observational data, including socially transmitted information communicated on Twitter. Both of these data sources rely only on text and overlook many important features of conversations and interpersonal communication, such as speech and tone (Knox and Lucas 2021; Damann, Knox, and Lucas n.d.; Dietrich, Hayes, and O'Brien 2019). The analyses that follow may reflect a conservative estimate of information distortion because they overlook these important features of communication.

SPARSE

Examining the decline in the amount of information flowing from the media to the actively informed to the casually informed is a relatively straightforward task and one that is best demonstrated visually. Figure 4.1 shows the decline in the number of words from news articles to socially transmitted messages about those news articles across the eight studies described in table 3.1. The articles examined in these studies were 3,943 words long on average, but the average socially transmitted message about those news articles was only 160 words long. This is a substantial decrease in the amount of information that could be communicated to another person. The patterns are just as striking when examining hand-coded units of information, which capture statements that communicate a single idea. Across all eight studies, news articles averaged about 59 units of information and messages about those articles

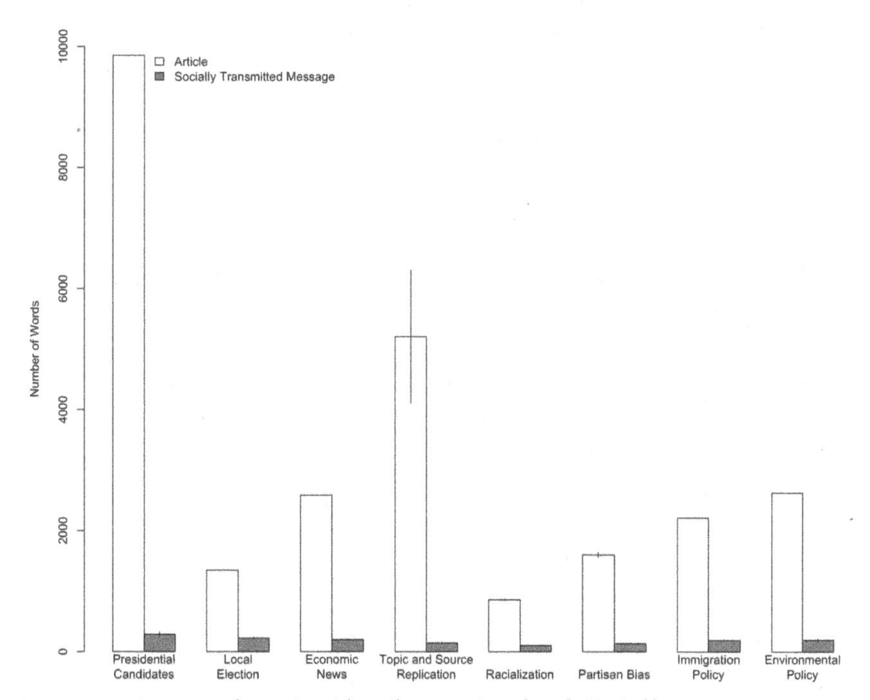

FIGURE 4.1. Average word count in articles and messages in each study. Vertical lines represent 95% confidence intervals, where appropriate. In the Presidential Candidates Study, the Local Election Study, and the Economic News Study, all participants read the same news article, so there is no confidence interval. The Topic and Source Replication Study had 23 different news articles. The Partisan Bias Study and the Racialization Study had only two news articles.

averaged about 3.4 units of information. This fits nicely with the notion that most messages contain about 7 (plus or minus 2) pieces of information that may or may not be useful to the casually informed down the line. The bottom line is that the amount of information available to the casually informed is substantially less (91 percent) than the amount of information available to the actively informed, even in just one news article.

Although the casually informed are exposed to substantially less information than the actively informed, they are still exposed to more than someone who is entirely uninformed, exposed to no information at all. This brings forth an important question: how does the content of what little information remains differ from the content of the full news article? The sections that follow begin to answer this question.

MORE BIASED

Measuring the degree of partisan bias in a message or news article is challenging, and there are many approaches one could take. In this case, a team of research assistants hand-coded the messages and articles for the number of units of information that favored and opposed Democrats and Republicans. This approach allows me to disentangle whether individuals were sharing more negative information about the out-party or more positive information about the in-party. Both would exhibit an overall bias in favor of their partisan preferences but driven by two different mechanisms.

Starting at the beginning of the two-step flow, I examine the partisan bias contained in the news articles participants read. Recall that these articles were selected from mostly nonpartisan sources. The articles may present information that favors one party or disparages another, but they should be *balanced* in the extent to which they present information favoring each party. According to the hand-coded data, the results suggest that nineteen of the thirty-two news articles examined favored Democrats and Republicans equally in the content covered, and only three articles favored one party by more than three units of information. One of these articles, which favored Republicans by 10 points, was a *New York Times* article about the 2016 presidential candidates at the primary stage. At the time, there were more than two dozen Republican candidates running for office, compared to only a handful of Democrats. It makes sense that this article would have more information about Republicans, much of which could be positive. The other two articles were about the "winners" of the GOP tax bill in 2018. These articles provided positive information about the bill, focusing more on Republicans than Democrats. Overall, the news articles in my studies began the two-step flow relatively balanced between Republicans and Democrats.

When people read and summarize the news, however, what comes out on the other side is less balanced. A simple difference of means test comparing the average partisan bias in the news articles to the average partisan bias in the social messages suggests that the social messages were significantly more biased than were the articles. Looking specifically at the proportion of biased units of information in a news article compared to the proportion of biased units of information in a message based on that article, social messages were more biased than the news articles. For example, a Reuters article about the GDP contained about 6 percent biased information, but social messages based on that article contained 13 percent biased information. Looking across all the articles and all the messages about them, social messages added about 5.2 percent more biased content.

These relatively short messages are not only dropping a lot of information, as shown in figure 4.1, but they are packing in more bias than was initially present. The differences, however, are subtle. It is not the case that individuals are reading nonpartisan news and passing on completely uninformative propaganda—at least not for the most part. But these subtle differences in how information is presented matter, as I show more fully in chapters 5 and 6. To give a sense of the bias in some of these messages, I provide examples in table 4.1.

These patterns vary by the partisanship of the actively informed person who wrote the message in the first place. Figure 4.2 shows the average percentage of message content that exhibited a Democratic or Republican bias, combining across favoring one party and going against the other. The results show that Democrats wrote messages that contained significantly more information that favored Democrats than that favoring Republicans. Similarly, Republicans transmitted more information that was biased toward Republicans than information that was biased toward Democrats. Both Republicans and Democrats exhibit an in-group bias, but this bias is slightly stronger for Republicans. Republicans transmitted messages that had about 7 percentage points more information that was favorable to Republicans than what was favorable to Democrats; Democrats transmitted about 5 percentage points more information favorable to Democrats than information favorable to Republicans. Although this difference is not statistically significant, it is worth further considering whether—and under what conditions—Republicans and Democrats differ in the degree to which they transmit biased information to others. There is strong evidence of in-group positivity: partisans pass along information that is more positive about their in-group.

TABLE 4.1. Example Messages and Partisan Bias

Study	*Bias*	*Message*	*Partisanship of Informant*
Economic News	Republican bias	It seems that our economy is slowly getting back to a good place despite having so many issues and roadblocks by the Democrats. Even though it's slow going, and not as fast as President Trump predicted, it is still going in a positive direction.	Republican
Economic News	Democratic bias	It seems that the economy is slowly knitting itself back together, no thanks to Trump and the GOP in congress.	Democrat
Economic News	Republican bias	It seems that consumer confidence has been up since Trump won. And that's even with the Democrats trying to dampen economic growth by slowing Trump down in his tax plan. Imagine how it will be once it is passed.	Republican
Economic News	Democratic bias	It seems like the economy is no longer stable. One minute the economy is doing great but then data reflects that is TRULY not! I wish Obama was back in office. At least we saw great improvements with the economy since his early presidency. By the way this article stated the economy has been bad since 2000 I beg to differ!!	Democrat
Immigration Policy Experiment	Republican bias	Joe Biden has screwed everything up at the border. He want to open the flood gates and has no plan to do anything about it.	Republican
Immigration Policy Experiment	Democratic bias	Biden's new immigration policy will help undocumented people inside the United States have a path to citizenship. It is a positive plan that will solve our immigration issues.	Democrat

LESS ACCURATE

While news outlets sometimes intentionally or unintentionally communicate false information, socially transmitted information is likely to be less accurate than information communicated by news outlets. Many news outlets have resources to engage in fact-checking, professional norms and training that promote accurate reporting, and know that they are subject to the scrutiny of third-party fact-checking organizations on publication. The actively

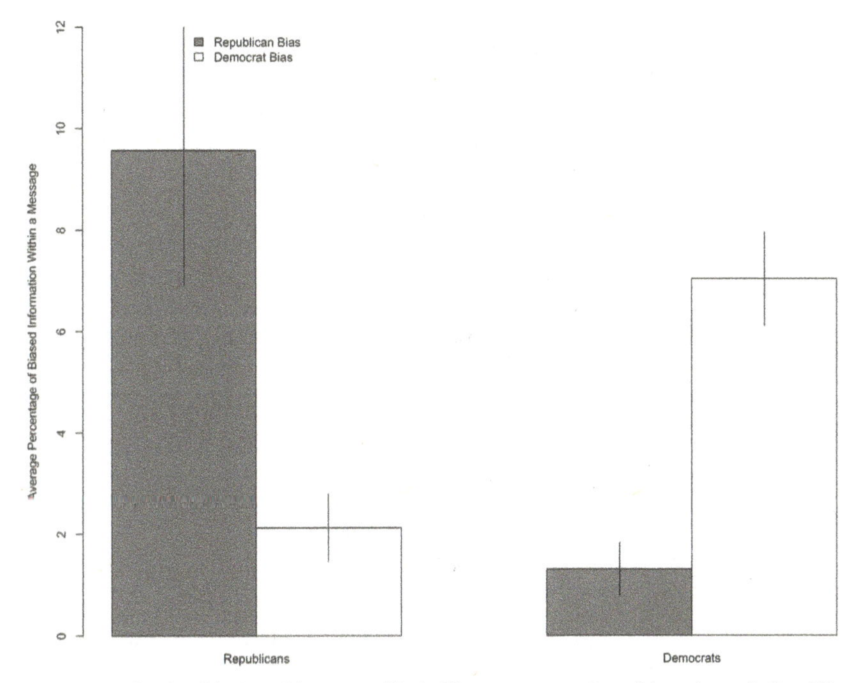

FIGURE 4.2. Partisan bias in social messages. Vertical lines represent 95% confidence intervals. Republican bias includes units of information coded as in favor of Republicans and units of information against Democrats; Democratic bias includes units of information coded as in favor of Democrats and units of information against Republicans. Independents who lean toward a party are coded as partisans. The Y-axis represents the average percentage of biased information within a message. This represents the average number of units of information in a message coded as biased toward Republicans or Democrats, relative to the total number of units of information in the message.

informed do not have these resources or norms holding them accountable, at least not to the same degree. Of course, there are social reputational costs for regularly communicating false information, but when the casually informed are less likely to be equipped to recognize the information as false, these reputational costs are less likely to be effective.

In the studies described in table 3.1, all participants read news articles that did not contain inaccurate information, at least at the time of the data collection and of this writing. How often does social communication introduce false information that was not initially present? Not very often. Across the eight studies, about 4.8 percent of socially transmitted messages contained at least one piece of false information. Is this a lot or a little? This is a normative question without a concrete benchmark. Table 4.2 provides examples of messages that contained false information.

TABLE 4.2. Example Messages with False Information

Study	*Message*	*What Is False*
Economic News	This government has not done anything it had promised. **The economy is slowing down** and even after tax cuts the spending has not gone up. Last year was much better. **The growth rate has decreased.**	The economy was not slowing down; the growth rate did not decrease.
Economic News	It looks like the economy has seen a boost in the **second quarter**, but it is less strong than both anticipated and Trump's promises. Retail and manufacturing are down, while consumer spending is up. The goal is 3% increase, but **it's 1.7%.**	The article was about the first quarter, not the second quarter. GDP was 1.4%, not 1.7%.
Presidential Candidates	There **only 4 democrats** and a lot of republicans. Some of the same familiar faces Hillary Clinton, Mike Hackubee [*sic*]. I personally hope that Rand Pau [*sic*] will win with his limited government.	There were more than four Democrats running at the time.
Presidential Candidates	There are basically two democratic candidates that we have heard about, Clinton and Sanders. Neither good choices, a socialist or a **fraud.** Unfortunately the republican ticket is too crowded, thus not yet creating a united front. Muddying the waters is Donald Trump, who seems to have nothing good to say about others from his party.	No information in the article described a candidate as a fraud.
Environmental Policy Experiment	. . . **climate change is a hoax** that government wants to further their socialist agenda while being so hypocrite about their actions. The democrats and the radical left wants to drain this country and make americans poor and the people.	Conspiracy theory about climate change being a hoax.
Immigration Policy Experiment	This President if undoing the mess your Republican President made of the immigration system. Biden is trying treat these people fairly by offering them paths to citizenship. All you President did was ridicule and shut them out of America. He is a hypocrite when **all he marries is Foreigners.**	Donald Trump has not been married to only immigrants.
Immigration Policy Experiment	That Biden is trying to let in anyone who wants to come in **regardless of their crimes and make them American.**	The policy described in the article still required background checks.

The degree to which the false information contained in these messages would be problematic for democracy is an open question. Typically, when we think about misinformation, topics like egregious political rumors come to mind. The examples in table 4.2 are mild by comparison to conspiracy theories. The false information in table 4.2 for the most part seems likely due to human error in comprehending the article in the first place or in remembering the fine details. Is telling someone that GDP grew at a rate of 1.7 instead of 1.4 going to dramatically change their perceptions of the economy? Probably not. Is telling someone that the economy is slowing down when in fact it is growing likely to affect their perceptions of economic performance? It very well could. These little slips in relaying information accurately to others change the information that the casually informed can use to update their attitudes and behavior. Little by little, these changes to information could have an impact on beliefs, as I demonstrate in chapter 5.

MORE MOBILIZING

I theorized that social messages would be more likely to contain calls to action, encouraging the casually informed to complete specific tasks such as doing additional research, voting, changing their minds, or engaging in some other form of political behavior. This could be because people are motivated to accomplish their political goals and therefore want to encourage others to do their part by taking action. It could also be because of a cognitive bias that favors action over inaction (Patt and Zeckhauser 2000). Regardless of the underlying reason, journalists are constrained by professional norms to avoid calling their readers to action,[3] but the actively informed are not. To investigate whether socially transmitted information is more likely to contain calls to action, a team of research assistants hand-coded the messages from the experiments for explicit calls to action. This coding revealed that about 4.4 percent of social messages included a call to action, compared to *none* of the news articles examined. Importantly, participants in the studies were not prompted to include calls to action in any way, which might make this a conservative estimate.

Although 4.4 percent seems low, it still presents an important shift in the spin the actively informed can place on information from the media. Although none of the articles examined in these experiments included an explicit call to action, they might indirectly mobilize people by providing information that triggers emotions necessary for political action or otherwise inspires political participation (Phoenix 2020). But social messages can similarly provide this information, *in addition to* encouraging people to engage.

TABLE 4.3. Examples of Social Messages with Calls to Action

Study	*Message*
Topic and Source Replication	I just read about the firearm related mortality statistics that there are more deaths related to guns than any other deaths and politicians refuse to do something about it. I think you **should research** about it.
Topic and Source Replication	I read some troubling news today that gun death rates are steadily climbing according to the CDC. They report deaths on the number of people who die by gunshot per 100,000 people. Surprisingly murder rates are noticibly [*sic*] up since 1999. Before you vote in this upcoming election **please educate yourself** in this matter and **vote** for a candidate who sees these statistics as a social priority.
Topic and Source Replication	**Please vote** Democrat at the next election. The rich will get richer and the rest of us will die.
Immigration Policy Experiment	**Please read** the Biden policy carefully. It is convoluted and pro illegal immigration. Also **be familiar** with the accuracy of the idea that possible terrorists and COVID infected individuals are allowed to come in to this country without adequate supervision of their status . . . **Consider how** this might affect our country, law and order and individual constitutional rights that we are fortunate to have in this country called America. **Make your own decision** of your agreement or disagreement with the policies presented by Biden administration.
Immigration Policy Experiment	**Please consider voting** against this Measure. First off they have been saying there are 11 Million Illegals in the Country for Over 20 Years. It's Probably Closer to 25 Million. The New Immigrants are going To Overwhelm are Schools, Hospitals and Welfare Services.
Environmental Policy Experiment	The time is now to **get involved** with climate problems. **Make your voice heard and your vote counted.**
Environmental Policy Experiment	Please understand that shutting down oil drilling effects every aspect of our economy from food prices, healthcare, and the cost of gasoline. It also causes our electricity and heating bills to rise. President is heading this country into a socialist government that is going to destroy America. **Please tell your representatives** in Congress to vote against his plans.

Given the influence that social networks can have on political engagement (Sinclair 2012; Bond et al. 2012), understanding how casual small talk about the news may be more powerful than previously thought. Table 4.3 gives examples of calls to action. They range from simple nudges encouraging people to consider some factors more than others when making political decisions to strong pleas for political action.

Observational Evidence from Twitter

So far I presented evidence that socially transmitted information is sparse, biased, less accurate, and mobilizing, at least relative to the news articles on which the socially transmitted information is based. However, all of this socially transmitted information was generated in an experimental setting in which participants were asked to read an article they might not otherwise choose to read and were asked to write a message to a vaguely described person they might not otherwise want to talk to. Moreover, in most of these studies, the only information the "actively informed" had about the person who would receive their message was their partisanship, which could have amplified partisan motivations (see the critique in Connors, Pietryka, and Ryan 2022).

Analyzing data from Twitter allows me to examine what socially transmitted information looks like "in the wild." Recall that this book is about socially transmitted information, not exclusively social media. Social media is, however, one important space where socially transmitted information is exchanged. I focus on two features available on Twitter at the time of data collection: replies and quote tweets.[4] Replies are similar to a comment on a tweet. If a news outlet tweets an article, for example, followers can comment on it by posting a reply. Depending on the users' privacy settings, other Twitter users can then view the replies (socially transmitted information) alongside the original tweet by the news outlet. Quote tweets are another form of socially transmitted information in which Twitter users can essentially retweet a tweet while adding their own commentary as well. Here other users can view the original tweet, as well as the content written by the Twitter user (the socially transmitted information). According to a 2021 Pew Research Center analysis, 21 percent of news-related tweets were replies and 7 percent were quote tweets (Shearer and Mitchell 2021). In my analysis, I focus specifically on replies to and quote tweets of tweets posted initially by news outlets.

This analysis is not a perfect extension of the two-step flow. But quote tweets and replies do represent an important source of socially transmitted information to which others can be exposed online. Although people choose to quote tweet content for a variety of reasons, it is likely that a quote tweet more closely captures an attempt to summarize the original tweet or article, whereas replies might more closely capture opinion sharing or discussion. Moreover, quote tweets may more closely capture summarizing behavior than the experiments.

In addition to the motivations for people to reply to or quote tweet news outlets online, the types of people who engage in these behaviors may be unique in important ways. Those who reply to tweets by news outlets online might be more interested in politics, stronger partisans, and follow the news more often. All of these characteristics also describe the actively informed, as I demonstrated in chapter 3. This means that the socially transmitted information generated in the replies and quote tweets likely reflects socially transmitted information created by the actively informed on Twitter.

The socially transmitted information on Twitter is, of course, going to differ from socially transmitted information communicated in my experiments and in real-world face-to-face conversations. This means that the analysis is important for two reasons. First, it provides a sense of whether even the broadest patterns of my expectations can be generalized to the social media context. Second, it provides an opportunity for future research to consider developing and testing theories about differences between socially transmitted information communicated on social media and face-to-face.

Finally, in this analysis I narrow my focus to socially transmitted information surrounding a single event. I focus on how the two-step flow shaped the narratives surrounding the Capitol insurrection.

On January 6, 2021, members of the House and Senate gathered to formally count and certify the Electoral College votes from the November 2020 presidential election. What should have been a standard, symbolic action that normally goes unnoticed quickly became international news. With 17 percent of American voters believing that Donald Trump definitely won the November 2020 election (Doherty et al. 2021), some Americans felt it was their duty to stop the certification of Joe Biden's victory. In an effort to "stop the steal," thousands of Americans left a nearby "Save America" rally and marched to the Capitol. Hundreds broke through police barricades, some making their way into the Capitol, vandalizing and looting the historical building for hours. News reporters documented the event as it unfolded, using social media as one way to communicate with the public. I analyze both how news outlets covered the event on Twitter and the related socially transmitted information to highlight the ways in which information became distorted through social transmission online.

Measuring Socially Transmitted Information in the Twittersphere

With teams of collaborators, I created two related datasets, one focusing on replies and the other focusing on quote tweets. To analyze replies, I worked with Erin Rossiter and Dominique Lockett to collect all tweets by a list of news outlets, as well as all replies to those tweets, in the thirty-six-hour period from 12:00 a.m. on January 6, 2021, to 12:00 p.m. on January 7, 2021. The dataset includes 4,753 tweets with nearly half a million (495,019) replies.[5]

I also analyze data collected for a separate research project with Carly Wayne, Erin Rossiter, and Cecilia Sui. We began with the same 4,753 news outlet tweets from the Replies dataset but then collected all publicly available quote tweets. In our dataset, 2,691 of the original tweets by news outlets had at least one publicly available quote tweet, which resulted in a total of 55,127 unique quote tweets.

In each dataset, I estimated how sparse, biased, accurate, and mobilizing the text of the socially transmitted information is compared to the text of the news content. In the Replies dataset, I primarily use dictionary-based methods. In the Quote Tweets dataset, we worked with a team of research assistants to hand-code 9,526 unique quote tweets for the presence of a wide range of ideological themes, topics, emotions, and other characteristics. We used 80 percent of this hand-coded data as a training set for supervised machine learning algorithms to predict the presence of these themes in the rest of the data. The remaining 20 percent of the hand-coded data was withheld for validation. We trained four algorithms (logit, naive Bayesian, support vector machines, and nearest neighbor), and each unlabeled tweet or quote tweet is considered to contain the theme if at least one of the four algorithms coded it as such.

Evidence of Information Distortion on Twitter

Is socially transmitted information on Twitter sparse, biased, less accurate, and mobilizing compared to tweets by news outlets? Answering this question requires a slightly different empirical approach than I applied in analyzing the experiments. With the experiments, it was feasible to hand-code all of the socially transmitted information for each quantity of interest. But hand-coding nearly half a million replies and over 55,000 quote tweets is not feasible. As a result, I relied on machine learning methods and coarse measurement strategies.

First, testing whether socially transmitted information on Twitter is sparse compared to news outlet tweets can be done by comparing the number of words in each. Using a simple measure of the difference between the number of words in the media tweet and the number of words in each reply, I find that replies are on average about six words shorter than the tweets on which they are based. Given that tweets can only be 280 characters,[6] a six-word drop in content is substantial. This provides externally valid evidence that socially transmitted information is sparse compared to information from the news.

Second, evaluating whether replies are more biased than tweets from the media is more challenging. I take two approaches to broadly examine variation in partisan bias and then dig deeper into the overall context of the insurrection to provide more thoughtful insights. First, analyzing the Replies dataset, I used a measure of partisan bias introduced by Kaufman (2014). The method uses congressional speech data from the *Congressional Record* to estimate how often Republicans and Democrats use a given word, giving each word a partisan score. The scores for each word in a document (a reply or original news tweet, for example) are then summed and scaled so that each reply is given a partisan bias score. Although replies to tweets are likely to be very different from the congressional speech to which they are compared, this measure provides at least some insight into the extent to which replies and news tweets are more similar to Democratic or Republican speech.

The results suggest that all tweets and replies during this period contained some degree of Republican bias, which could be shaped in part by the context of the event. The average partisan bias score for the original news tweets was .91, which indicated a stronger Republican bias than the replies, which averaged .87. Although my general expectation is that socially transmitted information (replies) would be more biased than the initial news tweets, the replies could appear to be more neutral simply because both Republican and Democratic Twitter users were actively producing replies, which could result in their respective biases canceling each other out.

Digging deeper into the actual content of the replies and news tweets reveals strong evidence of partisan bias on both sides of the political aisle. To broadly examine the content of these tweets and replies, I examined the top words used by news outlets in their tweets and, separately, the top words used in replies to those tweets. Table 4.4 shows the top words used in news tweets and the top words used in replies, after removing "stop words" such as "the," "and," and "an."

Given the context of the events that unfolded on January 6, the most common words used in tweets by news outlets make sense. All of the words describe the events at the *Capitol*, by *Trump supporters*, who entered the *building*, making their way into the *House* and *Senate* chambers to disrupt the certification of the *Electoral College votes*, despite efforts by *police* to stop them. The top words used in replies to those tweets were remarkably different. Although *Trump* was the most common word and *Capitol* made the list, the socially transmitted information about the insurrection mentioned terrorists and Antifa, a far-left extremist group.

Why would "Antifa" and "terrorist" appear in socially transmitted information about the events at the Capitol? Mentioning Antifa is likely rooted in false flag conspiracy theories. One theory, widely circulated on social media, suggested that the protesters were actually Antifa members trying to make Republicans and Trump supporters look bad. This theory follows a precedent of blaming Antifa for other events, such as mass shootings and wildfires (Dale 2021). The strongest piece of evidence supporting this conspiracy theory was

TABLE 4.4. Most Frequent Words in January 6 Tweets and Comments

News Tweets	*Replies*
Capitol	Trump
Trump	People
Senate	Antifa
President	President
Election	Police
Electoral	Time
Georgia	Capitol
Supporters	Election
Congress	America
House	Country
Live	White
Votes	Supporters
Police	BLM
Biden	Stop
Breaking	News
Joe	Terrorists
College	Biden
Results	Democracy
Trumps	Black
Building	Violence

that John Sullivan, who was known to add #antifa to his tweets, was present at the riots. However, Sullivan's affiliation with Antifa has not been widely accepted, and the theory that Antifa was behind the January 6 insurrection has been discredited by an FBI investigation. Yet the socially transmitted information circulating on Twitter—right next to information from the news—frequently mentioned Antifa. *Antifa* was the third most commonly mentioned word in replies to news articles on January 6. To further contextualize this finding, the word *Antifa* appeared in only 0.4 percent of tweets by news outlets in my dataset, which included right-wing sources, such as Sean Hannity, Breitbart, and Fox News, but *Antifa* appeared in 2.9 percent of all replies made to news tweets. The socially transmitted information circulating on Twitter on January 6 was about seven times more likely to discuss Antifa than the news, even though it was rare overall.

The dominance of Antifa in the socially transmitted information on January 6 most likely reflects how conservatives were discussing the news on that day. However, liberals were likely to change the narrative too but in a different direction. Another word that frequently appeared in replies, but not news tweets, was *terrorists*. On the left side of the aisle, some people considered the insurrection an act of domestic terrorism. Framing the rioters as terrorists instead of "Trump supporters," "protesters," or "patriots" may have important implications for how individuals think about the event. News outlets did not adopt this frame of considering the event an act of terrorism, at least not to nearly the same degree as did everyday users on Twitter. Only 0.5 percent of tweets by news outlets on January 6 included the word *terrorist*, but 2.8 percent of replies did. The socially transmitted information on Twitter about the Capitol insurrection was about six times more likely to discuss terrorists than were tweets by news outlets.

The socially transmitted information that circulated about the riots at the Capitol presented a very different picture of the events than that by news outlets across the political spectrum. The media, broadly construed, presented those involved in the riot as "Trump supporters," but everyday users on Twitter, perhaps largely representing the actively informed, presented them as terrorists and members of Antifa. Others exposed to socially transmitted information about these events could therefore walk away with very different impressions of what actually occurred. Some could become likely to think that this was all part of a big conspiracy theory on the left to hurt the right. Others could develop new fears of domestic terrorism.

Using the Quote Tweets dataset, I used different methods to uncover similar patterns regarding the extent to which socially transmitted information on Twitter is more biased than information communicated by news outlets. Using supervised machine learning, as described previously, we estimated whether quote tweets and the original news tweets were partisan in nature, appealing to partisan logic that clearly identified the two major parties or conservative or liberal ideology.[7] We found that 20.8 percent of quote tweets (socially transmitted information) were partisan, with 10.3 percent of quote tweets being partisan when the original news tweet was not. While the majority of quote tweets were *not* partisan, it was relatively common for users to add partisan content to originally nonpartisan news tweets.

Together, the partisan bias estimates of replies, the contextual analysis of replies, and the supervised estimates of quote tweets suggest that on January 6, 2021, the majority of socially transmitted information on Twitter was *not* biased, but socially transmitted information was *more* biased than information communicated by the media. Although the findings using the Kaufman (2014) measure in the analysis of replies are different from the results from the quote tweets analysis using supervised machine learning, the contextual analysis of the Replies dataset points to socially transmitted information having a more partisan narrative, compared to the narratives produced by news outlets.

Third, I examined whether socially transmitted information on Twitter was less accurate than information communicated by news outlets. Due to the scale of the dataset, this is difficult to accomplish without individually fact-checking each reply and quote tweet, as the team of research assistants was able to do for the experimental data. However, I test this argument to the best of my ability by using the Quote Tweets dataset. While research assistants did not fact-check each quote tweet, they did code for whether the quote tweets contained any conspiratorial content, such as references to QAnon, a specific conspiracy theory, or conspiratorial hashtags or phrases like WWG1WGA.[8] Using the estimates from the machine learning algorithm,[9] we found that 2.4 percent of quote tweets contained conspiratorial content, compared to 2.2 percent of tweets from news outlets. This difference is neither substantively nor statistically significant. However, 2.3 percent of quote tweets of nonconspiratorial news tweets referenced conspiracy theories. This suggests that even if the news is not discussing conspiracy theories, when people relay that information online they are more likely to add conspiratorial content to the conversation.

It is also important to consider these percentages in context. There were far more quote tweets than original tweets by news outlets, meaning that the denominator is much larger for the quote tweets than the parent tweets. Moreover, another way to think about the importance of conspiratorial content online is to consider the volume rather than the percentage. Figure 4.3 presents the average number of quote tweets and news tweets per hour that were classified as conspiratorial during the insurrection at the Capitol. The vertical dashed line shows the moment the protesters breached the Capitol. The figure demonstrates that socially transmitted information on Twitter (quote tweets, in this case) was more likely to reference conspiracy theories, especially in the moments immediately following the breach, reaching over one hundred conspiratorial quote tweets per hour at its peak. Of course, there are simply more quote tweets total than there are original news tweets, so the figure exaggerates the difference between socially transmitted information and information from news outlets. But the broader point remains that the conspiratorial content communicated on Twitter during the insurrection was dominated by socially transmitted information rather than the news.

There are two final points to consider with respect to the results in figure 4.3. First, the vast majority of tweets—whether they are from news outlets or quote tweets of news tweets—are not conspiratorial. The overall percentage of conspiratorial content on Twitter is low. Second, even over the course of a powerful event that resulted in part from conspiracy theories about election fraud, the amount of conspiratorial content in socially transmitted

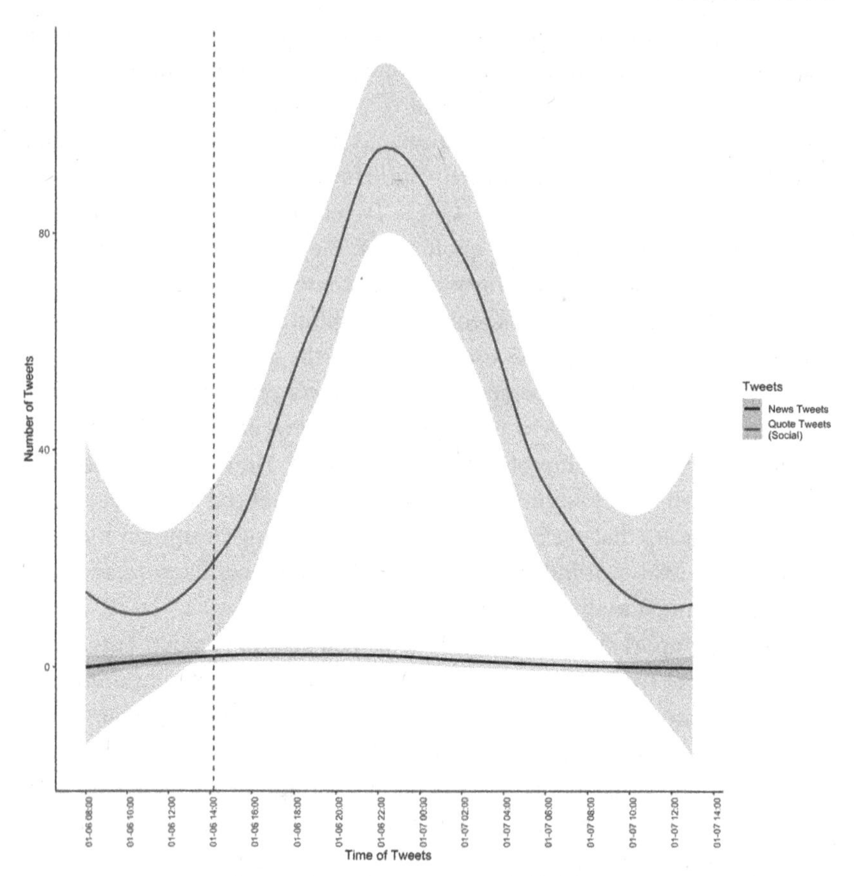

FIGURE 4.3. Conspiratorial tweets during the insurrection. The black line shows the number of tweets posted by news outlets that were classified as conspiratorial; the gray line shows the number of conspiratorial quote tweets of news tweets. Shaded gray bands reflect 95% confidence intervals. The dashed line at 14:10 represents the approximate time at which the protesters breached the Capitol.

information on Twitter declined quickly. Just as news stories wax and wane in their attention and coverage, so too do conspiracy theories online. Both of these points might lead to a more optimistic interpretation of socially transmitted information.

Finally, I investigated the presence of mobilizing calls to action contained in socially transmitted information on Twitter on January 6. First, in the Replies dataset, I created a list of mobilizing words based on the context of the insurrection and the results from the experiments. I then tabulated whether at least one of these words was present in each reply and each parent tweet in the dataset. I found that 12 percent of the original news tweets (572 unique tweets) contained at least one mobilizing word, whereas 6 percent of all replies contained at least one mobilizing word (29,796 total replies). While a greater percentage of news tweets were mobilizing, compared to replies, the raw volume of mobilizing content is remarkable. Moreover, there is an important growth in mobilization worth noting. Looking exclusively at news tweets that did not include a call to action, 4.5 percent of replies to these tweets included a call to action. Even when the original news tweet does not call people to action, 4.5 percent of the relevant socially transmitted information does.

In the Quote Tweets dataset, I have a bit more leverage on this question because our research team hand-coded the quote tweets for both whether they included an explicit call to action and whether they called people to *violent* action, which could have been particularly relevant in the context of the Capitol insurrection.[10] Just as with the Replies dataset, the vast majority of quote tweets did *not* contain calls to action. Only 3.1 percent of quote tweets called readers to action and 0.7 percent called readers to *violent* action. Importantly, looking only at the quote tweets of the 1,339 news tweets that were *not* mobilizing, 2.3 percent called people to action. This suggests that socially transmitted information can *add* mobilizing calls to action that were not initially present. Although explicit calls to violence are extremely rare in quote tweets overall, even on a day when we might expect this to be more common, there were still 1,568 quote tweets that included an explicit call to violence, compared to only 260 tweets by news outlets. Moreover, these percentages could underestimate the true amount of calls to violence because other quote tweets containing such calls could have been removed from Twitter before our data collection.

It is also worth noting that the calls to action in socially transmitted information occurred across the ideological spectrum. Some quote tweets encouraged the protesters, saying things like, "Get the job done." Others condemned the protesters and President Trump, calling on leaders to invoke the Twenty-Fifth Amendment, on law enforcement to "arrest these terrorists," and on the public to "stop spreading lies" and "get over it." Although the actions observed on January 6 were largely performed by Trump supporters, socially transmitted information on Twitter included calls to action from both the left and the right.

Altogether, a common theme across the analysis of socially transmitted information on Twitter is that the information distortions I examined, such as bias, inaccuracy, and mobilization, are rare overall but more common in socially transmitted information than in information from the news. This echoes a similar pattern uncovered in the experiments but in an entirely different context without researcher intervention.

Conclusion

In this chapter, I argued that as the actively informed transmit information about the news to their casually informed peers, the informational content becomes sparse, more biased, less accurate, and more mobilizing. In so doing, I attempted to paint a portrait of the ways in which information changes when it comes to the riveting tales of the news and political discussion. But just as two actively informed people can look at the same news article differently, there are different ways in which the results presented in this chapter can be interpreted. One interpretation takes on a dark view of just how distorted information really becomes; the other is more optimistic.

Those whose glasses are half empty might interpret the evidence in this chapter as appalling. I first showed that socially transmitted information is sparse relative to the news articles on which it is based. The evidence here is that socially transmitted information contains fewer words and fewer units of information than news articles, often orders of magnitude fewer. The casually informed are therefore exposed to far less information than their actively informed peers, and they could access far more information if they simply read the news themselves instead of relying on their peers. I then showed that what little information remains for the casually informed to learn is packaged in fresh, perhaps unexpected partisan bias. I showed that social messages contained significantly more partisan bias than the news articles on which they were based and that partisans tend to transmit information that benefits their party and disparages the other. While news outlets initially communicated information that was balanced between the two parties, that balance tilted to favor the actively informed partisan through social transmission. If we thought partisan news media was a problem for democratic functioning, we should expect partisan bias in socially transmitted information to be problematic too. I also showed that 4.8 percent of social messages contained at least one statement that was inaccurate, even when they were based on initially accurate news articles. This is a substantial increase from 0, which is the percentage of false information in the news articles used in my studies, and could contribute to the growth and spread of misinformation that currently plagues American democracy. Finally, the information communicated contains explicit calls to action alongside partisan bias, misinformation, and a dramatic loss of information. A pessimist might be most troubled by this finding because it may suggest that the casually informed are being mobilized to act based on questionable information.

However, people whose glasses are half full might interpret these results differently. Although the dramatic decline in the amount of information is hard to dispute, it is possible that the actively informed are able to sufficiently package information from news articles more succinctly. They might be able to identify and transmit key details without the nuance described in a news article. Whether this nuance is helpful or necessary for the casually informed remains to be seen, but perhaps simply having *less* information is not necessarily a problem. Furthermore, if the casually informed would otherwise be obtaining no information at all, perhaps even the sparse information communicated by the actively informed is the preferable alternative.

Thinking about bias, some might not be very concerned about these findings either. I found that social messages communicated about 5.2 percent more biased content than news articles, but this varied across studies, topics, and initial news sources. Perhaps 5.2 percent more bias is not large enough to provoke deep concern. Alternatively, perhaps these results echo a broader point raised by Soroka and Wlezien (2022) that the accuracy of information communicated by the news varies across different domains. Broadly arguing that partisan bias in information is always bad for democracy might be misplaced. Similarly, it is possible that the magnitude of the effect of the amount of inaccurate information communicated is negligible. While 4.8 percent of socially transmitted messages contained false information that was not initially present in the news article, 95.2 percent of messages did not communicate any false information.

Finally, when it comes to mobilization, optimists might not be very concerned that messages become more mobilizing because they might not be concerned about the quality of socially transmitted information to begin with. But let us assume that optimists are concerned about the quality of information. They might not be convinced that the information communicated is actually more mobilizing. Again, the percentage of mobilizing messages was relatively small, even if it was greater than in the news articles. Moreover, many of the mobilizing messages encourage people to do more research, which could counteract any of the informational quality problems raised by socially transmitted information. Ultimately, optimists might conclude that information changes through social transmission but not necessarily in ways that hurt American democracy.

How do we reconcile these two ways of interpreting the results from this chapter? The answer comes in the chapters that follow. Here I sought to characterize some of the ways in which information changes as it flows from the media to the actively informed to the casually informed. While some of the effect sizes and changes are subtle, it is hard to refute that the content changes in some way. To address whether these information distortions distort democracy, we need to consider the effect that socially transmitted information has on political learning, attitudes, and engagement. In the chapters that follow, I randomize exposure to socially transmitted information, as exemplified in this chapter, or information from the news, or sometimes no information at all to examine the extent to which the type of information to which someone is exposed affects their ability to learn about politics, develop opinions about related policies, and participate.

5
Underinformed

In 2013, the late-night TV personality Jimmy Kimmel and his team took to the streets to conduct their own public opinion survey. The team asked passersby whether they preferred the Affordable Care Act or Obamacare.[1] Respondents emphatically weighed in on their preference, failing to recognize that they are the same thing, even offering reasons they preferred one policy over the other. One respondent considered Obamacare "un-American" but not the Affordable Care Act. When asked if Obamacare was socialist, another person responded "yes" without hesitation. When asked if the Affordable Care Act was socialist, the same person replied "no."

While Kimmel's interviews certainly do not follow best practice techniques of random sampling and the most entertaining clips are chosen to air on the show, the segment highlighted a broader point about American politics that political behavior scholars have studied for decades. Far from the ideals of a democratic citizenry (Habermas 1984; Lipset 1960; Berelson, Lazarsfeld, and McPhee 1954; Campbell et al. 1960), the American public is often viewed as ill informed about politics (Delli Carpini and Keeter 1996; Campbell et al. 1960; Bartels 1996).[2] Consider this laundry list of ill-informed beliefs about the American political system:

- In 2019, only 39 percent of Americans could correctly name all three branches of government, the highest percentage in five years.[3]
- In 2019, about a quarter of Americans reported that they did not know which party controlled the House and the Senate.[4]
- In 2017, 39 percent of Americans incorrectly thought that the US Constitution gave the president (rather than Congress) the power to declare war.[5]

- In 2010, 72 percent of Americans could not correctly identify John Roberts as the Chief Justice of the US Supreme Court. Among this uninformed group, 53 percent openly reported that they did not know, 4 percent named the senator Harry Reid, and 8 percent named Thurgood Marshall, who had never served as chief justice and had been dead for seventeen years at the time of the survey.[6]

Despite the troubling nature of these statistics, some scholars argue that we should not be so worried about their consequences for the functioning of American democracy. It is possible that voters do not need to be well informed about politics to vote in line with their interests if they can use reliable heuristics, such as partisanship (Lau and Redlawsk 1997; Popkin 1991; Lupia 1994). But what if individuals were not just uninformed but misinformed? What if they were not just unaware of what was happening in the news or how government worked, but instead believed flatly false information to be true—and believed it passionately? Even heuristics could struggle to help a *mis*informed voter. Some argue that misinformation could be a more dangerous threat to American democracy than a lack of information (Flynn, Nyhan, and Reifler 2017).

Misinformation has been widely studied in recent years, and colorful examples abound. On March 12, 2016, President Donald Trump spoke at a rally, where a twenty-two-year-old political activist, Thomas DiMassimo, stormed the stage in an effort to make his voice heard. DiMassimo was quickly detained by the Secret Service, which Trump praised in a tweet later that day: "USSS did an excellent job stopping the maniac running to the stage. He has ties to ISIS. Should be in jail!" The fact is that there is not now, nor was there at the time, any evidence that DiMassimo had ties to ISIS.[7] This tweet containing some false information was "liked" over 20,000 times and retweeted more than 11,000 times. This wide-reaching, misinformative tweet quickly morphed into a twisted web of misinformation even more distanced from the truth.

On the other side of the political aisle, the 9/11 Truth Movement argues that the September 11 attacks were an "inside job." Movement supporters, primarily Democrats opposed to President George W. Bush, point to gaps in information in the National Institute of Standards and Technology report that appears to be a cover-up by government insiders (Byler and Woodsome 2021). The idea is that the attacks gave the George W. Bush administration justification to pursue the wars in Iraq and Afghanistan. While this theory has been widely discredited, it has not been without political consequence. Jeff Boss, a leader of the 9/11 Truth Movement, ran for president on a 9/11

Truth platform in several elections; he also ran for the US Senate and the New Jersey governorship.[8]

Misinformation takes many forms, not limited to conspiracy theories. Some misinformation is much less convoluted but potentially influential all the same. For example, in March 2021, some social media posts implied that Joe Biden was not really the president of the United States because he had not yet delivered the State of the Union address and had not been seen using the "real" Air Force One.[9] In December 2019, Democratic Speaker of the House, Nancy Pelosi, tweeted that a voter roll purge would mean "more than 200,000 registered Wisconsin voters will be prohibited from voting," which Politifact gave a false rating of "pants on fire."[10] The list goes on and on.

It is possible—even likely—that most Americans are unaware of or do not believe these rumors and false statements. But public opinion surveys indicate that nontrivial portions of the public are indeed misinformed. Below are some examples of misinformed beliefs held by members of the American public.

- In 2015, 17 percent of Americans believed that Barack Obama is Muslim.[11]
- In 2020, 15 percent of Americans believed that there was evidence that Barack Obama was not born in the United States.[12]
- In 2020, 29 percent of Americans believed that a group of unelected government officials in Washington, DC, referred to as the "Deep State," has been working to undermine the Trump administration.[13]
- In September 2020, 25 percent of Americans believed that there was widespread voter fraud in the 2016 election.[14]
- In 2020, 36 percent of Americans believed that corporations are promoting genetically modified foods (GMOs) that have been shown to be harmful to human health.[15]

Understanding both the lack of information (uninformed) and the prevalence of false information (misinformed) in American politics is important to the public, journalists, and scholars alike. These two aspects of the American political psyche form the first component of distorted democracy: being *underinformed*.

Americans can be underinformed for many reasons. They might pay too little attention to the news (Prior 2009; Wojcieszak et al. 2023; Kim 2023). They might engage in biased information processing that inhibits their ability to form and internalize accurate beliefs (Redlawsk 2006; Lodge and Taber 2013). They might also be exposed to biased reporting in the media or even deliberately false content (Garrett, Weeks, and Neo 2016; Weeks 2018; Weeks et al. 2021). Intertwined through these explanations is the idea that people can also become underinformed when they learn about politics via conversations with their friends and family.

I focus on the latter explanation: people become underinformed when they learn about politics via socially transmitted information. Recall from chapters 2 and 3 that the two-step flow was initially viewed as a process through which the public can be self-educating. For example, Berelson and colleagues (1954, 114) argued that the relationship between opinion leaders and their followers "is a useful instrument in democratic life," helping inform an otherwise ignorant public. However, this claim was made without much consideration for the content of the information that opinion leaders share with their peers. As I demonstrated in chapter 4, socially transmitted information is distorted in important ways, relative to information directly from the media, that might inhibit someone's ability to learn effectively. Considering how information changes through conversation might foster skepticism about the utility of the two-step flow for increasing political knowledge and awareness.

In this chapter, I build on the empirical findings presented in chapter 4 to examine the extent to which social transmission of political information affects the extent to which people are informed and misinformed. Using an experiment presented in a previously published article (Carlson 2019), I find that when individuals receive information from another person's summary of a news article, they learn significantly less than those who read the full news article, suggesting that socially transmitted information can lead individuals to be less informed. However, I find that if individuals receive information from someone who is more knowledgeable than they are and is a copartisan, they can actually learn just as much as if they had read the full news article themselves. This is good news for the two-step flow, for the self-educating public, and for the casually informed Americans who generally do not read the news. The findings suggest that some political conversations, between certain types of actively and casually informed people, can indeed substitute for reading the news, at least when it comes to how much individuals are able to learn.

Although the actively informed can help their casually informed copartisan peers learn, they also (ironically) have the power to *misinform* them. I use data from three nationally representative surveys to explore whether the casually informed are more likely to be misinformed. I find that the casually informed are often, but not always, more likely to believe false statements than are the actively informed. Moreover, when asked to specifically recall where they learned about whether a given statement was true or false, misinformed people were more likely to point to conversations with other people than were correctly informed people. I complement these correlational findings with experimental evidence that (1) exposure to socially transmitted information from a copartisan causes the casually informed to become misinformed; and (2) exposure to misinformative socially transmitted information on Facebook posts increases misbeliefs, even when presented alongside accurate information from a news outlet. I close the chapter by considering whether the evidence as a whole reveals a distorted or dysfunctional democracy.

Are the Casually Informed Uninformed?

In chapter 3, I showed that the casually informed pay less attention to politics than the actively informed, which is almost tautological. While this pattern could suggest that the casually informed are uninformed about politics, it could also be the case that they are simply good at using their actively informed peers as a shortcut.

The question of whether the casually informed are uninformed has been probed by two main lines of research, which both generally answer "no," suggesting that political conversations can at least partially substitute for directly reading the news. The first approach uses nicely controlled lab experiments in which some participants are given information about two candidates, such as their policy positions on issues, presented numerically on a scale, and other participants are not given such information. Participants can communicate back and forth. Researchers have used this general approach to introduce incentives to simply learn (accuracy) or try to get their preferred candidate elected (directional) (Pietryka 2016), to measure whether participants with information will send accurate information to others (Ahn, Huckfeldt, and Ryan 2014), and to ultimately measure whether initially uninformed participants are able to utilize socially transmitted information in a way that helps them vote in line with their interests. The results generally suggest that socially transmitted information can be a valuable shortcut: people can learn more than they would have absent any information at all, but they also open themselves to the possibility of being misled, especially if they receive information from someone who does not share their preferences. This line of research suggests that the electorate can be self-educating, but it happens through a process that is inherently *political* (Ahn, Huckfeldt, and Ryan 2014).

The second approach steps away from the controlled environment of the lab and measures the effects of political discussion networks on political knowledge. This research typically uses a name generator, where participants are asked to list about five people with whom they discuss politics or important matters (Sokhey and Djupe 2014; Klofstad, McClurg, and Rolfe 2009).

They then answer questions about those people, such as how frequently they discuss politics with them, whether they agree or disagree with each person, how knowledgeable they think the person is, and so forth. Researchers then use this information to analyze how the features of one's political discussion network correlate with their own political knowledge.

As many researchers note, however, these patterns are fraught with endogeneity issues. In this example, it is hard for researchers to know whether people who discuss politics more often are more knowledgeable because of these conversations or because they were already more knowledgeable in the first place and their political awareness leads them to have these discussions. But this line of research suggests that those who discuss politics more frequently have higher levels of political knowledge than those who discuss politics less frequently (Eveland and Hively 2009), especially when discussion networks are heterogeneous, meaning they have a mix of people with different partisan identities or preferences. Using a mix of the discussion network approach and the experimental approach, Ryan (2011) finds that political discussion can increase political knowledge but primarily when discussions are between people of differing knowledge levels. Importantly, he finds that people overestimate how knowledgeable their peers are, which could lead them astray.

While extant research suggests that political conversations can, under many conditions, increase political knowledge, there is reason to be cautious in encouraging everyone to discuss politics to save the nation from the low levels of political awareness noted at the opening of this chapter. First, some of the experimental work suggests that individuals can become misled by socially transmitted information. For example, Krupnikov et al. (2020) find that women are more reliant on socially transmitted information than men and are more likely to be misled when they rely on that information. Ahn, Huckfeldt, and Ryan (2014) find that individuals learn less when they receive information from someone who does not share their existing political preferences.

Second, the methods used in both approaches leave room for improvement in our theoretical understanding of the relationship between conversations and how much people know about politics. The network approaches suffer from endogeneity concerns, as the authors generously acknowledge. Those who talk about politics more often are likely already more politically knowledgeable, for example. The experimental approaches, as I argued in chapters 2 and 3, do not capture the complexities of language that can lead to different types of information distortions that can affect knowledge. Neither approach highlights the effect of the content of the information itself on political knowledge.

APPROACH: TELEPHONE GAME EXPERIMENT

In an effort to remedy some of these challenges to existing approaches used to understand whether conversations can substitute for the news in informing the public, I turn to an experimental design that I introduce and apply in two previous articles (Carlson 2018, 2019). As described in chapter 3, these telephone game experiments are not perfect, but they offer many advantages in trying to measure not only how information changes, but how it affects political learning.

The idea is that one group of participants first engages in a telephone game experiment like those analyzed in chapter 4. They read a news article and write a message to someone else telling them about the article that they just read. The instructions are kept intentionally vague to help participants feel free to pass along information that they would consider in reality. In this study, participants read an article published by Reuters, which Budak, Goel, and Rao (2016) identify as a relatively nonpartisan source. The article was about US economic performance, in terms of GDP in the first quarter of 2017. The gist of the article (if you trust me to deliver an accurate, unbiased summary!) is that GDP grew at a rate of 1.4 percent in the first quarter, which is revised up from previous estimates. Although this marks economic growth, the Trump administration promised 3 percent growth, a figure that falls short, as mentioned specifically in the article. Participants were then randomly assigned to write messages to a Republican, a Democrat, or an Independent.

I then fielded a second study on a fresh sample of participants. In this experiment, participants answered six true-or-false questions about the topic of the article that the participants in the first study read.[16] They then answered distractor questions and proceeded to the experiment. Here participants were randomly assigned to read the same news article that participants in the first study read (Media treatment) or one of the messages that the first study participants wrote summarizing that article (Social treatment). The experiment concludes by asking participants to respond to the same true-or-false questions posed at the beginning of the survey. By comparing performance on this "quiz" before and after exposure to information, I could measure how much participants learned, depending on the type of information they received.

ANSWER: YES, EXCEPT UNDER SPECIAL CIRCUMSTANCES

I consider learning in three layers. First, I examine whether participants answered more questions correctly after exposure to *any* information, regardless of whether they received that information via a full news article or another person's summary of that article. Participants learned! On average, participants answered 3.33 questions correctly at baseline and 3.54 questions correctly after exposure to an information treatment. This difference is statistically significant.

Information matters, but not all information is created equally. The second layer of analysis is to examine whether people learned more from the full news article or from the social summaries of those articles. I find that participants who read the full news article answered significantly more questions correctly than those who received a social message. This suggests that the casually informed are less informed than the actively informed. Information sources can cause some individuals to learn more than others, and in this case, it is those who receive socially transmitted information who are worse off.

This initial finding might lead readers to want to put an asterisk next to all the seminal research on the two-step flow. This is *not* what I would suggest, for two reasons. First, those who received socially transmitted information did show evidence of learning. This indicates that individuals still walked away from their "conversation," to put it generously, knowing more than they would have otherwise. While I did not directly compare participants who received socially transmitted information to participants who received no information at all, the within-subjects component of the design gives me some hope that socially transmitted information is not entirely useless; it is just not as influential on learning as is a full news article.

Second, there is yet another layer of analysis that needs to be interrogated to fully think through the conditions under which socially transmitted information might help people learn. The seminal research on the two-step flow suggests that the ideal informant is someone who shares the recipient's partisanship and is more knowledgeable than the recipient. It is this specific type of informant that should be a decent substitute for consuming the news directly. As shown in figure 5.1, this is exactly what I find in this study. If I break down the socially transmitted information treatment condition into groups based on features of the informant (the Study 1 participant who wrote the message) and the recipient (the Study 2 participant who read the message), I find that when individuals received information from someone who identified with the same political party *and* was more knowledgeable about the news topic than they were at baseline, they were able to learn just as much as those who received the full news article. In contrast, those who received information from someone who did not meet these two criteria showed no evidence of learning at all.

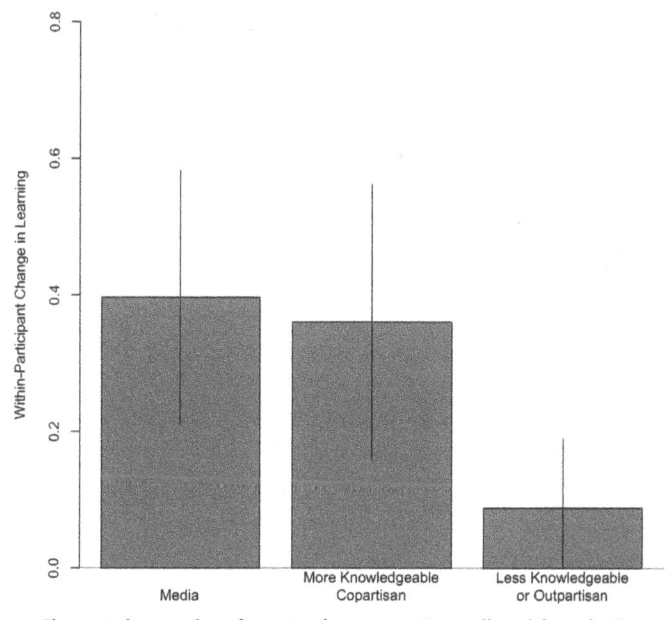

FIGURE 5.1. Change in learning by informational treatment. Data collected from the Economic News Study. Participants were randomly assigned to read the full Reuters news article (Media bar) or a message written by a Study 1 participant who read that article. Learning was measured as the difference in the number of correct answers to 6 true or false questions about economic performance before and after exposure to randomly assigned information. Vertical lines represent 95% confidence intervals.

Thinking through these layers to understanding how information source affects learning leads to a few important conclusions. Consistent with the two-step flow theory, individuals can indeed learn from their peers. This indicates that the casually informed are on average not entirely *uninformed*, but they are *less informed* than their actively informed peers who read full news articles. But when the actively informed are more knowledgeable and share the same partisan identity as their casually informed peers, they can essentially bring their casually informed peers up to their level of knowledge, compensating for the lack of attention to the news media.

Are these conditions likely to be met in reality? That is, are the casually informed most likely to receive information from their more knowledgeable copartisans? Most political conversations occur between copartisans. That criterion should be relatively easily satisfied in the real world. The challenge is to find conversations between people with different knowledge levels. In other work, Jaime Settle and I find that individuals are uncomfortable discussing politics with others who are more knowledgeable than they are (Carlson and Settle 2022). Moreover, there is evidence that individuals are not always able to figure out how knowledgeable people are about politics. For example, Ryan (2011) finds that individuals tend to overestimate how knowledgeable their friends are about politics. Jaime Settle and I also find evidence of this knowledge overestimation in a lab experiment reported in chapters 6 and 7 of our book (Carlson and Settle 2022). This means that even if someone was comfortable talking with someone who knows more and wanted to reap the benefits of the two-step flow, they might *think* they are talking to someone who is knowledgeable, but this might not be the case.

Are the Casually Informed Misinformed?

In this section, I unpack the consequences of socially transmitted information for becoming *misinformed.* As discussed at the beginning of this chapter, misinformed beliefs are widespread in the American public and scholars have dedicated significant attention to understanding these beliefs—and their consequences for democracy. Some of the research on political rumors, one particular type of misinformation, argues that a key feature characterizing rumors is that they spread socially. Yet little research to date has examined directly the extent to which individuals who believe these falsehoods actually become misinformed through interpersonal, social channels. I demonstrated descriptively in chapter 4 that social messages sometimes contain misinformation, even when they are based on articles that did not contain false information. Do political conversations facilitate misinformed beliefs? Are the casually informed more likely to be misinformed?

I argue that taking a step back to think about how individuals encounter misinformation in the first place is crucial. I argue that social information transmission is uniquely suited to facilitate the spread of misinformation while flying under the radar, escaping fact-checkers who try to set the record straight. Although the actively informed might be well intentioned, they can (and occasionally do, as shown in chapter 4) pass along false information to their casually informed peers. Without additional context, such as competing perspectives from other sources, fact checks, or information about what the original source was, the casually informed could be exposed to a stronger dose of misinformation than their actively informed peers.

APPROACH: SURVEY DATA

I test this argument using data from three nationally representative surveys. In each survey, I examine the correlational relationship between preferred information source (i.e., whether someone is casually or actively informed, using a variety of operationalizations unique to each survey) and the extent to which they report believing prominent political rumors and conspiracy theories. In each case, I consider those who reported the incorrect response to be misinformed and compare this group to everyone else, including those who knew the correct answer and those who reported that they were not sure.[17] These analyses are not causal. I have not randomly assigned participants to receive (mis)information from either another person or the news media. In each study I do my best to rule out confounding factors, but the results still need to be interpreted with caution.

ANSWER: YES, BUT IT'S COMPLICATED

How would we know if the casually informed are more likely to be misinformed? One simple, albeit imperfect, way is to ask them. I use survey data to simply measure whether the percentage of people who are misinformed on the wide range of misinformation measured across these surveys is higher among the casually informed than the actively informed.[18] I present the results in table 5.1, ordered by the percentage of the casually informed who believe each piece of misinformation.

Across almost all pieces of misinformation measured in these surveys, a greater percentage of the casually informed were misinformed, compared to the actively informed. However, these gaps are only statistically significant at conventional thresholds in a handful of cases. For example, in 2020, 28.7 percent of the casually informed believed that Obama was born outside the United States, compared to 16.5 percent of the actively informed. All three surveys measured beliefs that Obama was born outside of the United States and beliefs that Obama is Muslim. In all three cases, the casually informed were more likely to believe that these false statements were true, but the gaps between the casually and the actively informed varied, with most differences being statistically indistinguishable.

There are also two notable cases where the actively informed were more likely to believe the misinformation than were the casually informed: the Bush administration misleading the public about the presence of WMDs in Iraq and Obama removing the citizenship question from the 2010 census. Although previous research has used the WMD item (e.g., Miller, Saunders, and Farhart 2016), it is possible that the item wording here did not make it sound particularly conspiratorial and instead was more consistent with mass media narratives. As for the census item, more than half of the respondents reported that they did not know, including more than two-thirds of the casually informed, compared to only about half of the actively informed. Coding those who reported that they did not know as correctly informed dramatically shifted the outcome on this item. Indeed, when don't know responses are instead removed from this analysis, the gap is no longer statistically significant.

Examining the simple bivariate relationships in survey data is a useful starting place, but it presents a nuanced picture. One person might look at table 5.1 and think that the rightmost column is most troubling: nontrivial portions of Americans who actively consume the news are still misinformed. Another person might look at table 5.1 and feel underwhelmed given the problems of interpreting the results. After all, in the vast majority of cases, the casually informed and the actively informed are (statistically) equally misinformed. Another person still might want more than a simple bivariate analysis to be convinced one way or the other. For that, I turn to four additional tests, each tackling the question from a slightly different angle.

Confounds and Selection into Treatment

The top-line results in table 5.1 do not account for the many ways in which casually and actively informed Americans are different from each other in ways that can be correlated with their belief in misinformation. For example, the casually informed have lower levels of trust in mainstream media to report the news fairly, which has been previously shown to correlate with conspiratorial beliefs and misinformation (Pennycook and Rand 2019).

To address this concern about confounding variables like trust in media affecting the results presented in table 5.1, I conducted a series of regressions in which the dependent variable was whether the respondent was misinformed (1) or not (0) and the independent variable was an indicator for whether the respondent was casually (1) or actively (0) informed. As a first check, I simply controlled for a variety of political, demographic, and personality characteristics in the models, but I pushed this further and used matching to create a pruned dataset in which the actively and the casually informed were similar to each other on observable characteristics.[19] The observable characteristics available varied from one survey to the next. In the 2016 CCAP data, I matched on trust in media, trust in government, ideology, interest in politics, gender, ethnicity/race, education, and age. In the 2017 Original Survey, I matched on age, gender, ethnicity/race, education, and party identification. In the 2020 TASS data, I matched on age, gender, ethnicity/race, education, trust in media, urban residence, and party identification. The CCAP and TASS data include survey weights in the matching algorithm.

TABLE 5.1. Belief in Misinformation by the Casually and the Actively Informed

	Survey	*Percent of the Casually Informed who Believe*	*Percent of the Actively Informed who Believe*
The Bush administration misled the public about the presence of WMDs in Iraq.	2017 Original Survey	**42**	**53.3**
The government knew about 9/11.	2017 Original Survey	**35**	**26**
Obama is Muslim.	2017 Original Survey	**34.0**	**22.8**
Obama was born outside the United States.	2020 TASS	**28.7**	**16.5**
Obama was born outside the United States.	2016 CCAP	27.9	16.0
Obama was born outside the United States.	2017 Original Survey	27.3	21.9
Obama is Muslim.	2016 CCAP	26.7	24.3
Obama is Muslim.	2020 TASS	24.7	19.7
President Trump donates his salary to different government initiatives each quarter.	2020 TASS	19.5	24.8
Nancy Pelosi diverted Social Security money to the impeachment inquiry into President Trump.	2020 TASS	17.9	15.2
Obama removed the citizenship question from the 2010 census.	2020 TASS	**14.8**	**24.3**
Global warming is a hoax.	2017 Original Survey	13	17.5
Death Panels were part of the Affordable Care Act.	2017 Original Survey	13	16.5
Republicans stole the 2004 election via voter fraud in Ohio.	2017 Original Survey	12	16.3
The levee breach during Hurricane Katrina was intentional.	2017 Original Survey	12	12.5
Senate Majority Leader Mitch McConnell's biggest campaign donor is a Russian oligarch.	2020 TASS	7.8	10.3

Note. Boldface percentages reflect statistically significant differences at $p < .10$. Percentages from the 2020 TASS and 2016 CCAP surveys use weights provided by the survey vendor. No weights are available for the 2017 Original Survey. The measure for casually or actively informed for the 2017 Original Survey was calculated by taking the reported percentage of information respondents reported getting from other people and coding those who reported getting 50% or more of their information from others as casually informed and those getting less than 50% from others as actively informed, but results are generally similar if this threshold is changed to become more conservative (e.g., requiring a greater percentage of information to come from others to be considered casually informed).

Using this pruned, matched dataset, I estimated a logistic regression model for each piece of misinformation available in the dataset. I then simulated the predicted probability of being misinformed if one was casually or actively informed.[20] Because most of the matching variables are categorical, results from the simulations vary depending on the values selected. Holding variables at their modes seemed atheoretical in this context, and because the matching process obtained relative balance on these covariates, I simulated the predicted probabilities without controls.

After matching on observable characteristics, the casually and actively informed were equally likely to believe misinformation on most pieces of misinformation measured. However, where there are statistically significant differences between the groups, the casually informed were more likely to be misinformed than the actively informed. Figure 5.2 shows the predicted probability of believing Obama was born outside the United States and is Muslim from the 2016 CCAP data. The results show that the casually informed are about twice as likely to be misinformed on these topics as their actively informed counterparts. Figure 5.3 shows a similar pattern but examines more pieces of misinformation in the 2017 Original Survey. The casually informed were significantly more likely to (incorrectly) believe that 9/11 was an inside job and that Obama is Muslim. Figure 5.4 shows the results from the 2020 TASS data, which indicate that the casually informed were more likely to (incorrectly) believe that Obama was born outside the United States but that the actively informed were more likely to (incorrectly) believe that Obama removed the citizenship question from the 2010 census. Notably, on most of the pieces of misinformation examined, the difference between the actively and casually informed was not statistically significant.

Taken together, this analysis highlights at minimum a likely possibility that receiving information from others makes one more likely to be misinformed, even if the overall likelihood that one becomes misinformed is relatively low. However, even after using matching to make the casually and actively informed as similar to one another on observable characteristics as possible, there are still a host of unobserved traits that could be driving the patterns observed. I investigate some of these possibilities in the next section.

Alternative Explanations

One question stemming from these results is whether misbeliefs are really driven by someone's preferred information source or whether we would observe the same result by analyzing gaps based on other characteristics like trust in government or education. The matching analysis should rule out this

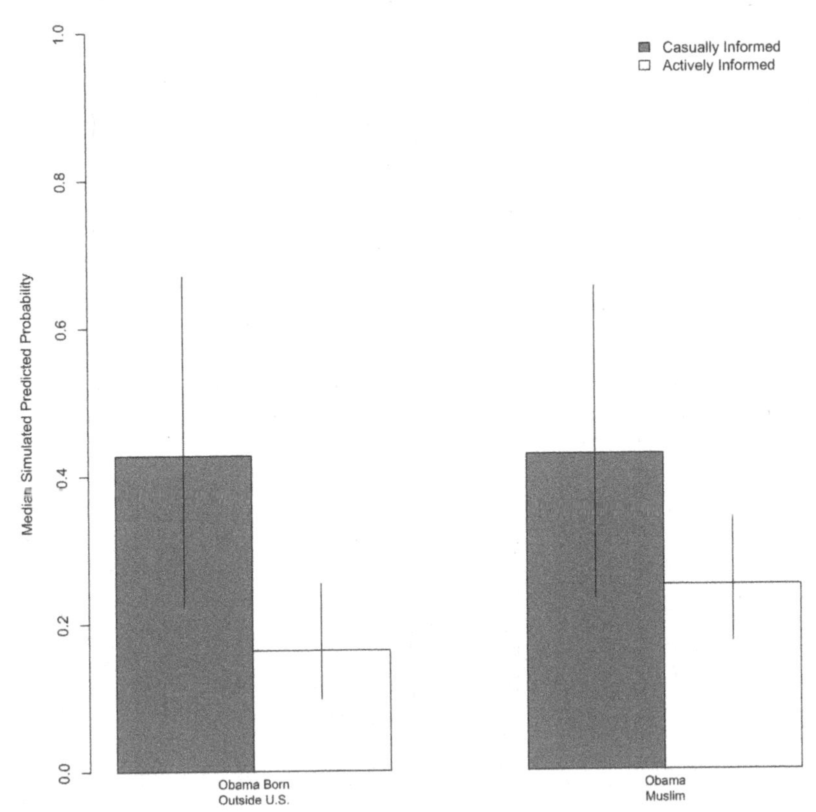

FIGURE 5.2. Predicted likelihood of believing misinformation by information source (2016 CCAP). Results were generated from simulations after matching on trust in media, trust in government, ideology, interest in politics, gender, ethnicity/race, education, and age. Survey weights incorporated in matching algorithm and regression. Vertical lines represent 95% confidence intervals. Regression results using the matched data reveal a positive, statistically significant coefficient between being casually informed and believing Obama was born outside the United States ($p < .05$) and believing Obama is Muslim ($p < .05$). Results hold when "don't know" responses are excluded and when survey weights are not used.

possibility to the extent possible, but I can also tackle this critique head-on by examining whether the gap in misbeliefs is larger between the casually and actively informed than it is between people in other demographic groups. If the gap remains largest between the actively and casually informed, we should be more confident that this is not simply a proxy for other variables like education, interest in politics, or trust in government. This would also give us more confidence that it is important to consider in future research.

In general, across the three surveys, the gap in misbelief is indeed wider comparing the actively and casually informed than it is comparing people from other groups. For example, the casually informed were 15 points more likely than the actively informed to believe that Obama was born outside the

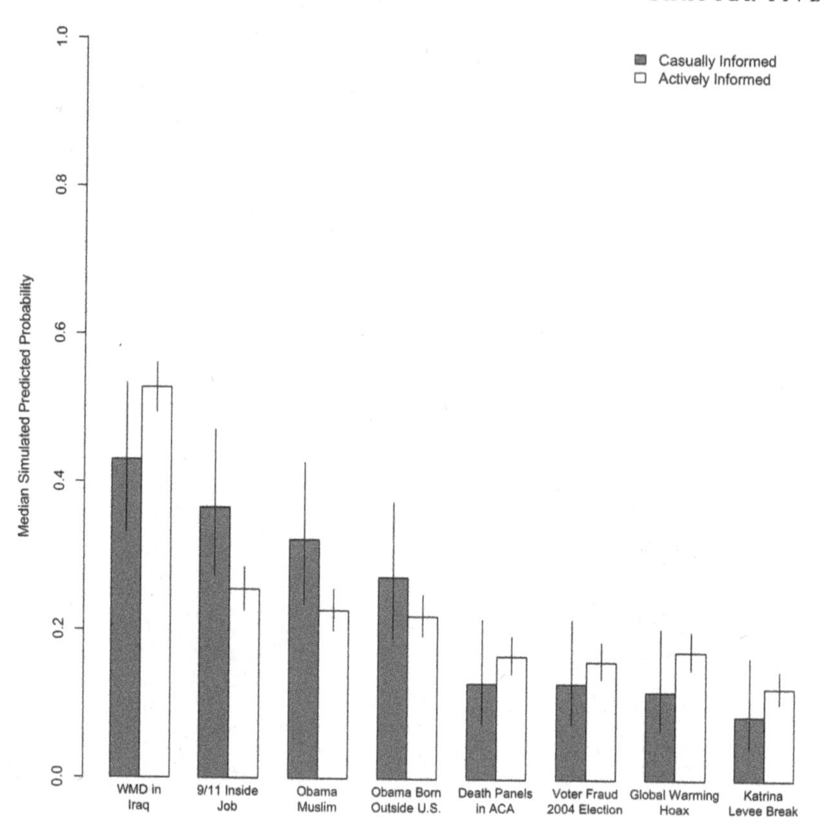

FIGURE 5.3. Predicted likelihood of believing misinformation by information source (2017 Original Survey). Results were generated from simulations after matching on gender, age, ethnicity/race, education, and party identification. Vertical lines represent 95% confidence intervals. Regression results using the matched data reveal a positive, statistically significant coefficient between being casually informed and believing Obama is Muslim ($p < .05$) and that the government knew about 9/11 ($p < .05$). Results hold when "don't know" responses are excluded.

United States, but people without college degrees were only 7 points more likely to be misinformed than people with college degrees. Even more striking, there is no evidence of a statistically significant difference in misbeliefs based on interest in politics, even on pieces of misinformation that the casually informed are significantly more likely to believe than the actively informed. People who distrust the government were more likely to believe that Obama is Muslim to a similar extent as were the casually informed. However, trust in government was not associated with believing that Obama was born outside the United States, but being casually informed was.

Although other individual characteristics are associated with beliefs in misinformation (Arechar et al. 2023; Flynn, Nyhan, and Reifler 2017; Anspach and Carlson 2022), being casually or actively informed still remains an important factor. This brief exploration indicates that relying on others for information about politics is not simply a proxy for interest in politics, education, or trust in government. It suggests something more, and future research on misinformation should consider information source preferences as key criteria to investigate further.

Identifying the Source

Another question that remains is whether socially transmitted information is actually responsible for misinformed beliefs. It could be the case that the casually informed are more likely to guess incorrectly, expressively respond, or

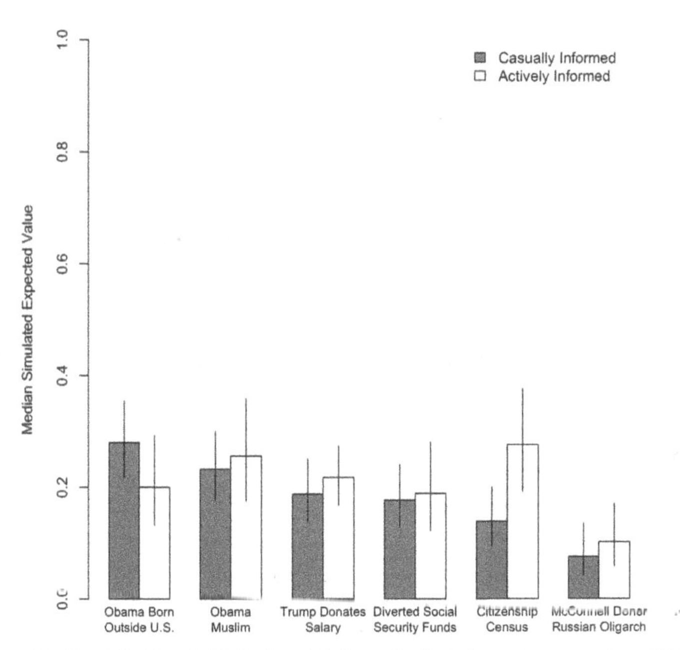

FIGURE 5.4. Predicted likelihood of believing misinformation by information source (2020 TASS). Results were generated from simulations after matching on gender, age, ethnicity/race, education, income, urban residence, internet access, trust in media, and party identification. Survey weights incorporated into the matching algorithm. Vertical lines represent 95% confidence intervals. Regression results using the matched data reveal a positive, statistically significant coefficient for being casually informed and believing Obama was born outside the United States ($p < .05$); negative, statistically significant coefficient for believing Obama removed the citizenship question from the 2010 census ($p < .05$). Results hold when "don't know" responses are excluded (though $p < .10$ for the census item) and when survey weights are not used. When "don't know" responses are excluded, the casually informed were more likely to believe Obama is Muslim ($p < .01$), that Pelosi diverted Social Security funds ($p < .01$), and that McConnell's donor was a Russian oligarch ($p < .05$).

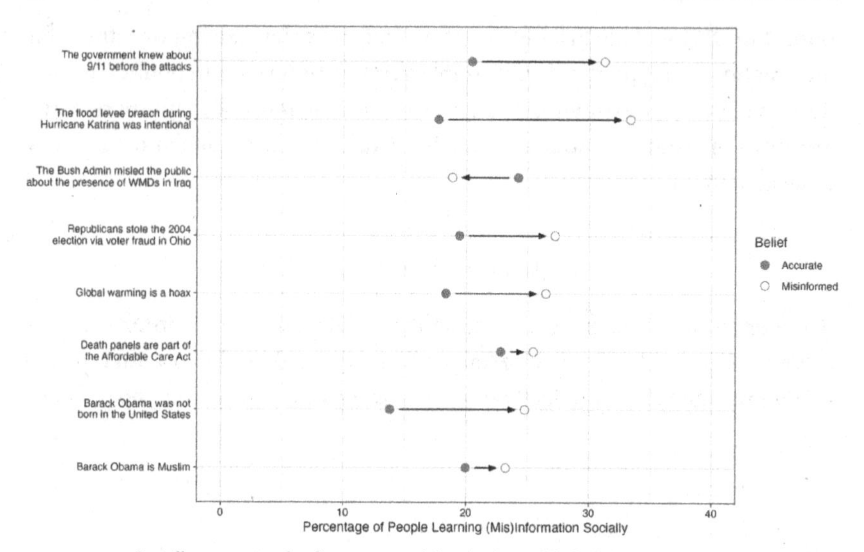

FIGURE 5.5. Socially transmitted information and (mis)informed beliefs (2017 Original Survey). Gray circles represent the percentage of accurately informed people who reported learning that information socially. White circles represent the percentage of misinformed people who reported learning that misinformation socially. Right arrows indicate that people who were misinformed were more likely to have learned socially than were the accurately informed. Left arrows indicate that the accurately informed were more likely to have learned socially.

be misinformed for reasons other than their primary information source. In an effort to examine this, I asked a follow-up question to respondents in the 2017 Original Survey. After respondents answered whether they thought each misinformation statement was true or false, I asked them where they recalled learning that the statement was true or false, piping in their previous (true or false) response.[21] Respondents could choose from a variety of sources, including television, radio, newspaper articles (online or in print) that they sought out on their own, newspaper articles (online or in print) that were referred to them by a friend, and conversations with other people (online or face-to-face). I then grouped these responses into conversations, social news (meaning that individuals learned about it from a news article that a friend sent them), and the news. The first two groups, friends and social news, would characterize how someone became casually misinformed, whereas the news group would characterize how someone became actively misinformed.

Although the vast majority of respondents reported that they learned the statement was true or false from the news, there are striking differences in the rates of casual information consumption between those who were misinformed and those who were correctly informed. Figure 5.5 shows the percentage of people who had accurate beliefs (gray circles) and the percentage of people who had misinformed beliefs (white circles) who reported learning socially. Arrows pointing to the right indicate that people who were misinformed were more likely to have learned socially than people who were accurately informed. This is the most useful comparison: the percentage of the misinformed who learned about the statement (incorrectly) socially and the percentage of the informed who learned about the statement (correctly) socially.

For all but one piece of misinformation, people who were misinformed were more likely to have learned socially than were people who were correctly informed. For example, among respondents who incorrectly believed that Barack Obama was not born in the United States, a quarter of them learned this falsehood from conversations. In contrast, only 14 percent of those who correctly knew that former president Obama was born in the United States learned this fact from conversations. However, a nontrivial percentage of people who had accurate beliefs reported learning those accurate beliefs socially. This suggests that conversations *can* be a method of correcting misinformation. While conversations can spread both fact and fiction, they could spread fiction more than they spread fact.

Experimental Evidence

The previous analyses have the advantage of looking at variation in misbeliefs between the casually and actively informed across a wide range of topics. Yet, as I have noted, the results need to be interpreted cautiously and only as correlations. Some might not be convinced that socially transmitted information can cause people to become misinformed. To address this important critique, I turn to two experiments.

First, I examine the Environmental Policy Experiment, a telephone game experiment I conducted in July 2021 that follows a design similar to the one described earlier. In short, I recruited a sample of self-identified actively informed Republicans and Democrats from Lucid and asked them to read a *USA Today* article about environmental policy. Then I asked them to write a message to another person who did not really follow the news on this topic. I then recruited a sample of self-identified casually informed people from Lucid and randomly assigned them to read either no information at all (control), the same news article the actively informed participants read (news), or one of the messages written by an actively informed participant (socially transmitted information). Those in the socially transmitted information condition were randomly assigned to receive information from a copartisan or an out-partisan. After reading their informational treatment, participants answered some questions, including one about whether they believed a common rumor about climate change—that oil and gas do not account for the largest portion of human-caused fossil fuel emissions from federal lands.[22]

The majority of participants were correctly informed on this topic, but there was an important partisan gap in misbelief. Democrats were more likely to be correctly informed on this point than were Republicans, with about 15.2 percent of Democrats being misinformed and 28.3 percent of Republicans being misinformed in the control group (those who received no information during the study). However, when individuals received socially transmitted information from a copartisan, they were significantly more likely to be misinformed ($p = .05$). Specifically, 21.5 percent of participants in the control group were misinformed, while 29.2 percent of participants who received socially transmitted information from a copartisan were misinformed. Notably, this result is driven by Democrats.[23] There were no differences in misinformation between those who received the news article and those who received no information, or between those who received the news article and those who received socially transmitted information. Together, these results suggest that exposure to socially transmitted information, relative to receiving no information at all, can cause people to become misinformed, but people are not necessarily better off when they read the news.

Second, I turn to an experiment I fielded with my colleague Nick Anspach in 2017 (see Anspach and Carlson 2020). We were interested in understanding how socially transmitted information on Facebook could facilitate misbeliefs. We randomly assigned participants on Mechanical Turk to one of four treatment groups: participants either (1) read a full news article, (2) viewed a Facebook post sharing the news article, (3) viewed a Facebook post sharing the news article with misinformative comments that favored Republicans, or (4) viewed a Facebook post sharing the news article with misinformative comments that favored Democrats. The news article was about former president Trump's approval ratings at the six-month mark of his presidency, which was shortly before our data collection began. The Facebook post conditions, just like the full article condition, contained accurate information about Trump's approval rating, which was 36 percent at the time. The two socially transmitted information conditions included false information about Trump's polling numbers. The socially transmitted information congenial to Republicans suggested that Trump's approval rating was closer to 49 percent, whereas the socially transmitted information congenial to Democrats suggested that his approval rating was closer to 23 percent. After exposure to their information treatment, participants were asked some questions about Trump's approval rating, including what they thought it was.

Although all participants were exposed to the correct information about Trump's approval rating, the misinformation communicated socially in the comments caused people to become misinformed. Over 80 percent of participants who were not exposed to any socially transmitted information (i.e., those who read the full article or those who received the article preview without commentary) correctly identified Trump's approval rating as 36 percent. In contrast, only 49 percent of participants who viewed the post with conservative misinformative commentary and only 36 percent of participants who viewed the post with liberal misinformative commentary correctly answered the question. Indeed, those exposed to socially transmitted *mis*information were more likely to report that Trump's approval rating was whatever that person said it was, instead of what the article preview said it was.

Together, these two experiments powerfully demonstrate that socially transmitted information—both in an abstract context and in a social media context—can cause people to become misinformed. In the first case, the context is abstract, but the result shows that even people ideologically inclined to reject a given piece of misinformation can be led astray by socially transmitted information, compared to receiving no information at all. In this case, being casually informed might actually be worse than being completely uninformed. The second experiment (Anspach and Carlson 2020) suggests that in a social media context where people can be exposed to information from the news at the same time that they are exposed to socially transmitted information about it, people pay more attention to and can be misled by socially transmitted information.

Conclusion

How does social information transmission affect what people know about politics? In this chapter, I presented experimental evidence that individuals can indeed learn from socially transmitted information, as long as they are receiving information from a more knowledgeable copartisan. This is consistent with what classic theories of opinion leadership predict (e.g., Downs 1957; Lupia and McCubbins 1998), but it is tested in a way that allows for more nuance in what information is actually being communicated. This could generally be viewed as an efficient way in which the public can be self-educating and democracy becomes a little less distorted. People learned *more* when they received information from a full news article, but they still learned something from their peers. Perhaps this is a better outcome than people simply not consuming the news at all.

To some, however, the bigger problem distorting American politics today is not the public's lack of awareness but the public's steadfast beliefs in false information. When it comes to *misinformation*, the casually informed do not fare as well. I presented correlational survey evidence of a general pattern that *if* there is a difference in misbeliefs based on information source, the casually informed are more likely to be misinformed than are the actively informed. Moreover, when asked to recall specifically where they learned various "facts," individuals who were misinformed were more likely to point to conversations with others than were people who were accurately informed.

I also presented evidence from two experiments that exposure to socially transmitted information can cause people to become misinformed. One way in which this can happen is by direct exposure to false information communicated socially. Anspach and I demonstrated that people are more likely to believe false information communicated socially on Facebook than accurate information communicated by news outlets, even within the same post (Anspach and Carlson 2020). However, this might also happen in a less direct fashion. Yes, the actively informed can and do communicate false information directly. Recall from chapter 4 that about 4.8 percent of messages generated in my experiments contained at least one piece of false information. In the experiment I presented in this chapter, some participants became misinformed after exposure to socially transmitted information from a copartisan even when the message itself did not contain the specific piece of misinformation measured. It could be the case that the ambiguity in socially transmitted information leads people to be generally skeptical or more confused to the point that they become misinformed.

Where does this leave us in thinking about the extent to which political conversations can distort democracy? Reconciling the results from this chapter suggests that socially transmitted information can help people learn, but it might also help people learn *misinformation*. When individuals choose to forgo active news consumption in favor of secondhand information, they might save themselves some time and effort and learn some valuable information, but they do so at the cost of potentially becoming misinformed.

The findings in this chapter push back against the rosy view of political conversations and the opinion leader relationship as being important for democratic functioning. While early seminal social science research pointed to the two-step flow as a process that would help educate an otherwise ill-informed public, I join more recent scholars in arguing that this conclusion might be too optimistic. Ahn, Huckfeldt, and Ryan (2014) importantly caution that political discussion is not an antiseptic, reminding us that it is an inherently political process. Although I use a different methodological approach, my conclusion is similar.

The importance of this finding rests on the assumption that individuals are able to accurately translate beliefs into preferences and preferences into action (Huckfeldt, Johnson, and Sprague 2004; Ahn, Huckfeldt, and Ryan 2014). That is, if individuals do not update their preferences in light of the (mis)information they obtain, it is possible that there is no need to worry. But if the casually informed are more likely to be misinformed, in part due to the content of the information to which they are exposed, we need to consider how they in turn update their preferences. In the next chapter, I examine the extent to which individuals update their preferences in response to socially transmitted information. I focus on the extent to which political conversations can further polarize political preferences, finding that exposure to socially transmitted information leads individuals to hold more extreme preferences.

6

Polarized

The word *polarization* has occupied news headlines in the United States for decades. It seems everyone, from politicians to our neighbors to scholars to celebrities, has something to say about polarization. During his remarks on the twenty-year anniversary of the September 11 attacks, former president George W. Bush stated, "A malign force seems at work in our common life that turns every disagreement into an argument, and every argument into a clash of cultures. So much of our politics has become a naked appeal to anger, fear, and resentment. That leaves us worried about our Nation and our future together."[1] Barack Obama echoed this point in his final State of the Union address as he lamented his inability to bridge divides during his presidency: "The rancor and suspicion between the parties has gotten worse instead of better."[2] While these two presidents would not have seen eye to eye on most policy issues, their comments on polarization similarly reflect critical dialogues about polarization among social scientists.

Research leaves little doubt that political elites are indeed polarized, meaning that Republicans and Democrats in Congress are ideologically further apart now than they have been in other points in history (McCarty, Poole, and Rosenthal 2016). This polarization may or may not extend to the general public. A fierce debate over the past few decades examines whether Republican and Democratic *voters* have opinions that are further apart now than they were before or whether they are simply better sorted ideologically, leaving fewer conservative Democrats and liberal Republicans (cf. Fiorina, Abrams, and Pope 2008 and Abramowitz and Saunders 2008).

There is also a social component of polarization, which the public experiences on a day-to-day basis. Republicans and Democrats are socially polarized, meaning that they prefer not to associate with one another even in nonpolitical interactions (e.g., Mason 2018). Dozens of papers point to examples of other ways in which Republicans and Democrats have distanced themselves from each other, defriending each other on social media (Settle 2018), cutting social ties altogether (Carlson and Settle 2022), preferring not to date or marry each other (Huber and Malhotra 2018; Easton and Holbein 2021), and avoiding neighborly favors (Webster, Connors, and Sinclair 2022).

But what causes, or at least amplifies, this polarization? The list of potential culprits is long: social scientists have shown that partisan media (Levendusky 2009, 2013; Arceneaux and Johnson 2013), social media (Settle 2018; Bail et al. 2018; Lee et al. 2014; Sunstein 2018; see also Boxell, Gentzkow, and Shapiro 2017), elite polarization (Hetherington 2001), and political discussion (Klar 2014; Druckman, Levendusky, and McLain 2018; Hutchens, Hmielowski, and Beam 2019) all share some responsibility for polarization. But in this new information environment where people are exposed to both news content and socially transmitted information simultaneously via social media, it is essential to understand how the social transmission of information from the news contributes to polarization. In this chapter, I argue that socially transmitted information, even when based on nonpartisan news, can polarize political attitudes.

Previous work has shown that political conversations between copartisans can amplify the polarizing effects of *partisan* media (Druckman, Levendusky, and McLain 2018). I take this work a step further to examine the extent to which socially transmitted information from *nonpartisan* media can polarize attitudes toward policy and one another. This distinction is subtle, but it matters. If most Americans are consuming more moderate, balanced news diets rather than exclusively (co)partisan media (Guess 2021), then we need to understand the downstream consequences of political conversations based on nonpartisan media.

I argue that when the actively informed consume nonpartisan news, they add partisan bias as they pass the information along to the casually informed. I presented evidence of this pattern in chapter 4: individuals pass along more information that benefits their party. By screening out information that makes their party or preferred policy position look bad, and by adding their own spin to make their perspective look even better, the actively informed essentially create partisan "media" as they pass information to the casually informed. As a result, the casually informed are exposed to partisan content, whether they know it or not, and are more likely to update their political attitudes accordingly. This means that polarization can happen even without partisan media; it can happen as a consequence of simple conversations about the news with peers.

Using two telephone game experiments, I show that socially transmitted information from copartisans can indeed polarize policy attitudes. For both salient (immigration policy) and relatively dormant (environmental policy) polarized issues, when individuals receive information from copartisans, they become better "sorted" in their policy preferences, widening the policy gap between Democrats and Republicans. On less salient issues, where individuals' attitudes should be more pliable (e.g., Druckman, Peterson, and Slothuus 2013), socially transmitted information from copartisans leads individuals to be better sorted and more likely to adopt more extreme preferences. Despite these important findings for the impact of socially transmitted information on attitudinal polarization, I find no evidence that social information transmission increases affective polarization.

Together, these results suggest that socially transmitted information can help fuel the polarization component of distorted democracy. While it does not appear to fuel distaste for out-partisans—and in fact, could help remedy affective polarization—it can lead people to adopt more extreme policy preferences and to widen the gap between Democrats' and Republicans' policy preferences.

How Does Information Lead to Polarization?

My focus in this book is on the role that information plays in shaping attitudes and behavior. In order to evaluate the role that information, whether from the media or from other people, plays in political polarization, I first take a closer look at what previous research says on the topic. I discuss three means through which people are exposed to political information: (partisan) media, social media, and political discussion.

PARTISAN MEDIA AND POLARIZATION

For decades, partisan media was viewed as the biggest scapegoat for many of American democracy's ailments. As cable news became widely viewed among American families, people had *choices* about what news to watch instead of being limited to only a few channels, as they were in the broadcast era. Cable news channels, such as Fox News and MSNBC, offered viewers a twenty-four-hour news cycle that presented information in a way that was, to some, refreshingly congenial. Right-leaning conservative Republicans could tune into Fox News and left-leaning liberal Democrats could tune into MSNBC, each group hearing similar stories presented with very different framing.

Concerned about the impact that this fractionalized media environment would have on American politics, many researchers jumped at the chance to examine whether this fundamental shift affected political behavior. One of many outcomes scholars investigated was polarization. The general idea is that the availability of conservative and liberal media might lead people to sort into echo chambers, only hearing the news from a network with a similar perspective. This could serve to deepen the partisan divide, pushing Republicans and Democrats further apart through both sorting and adopting more extreme attitudes. Moreover, if moderates, who are less strongly tied to a party, were exposed to either Fox News or MSNBC, the question among scholars was whether the ideological bias in the news programming could nudge their attitudes and turn them into ideologues.

There have been dozens of studies on the impact of partisan media and polarization. Exposure to partisan media has been shown to affect several different indicators of polarization, such as vote share (Della Vigna and Kaplan 2007; Martin and Yurukoglu 2017), policy preferences (Broockman and Kalla 2023), and elite position taking (Arceneaux et al. 2016). Media effects research typically needs clever research designs to measure the causal effect of exposure to partisan media on polarization because selection into treatment is so important. That is, simply observing that people who watch conservative media are more conservative and that people who watch liberal media are more liberal does not definitively suggest that partisan media causes polarization. It could simply be that people are selecting into consuming ideologically consistent media.

To address this limitation, many scholars have investigated natural experiments in the availability of partisan media exposure. For example, some have leveraged the exogeneous geographic variation in availability of Fox News during its rollout (e.g., Clinton and Enamorado 2014), while others have leveraged channel positioning (Ash et al. 2022). These aggregate-level patterns are not able to measure individual-level exposure, however. Addressing this concern, Broockman and Kalla (2023) partnered with a media firm to conduct a randomized experiment in which Fox News viewers were randomly incentivized to watch CNN for a month, finding that exposure to more moderate media led to more moderate political views.

With the exception of Broockman and Kalla's (2023) study, most experimental research on partisan media effects takes place in the context of a lab or survey experiment. Participants are often randomly assigned to view or read partisan media, nonpartisan media, or entertainment media. Researchers then examine variation in political views before and after exposure to partisan media. Experiments such as these have revealed an important debate. On the one hand, some studies suggest that even after accounting for preferences for partisan content, people develop stronger partisan attitudes after exposure to ideologically congruent partisan content (Levendusky 2009, 2013). In contrast, other work argues that when given the choice, Americans prefer to watch entertainment instead of news, and those who do prefer to watch news already have such strong attitudes that exposure to partisan media content does not do much to change their minds (Arceneaux and Johnson 2013, 2015, 2019). Aggregate-level analyses struggle to highlight this important tension around the importance of selective exposure to partisan media.

This debate is important for thinking about the role of socially transmitted information. In chapter 3 I showed that the actively informed are stronger partisans who consume news more frequently. They are the types of people most likely to consume (at least some) partisan media in the first place. While their attitudes may or may not be likely to polarize after exposure to the news content, the way that they interpret the information and transmit it to others could still affect whether the casually informed become polarized through exposure to biased socially transmitted information (cf. Levendusky 2013 and Arceneaux and Johnson 2013). In fact, Druckman, Levendusky, and McLain (2018) argue that the conflicting evidence over the relationship between partisan media and polarization could be due in part to the two-step flow amplifying the polarizing effects of partisan media.

SOCIAL MEDIA AND POLARIZATION

While scholars continue to stew over the impact of televised partisan media on polarization, another fundamental shift in the information environment begged for scholars to reevaluate the causes of polarization. With the growth of social media, Americans had even more choice about where to consume news, which could foster even deeper echo chambers than televised media could create. Social media had the power to amplify the selective exposure scholars observed with partisan cable TV news (Bakshy, Messing, and Adamic 2015; Prior 2013; Pariser 2012).

While some feared that social media could enable people to curate an ideologically friendly social network and information environment, others were less convinced. People could also use social media to easily access counterattitudinal information. Even if people are not deliberately choosing to consume counterattitudinal information, many become inadvertently exposed to counterattitudinal content online (for a review, see Barberá 2020). People form their online social networks for many reasons, most of which are likely completely unrelated to politics (Settle 2018; Minozzi et al. 2020). But if even a minority of someone's social contacts disagree and post counterattitudinal content, that person could become inadvertently exposed to disagreeable information. This partially addresses the selection problem raised by Arceneaux and Johnson's work on televised partisan media.

But what effect does social media ultimately have on polarization? Just as the jury is still out on whether partisan cable news channels cause polarization, so too is the jury over whether social media causes polarization. There is mixed observational evidence about the extent to which individuals are embedded in ideological echo chambers. Early work in this area found strong observational evidence of polarization in the conservative and liberal blogosphere (Adamic and Glance 2005), but other work finds that online discussion spaces are filled with a diverse mix of political views (Wojcieszak and Mutz 2009).

Increased access to data from major social media platforms like Facebook and Twitter has allowed for even more insights into—and even more conflicting evidence on—the relationship between social media and polarization. In contrast to previous work on political blogs and online discussion platforms, most people are not spending time on social media for political reasons (Settle 2018), and this matters because patterns of selective exposure vary depending on the political nature of the content. For example, Barberá and colleagues (2015) found that on Twitter, conservatives and liberals are mostly separated from each other when they engage with news about purely political events, such as elections or government shutdowns, but most other news stories have more blended conversations. These patterns uncovered using observational data mirror what has been observed using self-reported survey data. Evidence from Pew Research Center suggests that most people report that they are exposed to a variety of political views on social media (Duggan and Smith 2016). Moreover, Boxell, Gentzkow, and Shapiro (2017) find that polarization has increased the most among groups least likely to use the internet at all, such as the elderly, raising a question about the role that social media plays in causing polarization.

While observational and survey data reveal mixed findings about the ways in which social media forces people into ideological echo chambers, these studies have weak causal identification. Just as Arceneaux and Johnson (2013, 2015) pointed out this problem with televised partisan media, when it comes to social media, it is hard to tell whether people who are polarized create their own echo chambers or if there is something about social media that leads people to become more sorted and more polarized. Little knowledge of the inner workings of social media platforms' content algorithms makes this even harder to evaluate. One important paper on this subject tried to address the problem by conducting a field experiment in which participants were incentivized to follow bot Twitter accounts that were either liberal or conservative (Bail et al. 2018). The researchers found that conservative participants actually became more polarized after forced exposure to counterattitudinal information, but liberals seemed unaffected by the ideological content.

Altogether, the relationship between social media and polarization is difficult to unpack and shares a similar series of challenges with the partisan media literature. Much like cable news networks give viewers choices—and that freedom of choice brings with it the possibility of polarization—so too does social media. But social media offers users even more choices. Cable TV and the internet offer political and nonpolitical (or entertainment) options, as well as (conditional on choosing political content) options on the ideological slant of the coverage. These choices exist on social media too, but they are not limited to content generated by professional journalists. On social media, people are exposed to content from their friends, family, frenemies, and foes alike. On social media, people can create echo chambers based on the explicitly political content to which they expose themselves, but they can also create echo chambers (intentionally or not) by pruning their social networks to be more and more homogeneous.

To fully understand the impact of social media on polarization, it is important to understand how the collision between socially transmitted information and information from the media fosters polarization. To do that, we need to consider the social side of social media. We need to evaluate the content generated by everyday social media users and understand how social interactions about politics can facilitate polarization. To answer this, I turn to the political discussion network literature in the next section.

POLITICAL DISCUSSION AND POLARIZATION

Up to this point, I have discussed conflicting evidence on the role of televised partisan media and social media in polarization. Considering the role of political discussion in polarization is important because it lays the groundwork for why I expect political discussion to contribute to the polarization arm of distorted democracy. More specifically, it helps contextualize the conditions under which political discussions about the news might increase or decrease attitudinal polarization.

The general consensus in the political discussion and polarization literature is that homogeneous political discussions (i.e., between politically like-minded people) can cause polarization (Klar 2014; Druckman, Levendusky, and McLain 2018), while heterogeneous political discussions (i.e., between people who disagree politically) can reduce polarization (Druckman, Levendusky, and McLain 2018; Mutz 2006), including *perceptions* of polarization (Lyons and Sokhey 2017). Much like the studies on televised and social media, the ideological congruence between the informational content and the person under study is the key. In the case of political discussion, the goal is to test the effects of exposure to like-minded, ideologically congruent information communicated via discussion with others rather than via a news outlet directly.

Using observational data on political discussion networks, previous work has found that people who are in more homogeneous discussion networks tend to have more polarized political attitudes than those in more diverse networks. But just as with the studies on social media, political discussion network composition is likely endogenous to political attitudes. It is unclear whether people with more polarized attitudes are choosing to discuss politics with those who agree, deliberately seeking them out, or forming networks for some other reason and whether it is these conversations that have pushed people's attitudes to become more extreme.

Innovative group discussion experiments have examined the causal effect of discussion network composition on polarization. Klar (2014) finds that homogeneous political discussions cause people to engage in more partisan-motivated reasoning and have more "sorted" political attitudes, leading to more opinion polarization. In contrast, she also finds that heterogeneous political discussions, in which people engaged with those who agreed and disagreed with them, caused people to moderate their preferences and engage in less partisan-motivated reasoning. Randomly assigning people to homogeneous or heterogeneous political discussion networks suggests that like-minded political discussion can cause polarization, whereas non-like-minded political discussion can reduce it.

But these studies do not closely examine the ways in which the news filters through these conversations. They do not engage with the important findings on the relationship between partisan media exposure and polarization or with the impact of social media on polarization. Yet presumably *someone* in these discussions learned political information from the news and brought it into the conversation.

Druckman, Levendusky, and McLain (2018) evaluated the relationship between partisan media and the two-step flow. They conducted an innovative group discussion experiment in which participants were randomly assigned to be exposed to partisan media (or not) and then have a group discussion that was either homogeneous or heterogeneous or no discussion. By leveraging variation in who was previously exposed to partisan media and who was not within the political discussions, they were able to reveal the extent to which partisan media bias can propagate through social interactions. They find that people who did not read partisan media themselves but had a discussion with someone who did had significantly more polarized political attitudes than those who were simply exposed to partisan media. This suggests a powerful downstream effect of partisan media: political discussion is a key mechanism through which attitude polarization develops in American politics.

My theoretical expectations in this chapter are largely built on the work of Druckman, Levendusky, and McLain (2018). While their paper lays the foundation for the notion that the two-step flow can amplify partisan media bias, it leaves some important lingering questions unanswered that I address in this chapter. First, I examine whether partisan bias can *develop* and grow from initially nonpartisan media and whether that biased socially transmitted information can polarize political attitudes. Second, I examine whether a much weaker stimulus, that is, simple exposure to someone's summary of a news article rather than a full conversation, can cause polarization. The stimuli in my studies in this chapter more closely emulate exposure to political content on social media or short comments from others rather than the effect of engaging in a thoughtful conversation.

Altogether, there is conflicting evidence about whether partisan media, social media, and political discussions cause polarization. However, there is considerably more consensus that homogeneous political discussion causes attitudinal polarization than there is that partisan media or social media cause polarization. This increases my confidence that one of the fundamental challenges of political discussion in American politics today is that it can contribute to divisive attitudinal polarization. Ultimately, I show that when the casually informed are exposed to socially transmitted information about nonpartisan news, they develop more extreme policy preferences that show more evidence of partisan sorting. Thus this chapter shows that socially transmitted information can contribute to distorted democracy by causing shifts in attitudinal polarization.

Does Socially Transmitted Information Increase Polarization?

In chapter 4, I showed that the actively informed add partisan bias to initially balanced information from the media as they summarize it for their casually informed peers. Here I want to test whether this biased information can have the effect of polarizing attitudes, much like partisan media. In creating social messages, Democrats essentially turn nonpartisan information from *USA Today* to a clip from the *Rachel Maddow Show*, while Republicans take the same information and turn it into a clip from *Tucker Carlson Tonight*.

Previous studies on partisan media suggest that, at least in a forced exposure design, people exposed to ideologically congruent partisan media will develop more polarized attitudes. I expect to observe the same pattern when the casually informed obtain information from the actively informed. When someone learns about the news from a copartisan peer, they (intentionally or unintentionally) expose themselves to congenial partisan bias. Republicans get the Tucker Carlson spin; Democrats get the Rachel Maddow twist. In this case, partisans should be more likely to update their preferences to align more with their party's position—both through sorting and through adopting more extreme preferences. In contrast, when someone learns about the news from an out-partisan peer, they might not update their preferences at all or might even moderate them. Exposure to cross-cutting information can reduce attitudinal polarization (Mutz 2006), but people might also just dismiss it altogether since it comes from a less trusted source (Zaller 1992).

As I discussed above, *partisan* media has been shown to increase polarization, but there is limited evidence that nonpartisan media can do the same. On the one hand, we might expect that people will not change their attitudes at all in response to this nonpartisan information. On the other hand, it is possible that people pay attention to the information in the article that supports their prior beliefs (or interpret it that way) (Zaller 1992; Lodge and Taber 2013). As a result, even exposure to nonpartisan news can increase partisan sorting and attitudinal polarization, especially for less salient topics.

Given the ongoing debate about whether polarization is best captured by partisan sorting or adopting more extreme policy preferences, I examine both types of polarization in this study (cf. Abramowitz and Saunders 2008 and Fiorina, Abrams, and Pope 2008). Partisan sorting might have stronger implications for how we think about vote choice and representation as a downstream consequence of policy preferences. Attitude extremity might be more relevant for considering the implications of these findings for voting in primary elections (e.g., Hall 2015; Lau 2013), stereotypes about the out-party (Rothschild et al. 2019; Busby et al. 2021), and policy making more broadly. Both forms of polarization are important, and my expectations for both are similar.

In summary, I expect that individuals who receive socially transmitted information from copartisans will have more extreme policy preferences and more sorted policy preferences than will those exposed to no information and those exposed to information from the media. I test these expectations using two experiments, one focused on immigration policy and another focused on environmental policy, which I describe in detail next.

APPROACH: TWO TELEPHONE GAME EXPERIMENTS

To test whether socially transmitted information based on nonpartisan media causes polarization, I conducted two experiments. The research design in both studies follows from the design used in chapter 5 to study whether socially transmitted information leads individuals to learn less than they would by reading a news article. However, instead of focusing on the facts participants learned, I focus on their subjective attitudes. I also added another treatment condition, a pure control group, in which participants were not exposed to any information. This addition changes the counterfactual driving the key comparison in this chapter. In chapter 5, the key comparison was between the actively informed (those who received a news article) and the casually informed (those who received a social message based on a news article). Here, however, as I turn to investigating polarization rather than learning, I examine the difference between receiving socially transmitted information and receiving no information at all.

The first study focused on immigration policy, which is a highly polarized, salient topic, about which most respondents have strong, crystallized preferences. This is a topic for which it should be hard to observe attitude change, especially in the context of a relatively mild treatment in a survey experiment. The second study focused on environmental policy, a polarized topic that is less salient, with more malleable attitudes. This should be a case where it would be easier to observe a treatment effect, setting a sort of "upper bound" on the impact of socially transmitted information, at least in the context of experiments like these.

Stage 1: Generating Socially Transmitted Information

For each experiment, I first recruited a sample of participants from Lucid, an online survey panel aggregator, to answer basic demographic questions, read a news article, and write a message to someone else about that news article. Importantly, all participants recruited to this sample were *actively informed*, meaning that they reported that they actively seek out news and information rather than bump into it as they do other things or hear about it from others. This sample, therefore, more accurately reflects the types of people who are doing the information transmitting in the real world. I recruited one thousand actively informed respondents in the Immigration Policy Experiment and five hundred actively informed respondents in the Environmental Policy Experiment.

All participants read the same news article, which was an excerpt from a *USA Today* article. *USA Today* has generally been shown to be a nonpartisan outlet (Budak et al. 2016), much like the Reuters article that was used in chapter 5. In the Immigration Policy Experiment, the article discussed President Biden's proposed immigration reform, which included a path to citizenship for undocumented immigrants currently living in the United States. At the time of data collection (July 2021), immigration was a polarizing issue, especially regarding citizenship for undocumented immigrants. Republicans, generally speaking, opposed paths to citizenship for undocumented immigrants and increased immigration, whereas Democrats, generally speaking, supported paths to citizenship and increased immigration. For example, results from an April 2021 Pew Research Center survey indicated that 56 percent of Democrats supported a path to citizenship for undocumented immigrants, compared to only 26 percent of Republicans.[3]

In the Environmental Policy Experiment, participants read an excerpt from a *USA Today* article about the Biden administration's ban on oil and gas lease sales. The article discussed the potential for this policy change to reduce carbon emissions and improve environmental outcomes while also discussing the potential economic impact of unemployment in local communities. At the time of data collection (September 2021), environmental policy was a polarizing issue, with Republicans generally preferring to prioritize economic over environmental concerns and Democrats preferring the opposite. Democrats were generally more supportive of Biden's ban on oil and gas lease sales, with some arguing that it did not go far enough, and Republicans opposed the ban.

After participants read the news article, they were asked to write a message to someone else, telling them about the Biden administration's recent policy actions. The prompts are largely similar to the one used in chapter 5, but a key difference is that I provided more details about the intended recipient of the information to make it clearer that they were casually informed. I described the person as one who is not totally disengaged from politics but is not particularly active, does not follow the news, and has not yet learned about the proposal.

The vast majority of respondents were attentive and completed the writing task thoughtfully. After removing nonsense responses in which participants wrote gibberish or otherwise rushed the survey (about 15 percent of the sample), the median message was twenty-seven words long in the Immigration Policy Experiment and twenty-eight words long in the Environmental

Policy Experiment. In the Immigration Policy Experiment, Republicans and Democrats wrote a message of the same length on average. However, in the Environmental Policy Experiment, Republicans wrote longer messages than did Democrats.

The content of the messages follows the patterns broadly described in chapter 4. The messages were, of course, much shorter than the news article and contained much more opinion. Table 6.1 provides example messages to provide a sense of what information was passed along in Stage 2 of the Immigration Policy Experiment, and table 6.2 provides example messages from the Environmental Policy Experiment.

TABLE 6.1. Example Messages from the Immigration Policy Experiment

	Actively Informed Republican	*Actively Informed Democrat*
Casually Informed Republican	This administration is about to screw the legal citizens of this country by giving amnesty to 11 million plus illegal criminals so they can have continuous democrat in the political arena while using AMERICAN citizens money to pay for all the crimes and future welfare for the illegals.	President Biden's proposal offers a legal pathway to citizenship for those currently in our country. It's an eight year process filled with vetting of those applying and background checks. Immigrants make our country great and help our country succeed. It's vital that we have plans in place to help them obtain citizenship.
Casually Informed Independent	Well get ready for taxes to go up Biden is trying to pass a new bill to take care of all the illegals that come into our country. This is not right and our responsibility. We have millions of Americans that have no health care their homeless and were suppose to take in millions coming from Mexico that Biden wants to take care of.	So the Biden Administration wants to reform immigration in a way that will help so many people. There will be an eight year path to citizenship for the millions of undocumented workers. There's also a plan to give green cards to children brought here, refugees and agriculture workers. It's a fair plan to benefit people who deserve to stay in this country. There hadn't been something this big on immigration done in this country in a very long time. I think it's super important for everyone that it passes. It will help so many families.
Casually Informed Democrat	This is a bad bill. It doesn't solve the problem of border crossings. They need to be vetted before entering our country. Those that are born here as anchor babies should be allowed u. s. citizenship as they were born here, parents should go through the immigration processes to become legal citizens.	The Biden Administration has developed a pathway to citizenship for immigrants coming into the country. The process would take about 8 years and immigrants would be allowed to be in the country. Children who are brought to the USA as children would be allowed to get a green card right away.

TABLE 6.2. Example Messages from the Environmental Policy Experiment

	Actively Informed Republican	*Actively Informed Democrat*
Casually Informed Republican	Did you hear that Biden shut down the pipeline and illegally suspended oil and gas leases. Oil dependent states are going to be hurting fast and the pipeline just killed thousands of jobs. Very callous as none of those workers have any "clean" energy jobs to go to as Biden told them to do. Maybe they could move to China? Gas is going to Skyrocket and so is e every around it. Hang on to your hat, here comes massive inflation, and it will be quick.	Look at what's happening tonight and tomorrow in New Orleans. Look what happened in Tennessee last week with unprecedented flooding. Watch how the fires are consuming thousands of acres of bone-dry forests in the West - even Lake Tahoe is threatened, and much of the forests in Mount Lasen [*sic*] National Park have been burned. Glaciers are melting rapidly. Why? Because humankind has been burning fossil fuels like gas and oil for the past almost 200 years, and the only way we can stop such changes in our climate is to stop using fossil fuels. That's why the President has placed the temporary (I hope it will become permanent) ban on oil and gas leases, aside from the other environmental impacts on nearby rivers, etc. Sure, some jobs may be lost, but it will take new jobs to develop alternative energy sources.
Casually Informed Independent	Please understand that shutting down oil drilling effects every aspect of our economy from food prices, healthcare, and the cost of gasoline. It also causes our electricity and heating bills to rise. President is heading this country into a socialist government that is going to destroy America. Please tell your representatives in Congress to vote against his plans.	Climate change is a reality. We must focus our efforts on reducing fossil fuels and start looking at renewable energy. Shutting down the oil pipeline only effects 1% of the global emissions, but it is a start. Renewable energy will create jobs to offset the loss of jobs. This will also put people back to work from the pandemic.
Casually Informed Democrat	That the Biden Administration has halted oil drilling and natural gas lease's on Federal land. This is supposed to make some sort of difference in greenhouse gases but, it is only going to have a net affect of 1%, which is negligible. It is going to cost somewhere between 60,000 and 300,000 Gas and Oil jobs. No one is really sure.	Biden and his administration is very concerned over climate control. The previous administration was not. Oil production was stopped early on with Biden. Some jobs will be lost. If we are not concerned with climate control there will be more things to deal with.

Stage 2: The Effect of Information on Polarization

In the second stage of the experiment for both studies, I recruited a second sample of respondents from Lucid, this time only with respondents who reported that they bump into the news as they do other things or hear about it from other people. Thus the participants in Stage 2 identify themselves as casually informed. Each study had approximately one thousand casually informed participants. Stage 2 participants first answered some pretreatment questions, which included policy preferences on immigration or environmental policy, depending on the study. Next they completed a distraction task and attention check, which included simple logic puzzles designed to provide some separation from the pretreatment measures and the treatment. Some researchers call this the "washout period" (de Benedictis-Kessner et al. 2019).

Next came the information treatment. Participants were randomly assigned to one of three conditions: (1) control, (2) news, or (3) social. In the control condition, participants did not receive any information at all and instead moved on to the post-treatment questions. In the news condition, participants were asked to read the same *USA Today* article that Stage 1 participants read. In the social condition, participants were only shown a message written by one of the Stage 1 participants, based on the *USA Today* article.

Participants in the social condition were randomly shown a social message from either a Republican or Democratic Stage 1 participant. However, they were all given a message that was written *to* someone of their partisanship. Because the actively informed might tailor the information they share to the partisanship of the intended recipient, it makes sense to give Stage 2 participants a message that was intended for someone like them. Just as in the experiment presented in chapter 5, participants could view any one of the hundreds of messages generated in Stage 1. I ensured that all messages were actually about the topic at hand (immigration or environmental policy), and lightly edited them to remove phrases like, "I would tell them that . . ." I otherwise left the messages with typos and grammatical errors intact.

Participants in both of the information conditions—but not those in the control group—received some context about their information source. Table 6.3 summarizes the prompts given to each group.

Measuring Attitudinal Polarization

After exposure to information (or not), participants were asked a handful of post-treatment questions. In the Immigration Policy Experiment, partici-

TABLE 6.3. Prompts for Each Treatment Group

	Immigration Policy Experiment	*Environmental Policy Experiment*
News	On the next screen, we will show you a news article from *USA Today* about the Biden Administration's immigration reform proposal. We'd like you to read the article as if you were reading the news in your daily life.	On the next screen, we will show you a news article from *USA Today* about the Biden Administration's recent climate change actions. We'd like you to read the article as if you were reading the news in your daily life.
Social	On the next screen, we will show you a short message written by another person who read a news article from *USA Today* about the Biden Administration's immigration reform proposal. The person who wrote the message is a [Republican / Democrat] who generally reads a lot of news.	On the next screen, we will show you a short message written by another person who read a news article from *USA Today* about the Biden Administration's recent climate change actions. The person who wrote the message is a [Republican / Democrat] who generally reads a lot of news.
Control		

pants were asked to report their opinion on a path to citizenship for undocumented immigrants and how strongly they held that opinion. In the Environmental Policy Experiment, participants were asked to report their support for the ban on oil and gas lease sales, as well as other environmental policy questions used in previous polarization studies (e.g., Druckman, Levendusky, and McLain 2018).

In the Immigration Policy Experiment, I measured immigration policy preferences by asking a branched question used by the Pew Research Center. Participants were first asked, "Which comes closest to your view about how to handle undocumented immigrants who are now living in the U.S.?" Participants could choose between "they should not be allowed to stay in the country legally" and "there should be a way for them to stay in the country legally, if certain requirements are met." Those who reported that there should *not* be a way for them to stay in the country legally were then asked whether they thought there should be a national law enforcement effort to deport all immigrants who are now living in the United States illegally. Those who reported that there should be a way for them to stay in the country were asked if they should be eligible to apply for US citizenship or permanent residency but not US citizenship. I used responses to this question to create a four-point scale that ranged from 0 (national law enforcement effort to deport) to 3 (eligible for citizenship).

In the Environmental Policy Experiment, I measured policy preferences using questions taken directly from previous research on polarization. Environmental policy positions are not as easily ordered in terms of how extreme they are as in the immigration policy case. Moreover, part of the goal with the Environmental Policy Experiment was to figure out what the "upper bound" of socially transmitted information's effect on attitude polarization might be. As such, I wanted to use questions that have previously been shown to have large treatment effects using other study designs, such as in-person group discussions. Participants were asked a series of questions about how much they favor or oppose efforts to increase onshore and offshore drilling, as well as a question about how they weigh the tradeoffs between economic and environmental concerns (Druckman, Levendusky, and McLain 2018). Finally, I added a question—the main outcome of interest—that was tied specifically to the topic covered in the article: support for Biden's ban on oil and gas lease sales. In all of these policy questions, respondents reported their support on a seven-point scale.

I examined two operationalizations of polarization: sorting and attitude extremity. In the Immigration Policy Experiment, Republican respondents who scored a 0 (national law enforcement effort to deport undocumented immigrants) or 1 (undocumented immigrants should not be allowed to stay but no law enforcement to deport) were considered to be sorted. Democrats who scored a 2 (undocumented immigrants should be allowed to stay legally but no path to citizenship) or 3 (path to citizenship) were considered sorted. In the Environmental Policy Experiment, Republicans were considered sorted if their scores were greater than 4, indicating that they opposed Biden's oil and gas lease ban, supported drilling, or prioritized jobs over the environment. Democrats were considered sorted if their scores were less than 4, indicating that they supported Biden's oil and gas lease ban, opposed drilling, or prioritized the environment over jobs.

In the Immigration Policy Experiment, 65 percent of respondents were sorted prior to exposure to information. This reflects the vast degree of polarization over immigration in the United States. In contrast, prior to exposure to any information, only about half of respondents were sorted across the four issues examined in the Environmental Policy Experiment. However, when given a direct partisan cue in reporting support for Biden's ban on oil and gas lease sales, 58 percent of respondents were sorted at baseline. Ultimately, in the analysis that follows, I created a variable that indicated whether respondents were *not* sorted before treatment but became sorted after exposure to information (1) or not (0).

The second way to capture polarization is by measuring attitude extremity. Did people have more extreme policy preferences after exposure to socially transmitted information? In the Immigration Policy Experiment, this test is straightforward. If respondents moved from a more moderate preference (e.g., 1 or 2 on the scale) to a more extreme preference (e.g., 0 or 3), this would be clear evidence of participants preferring a more extreme policy solution. For example, we can observe participants shifting from preferring that there be no way for undocumented immigrants to stay in the United States legally but not wanting law enforcement to deport them to preferring that law enforcement get involved. In the Immigration Policy Experiment, I code whether participants adopted more extreme preferences if they moved from 2 to 3 or from 1 to 0 after exposure to information.

Attitude extremity is harder to measure in the Environmental Policy Experiment. In this study, I borrowed questions from previous polarization research that examined environmental policy. These questions measure support for policies on seven-point scales but do not clearly specify policy alternatives that might be more extreme or more moderate solutions to the same problem. That said, I measure attitude extremity by capturing whether individuals strengthened their support for or opposition to environmental policy before or after exposure to information. Specifically, if someone's preference was 5 or 6 at baseline but increased after exposure to information or if someone's preference was 2 or 3 at baseline but decreased after exposure to information, they were considered as adopting a more extreme preference. If someone was a 4 at baseline (the midpoint on the scale) but moved in either direction after exposure to information, they were also considered to have more extreme preferences. While this approach is not as clean as the Immigration Policy Experiment, as it more accurately captures preference intensity than a specific policy preference, it largely follows previous polarization research.

ANSWER: INFORMATION FROM COPARTISANS INCREASES POLARIZATION

The results from the immigration and environmental policy experiments largely support my expectations that socially transmitted information from copartisans polarizes attitudes. Starting with partisan sorting, figure 6.1 shows the percentage of participants who became sorted after exposure to information by the treatment group. The results show that participants were more likely to become sorted when they received information from a copartisan or from the news, compared to receiving no information at all. In the

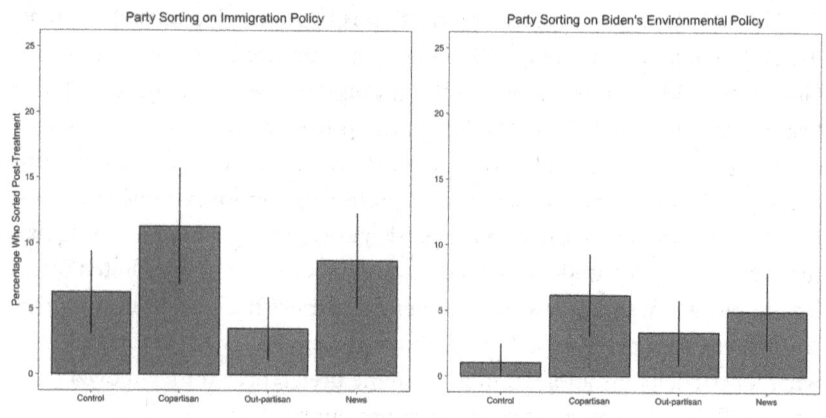

FIGURE 6.1. Partisan sorting by information treatment. Plots show the percentage of participants in each treatment group whose policy preferences were not sorted before exposure to information but became sorted after exposure to information. Data come from Stage 2 of the Immigration Policy Experiment and Stage 2 of the Environmental Policy Experiment. Vertical lines represent 95% confidence intervals. In both studies, the difference between the copartisan condition and the control condition is statistically significant. The difference between copartisan and out-partisan is only statistically significant in the Immigration Policy Experiment. Independent leaners are treated as partisans.

Immigration Policy Experiment, 11 percent of participants became sorted after exposure to information from a copartisan, compared to 6 percent who received no information ($p < .10$), 9 percent who received nonpartisan news information, and 4 percent who received information from an out-partisan. In the Environmental Policy Experiment, 6 percent of participants who received information from a copartisan became more sorted than they were at baseline, as did 5 percent of those who read the *USA Today* article directly. Both of these percentages are significantly greater than the percentage of participants in the control group who sorted, which was only 1 percent. Only 3 percent of participants who received information from an out-partisan became more sorted after exposure to the information. In both studies, socially transmitted information from copartisans caused individuals to shift their attitudes to be more sorted in line with their party, providing the first piece of evidence that socially transmitted information can contribute to polarization.

Although these differences are statistically significant, as described, they might seem substantively small. Indeed, it is not the case that the *majority* of people exposed to socially transmitted information from copartisans suddenly became sorted: only 11 percent in the Immigration Policy Experiment did, and only 6 percent in the Environmental Policy Experiment did. However, when considering that 65 percent of participants in the Immigration Policy Experiment and 58 percent of participants in the Environmental Policy

Experiment were already sorted *prior to* receiving any information, these effect sizes are quite remarkable. This means that in the Immigration Policy Experiment, among people who were not sorted at baseline, about one-third became sorted after exposure to information. For comparison, strength of partisanship was not significantly associated with sorting after exposure to information at all in either study. In the Environmental Policy Experiment, about 5 percent of weak partisans, 3 percent of moderate partisans, and 4 percent of strong partisans sorted after exposure to information. In the Immigration Policy Experiment, about 6 percent of weak, 7 percent of moderate, and 9 percent of strong partisans sorted after exposure to information. Thus the effect of socially transmitted information from copartisans on sorted policy preferences remains strong and substantively important.

Next, I tested whether participants adopted more extreme policy preferences after exposure to socially transmitted information from a copartisan. I find support for this expectation in the Environmental Policy Experiment but not the Immigration Policy Experiment. As shown in figure 6.2, in the Environmental Policy Experiment, I found that 11 percent of participants who received information from a copartisan developed more extreme policy preferences, compared to their baseline policy preferences. Participants who received information from the news also developed more extreme preferences, with 14 percent of participants becoming more extreme. These percentages are not statistically distinguishable, but they are both significantly greater than the percentage of people in the control condition who had more extreme preferences by the end of the study.

Why did information from copartisans push people to become more extreme in the Environmental Policy Experiment but not the Immigration Policy Experiment? There are two possible reasons. One explanation is that attitudes about immigration policy are more crystallized than attitudes about the environment. Although I observed some movement on immigration policy preferences in measuring partisan sorting, there was not much movement overall. It could be the case that the actively informed can make their casually informed peers more extreme only on topics that are less salient.

However, another explanation rests in measurement. In the Immigration Policy Experiment, participants only had four policy options, which were estimated by combining responses to two branched questions. In contrast, participants in the Environmental Policy Experiment reported their support for or opposition to a given policy on a 7-point Likert scale. As a result, participants in the Environmental Policy Experiment not only had the ability to move more because of the longer scale, but they were also simply reporting their degree of support for one policy option rather than directly weighing more than one.

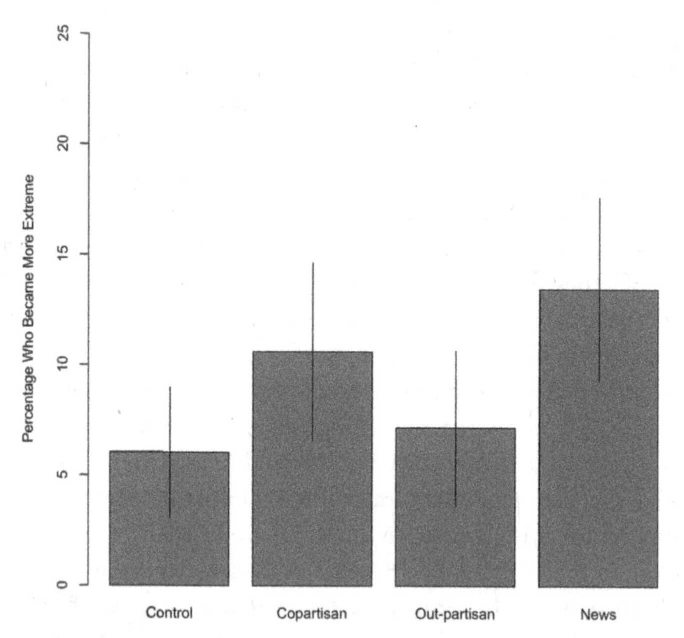

FIGURE 6.2. Attitude extremity by information treatment in the Environmental Policy Experiment. Bars reflect the percentage of participants in each treatment group whose attitudes became more extreme after treatment compared to their pretreatment, baseline attitudes. Vertical lines represent 95% confidence intervals. The difference between copartisan and control is statistically significant ($p < .10$), as is the difference between the news and control ($p < .05$).

Conclusion

In this chapter, I argued that the political conversations that characterize the two-step flow can contribute to the polarization arm of distorted democracy. The results suggest that socially transmitted information based on nonpartisan news can polarize political attitudes among the casually informed, in the form of both sorting and adopting more extreme policy preferences. This adds more evidence that the political conversations that characterize the two-step flow can contribute to attitude polarization.

While the findings I present in this chapter are not directly modeled after a social media setting, I hope that the results shed light on the influence that user-generated content on social media can have on polarization. The experiments I present in this chapter in some ways mirror what happens when people post about the news on social media, particularly in the form of quote tweets on Twitter or shares on Facebook, where they add their own take on the article as they pass it along to their social networks. Previous work on social media and polarization has not adequately engaged with the influence of user-generated content in shaping polarization online. I hope that the results in this chapter can help address this gap and open the door for future research. Regardless of the context that best reflects the experiments presented in this chapter, the results challenge researchers to rethink important features of how we understand polarization and the media's role in it. I conclude this chapter by making two key points about what these results mean for our broader understanding of polarization.

RETHINKING POLARIZATION WITHOUT THE MEDIA

Beyond the contribution to my central argument that socially transmitted information from copartisans can cause attitudinal polarization, the results speak to a broader debate about what drives polarization. Given the conflicting evidence about whether partisan media drives polarization, a major question nags political communication scholars: How do we explain polarization without partisan media? Kim and Kim (2021) answer this question by suggesting that people selectively tune in and out of political news when the news coverage of their party is good or bad. Druckman, Levendusky, and McLain (2018) argue that the content of partisan media is amplified by the two-step flow, polarizing people who were only indirectly exposed to partisan media from others. Somewhere between these two explanations, my results suggest that polarization can arise even from nonpartisan media. When the actively informed transmit information from nonpartisan news to their peers, it can have a polarizing effect. These findings contribute to the conversation on what causes polarization by demonstrating that it can occur *even without partisan media.*

If this is the case, who are we to blame (or thank)? It is simple to blame "the media" or "the partisan media" for the problems in American politics. And the media surely deserves some responsibility for contributing to polarization. But the results in this chapter are provocative because they put some of the blame on us. We, collectively, share responsibility for contributing to polarization. The results here suggest that when people discuss politics with others, they may be inadvertently polarizing their attitudes, though the extent to which this attitude polarization is inadvertent or intentional may depend on the motivations of both the actively and casually informed (Connors, Pietryka, and Ryan 2022). The bottom line, however, is that everyday people, not just the media or political elites, share some responsibility for shaping attitude polarization. This is an uncomfortable reality that we must continue to understand if we are to try to change it.

I want to challenge us to think harder about whether this is all bad. While the results here do present substantively and statistically significant results showing that simple socially transmitted information can push attitudes to become more sorted and more extreme, some researchers suggest that polarization can be *good* for democratic functioning. Indeed, the now-famous 1950 American Political Science Association (APSA) report begged for more polarization. Polarization can make it easier for voters to identify candidates and parties who support their policy preferences, facilitate political engagement, and yield other benefits that might actually help democracy function. This book is not about whether polarization is necessarily good or bad for democracy, but the results—and my overarching argument—suggest that socially transmitted information can contribute to attitudinal polarization and sorting in a way that has been previously unexplained.

Setting aside the debate over whether attitudinal polarization is good or bad for democracy, next I consider another form of polarization that might leave us with a more pleasant view of the two-step flow.

IS IT REALLY THAT BAD?

The picture might not be so grim. There is another form of polarization that the public has become increasingly concerned about in recent years: affective polarization. Affective polarization refers to the extent to which Republicans and Democrats dislike one another. While there is much debate over the best ways to measure affective polarization and the degree to which it exists (e.g., Druckman et al. 2022; Druckman and Levendusky 2019), there is a rapidly growing body of research suggesting that, at least to some degree, Republicans and Democrats do not like each other, and this distaste has been growing over time (Iyengar, Sood, and Lelkes 2012; Iyengar et al. 2019).

In contrast to its effects on attitude polarization, political discussion has been viewed as a potential *remedy* to affective polarization. Recent work has shown that interacting with the other side can reduce out-party animosity and increase out-group tolerance (Mutz 2006; Gibson 1992; Rossiter 2020; Rossiter and Carlson 2023; Levendusky and Stecula 2021; Levendusky 2023). But these studies either focus on repeated interactions with the out-party in real social networks (e.g., Mutz 2006) or experiments specifically designed to facilitate meaningful conversations between out-partisans (e.g., Rossiter 2020; Levendusky and Stecula 2021; Rossiter and Carlson 2023). Can simple information from an out-partisan work to reduce out-party animosity? Does information from a copartisan increase out-party animosity?

Social information transmission can highlight the very features of politicized social experiences that drive affective polarization. For example, Druckman and colleagues (2022) find that feelings toward the out-party are much cooler when individuals are thinking about out-partisans who are ideologically extreme and politically engaged, the very features that also characterize the actively informed. Socially transmitted information from copartisans might also be dressed with the very type of partisan cheerleading that pushes people into their corners, leading them to feel more negative about the other side. It could also be the case that exposure to a message from an out-partisan reveals deeper policy disagreement that in turn triggers out-party animosity (Orr and Huber 2020).

I examined the relationship between exposure to socially transmitted information and change in out-party animosity in both the immigration policy and environmental policy studies. I measured affective polarization using a standard 100-point feeling thermometer, in which people report how warm or cold they feel toward other groups. Following recent evidence that out-party animosity can be exaggerated when people are thinking about the ideologically extreme, politically active members of the out-party rather than the ideologically moderate, less active members of the out-party, I asked participants to report how they felt about all of these combinations for both Democrats and Republicans. I then created a variable for out-party animosity by using the ratings when Republicans reported how they felt about Democrats and when Democrats reported how they felt about Republicans. I dropped Independents from these analyses but treated Independents who leaned toward one party as partisans.

For better or for worse, it turns out that feelings toward the out-party are incredibly strong and not particularly malleable. Even on a feeling thermometer, which should have some variability because of the wide range of response options, 24 percent of respondents gave the exact same rating before and after treatment, and 40 percent of respondents did not move their ratings by more than 2 points in either direction. Regardless of whether I examined within-subject change in feelings, only post-treatment feelings, or the difference between in- and out-party evaluations, I find no evidence that the informational treatments caused individuals to update their feelings toward the out-party in either direction.

These null findings suggest that socially transmitted information does not seem to affect the way people feel about the other side. This stands in contrast to experiments demonstrating that face-to-face (Levendusky and Stecula 2021), video chat (Santoro and Broockman 2022; West 2022), and online text chat (Rossiter 2020) conversations between out-partisans can make people feel warmer toward the other side. A key difference might be that the conversations in the experiments allowed for a more personal, social interaction than the one-shot exposure to a single message in my experiments. It might be the case that my treatment was simply not strong enough to change people's attitudes toward the other side. Alternatively, these conflicting findings could reflect the importance of the social connection for influencing affective polarization, which might be less essential for influencing attitudinal polarization. This is something for future research to grapple with, especially when considering the nature of social interactions on social media, which might have less back-and-forth than face-to-face conversations.

Socially transmitted information can indeed contribute to attitude polarization, which may bring its own challenges, but it does not affect the deep tension between Republicans and Democrats. This presents yet another paradox in considering whether socially transmitted information helps or hurts democratic functioning.

7
Engaged

In fall 2019, Facebook founder, Mark Zuckerberg, gave a speech at Georgetown University in which he highlighted the importance of free expression for democracy. In doing so, he explained the ways in which his social media platform enabled more people to have a voice, viewing the platform as a crucial way to uphold political participation and democratic values. Zuckerberg remarked, "The power of democracy in these systems is that when you give everyone a voice and give people power, the system usually ends up in a really good place, so what we view our role as is giving people that power."[1]

Many have debated the role that social media platforms, including but not limited to Facebook, play in helping or hurting democracy (e.g., Sunstein 2018). This debate is likely to continue as platforms change and add new features or terms of use for user engagement, as legislators change the rules that govern how platforms operate, and as political events unfold around the world. But one thing that is particularly important to focus on in considering this debate is the role that everyday people play in contributing to the content shared on the platforms as they express their voices and the intimate connection this may have with political participation.

Facebook is an important vehicle through which socially transmitted information can increase participation in elections. Thousands of people turned out to vote in 2010 as a direct result of content they saw about their friends' voting behavior on Facebook (Bond et al. 2012). Facebook is a digital space through which socially transmitted information spreads among 2.89 billion people worldwide. Perhaps Zuckerberg is right to describe his company as one that gives people the power to express their voices and participate in democracy.

At this point in the book, I have shown that socially transmitted information can sometimes make people less informed, lead them to be misinformed, and hold more partisan political attitudes. But perhaps these informational and attitudinal outcomes are irrelevant if people do not *act*. Does socially transmitted information have behavioral consequences too?

A wealth of existing research has shown that peers have a tremendous impact on political engagement. People are more likely to vote when their friends vote (Kenny 1992; Fowler 2005; Nickerson 2008; Sinclair, McConnell, and Green 2012; Bond et al. 2012). People are more likely to turn out to vote when they are encouraged by a face-to-face conversation with a canvasser than when they receive a phone call or mailer (Gerber and Green 2000). Beyond voting, social networks are especially influential for increasing public forms of participation, such as donating to campaigns (Sinclair 2012). The more people discuss politics with their peers, the more likely they are to participate in political campaigns (McClurg 2003). The list goes on, but suffice it to say that political engagement is largely shaped by social networks.

Research on social networks and political participation does not have a strong grasp on the mechanism that drives these important shifts in engagement. One possible mechanism is social pressure. Humans have a strong desire to fit in with others, and they might take political action because of pressure from their peers (e.g., Gerber and Green 2000; Gerber, Green, and Larimer 2008). An alternative explanation involves the endogeneity and homophily in social networks. Measuring causal effects of social networks on political behavior is incredibly challenging (Fowler et al. 2011; Rogowski and Sinclair 2012; Minozzi et al. 2020). It could be the case that people who were already politically engaged are friends with one another and discuss politics together rather than the engagement of one person causing another to become more engaged as a result of their social interactions.

All of these explanations are at least partially true given the state of the evidence in the field. But another explanation focuses on the *information* exchanged within social interactions as the key driver of political participation. In developing his social network model of participation, Scott McClurg wrote:

> The main tenet of this approach is that informal conversations between network partners expose people to political information from the surrounding social environment. . . . People also may be exposed to information about the mechanics of electoral politics and involvement. Information about which candidate to support, why to support that candidate, when the candidate is holding a rally, or even how to just get involved are all types of information that can be effectively exchanged by word of mouth. (2003, 7)

Communication scholars make a similar point, asserting that political discussion networks influence political behavior because of the information that is exchanged in these discussions. While these studies articulate an interesting (and likely) mechanism that could drive political participation, they do not actually record, measure, or analyze the substance of the information exchanged in political discussions. This is a hard task to accomplish, but if we are to understand the role that socially transmitted information plays in shaping political participation, we need to examine these conversations directly.

Throughout this book, I have developed new methods for capturing the content of socially transmitted information. While my studies do not fully capture the content of informal political discussions, they provide a sense of the type of information that might be conveyed in these conversations and, importantly, how it differs from the alternative of acquiring that information from the news. In chapter 4, I showed that socially transmitted information is sparse, contains more partisan bias, contains more false information, and contains more mobilizing calls to action than information communicated by the media. In addition to providing information that might be essential to participation, such as that outlined by McClurg (2003), socially transmitted information also contains explicit calls to engage in politics. These calls to action are an important addition to the information environment, one that is distinct from most news coverage.

Does socially transmitted information increase political engagement? Yes. Because political engagement is difficult to measure, I use three approaches to answer this question. I begin by revisiting the experiments discussed in chapter 6 to examine whether exposure to socially transmitted information causes individuals to become more engaged in politics. The experiments reveal that when people receive socially transmitted information from a copartisan, they are more likely to report that they would contact their legislator, donate to relevant organizations, and sign up to receive emails from relevant organizations. Although the experiments allow me to estimate the *causal* effect of socially transmitted information on political engagement, they have limited external validity. To address this concern, my second approach is to use nationally representative cross-sectional survey data to show that when people increase their exposure to socially transmitted information, they are more likely to engage in politics. I find, for example, that people who learned about politics from conversations a lot more than usual leading up to the 2022 midterm elections were about 9 points more likely to contact a legislator with concerns about election integrity than were people who learned from conversations a lot less than usual.

The results from the experiments and survey data suggest that socially transmitted information is associated with increased political engagement. However, both approaches rely on self-reported political engagement. I therefore add a third approach to understanding this relationship. I describe several real-world cases in which socially transmitted information has facilitated political engagement. I use examples from across the ideological spectrum to highlight how both online and face-to-face communication led people to participate politically. These examples demonstrate political engagement in the real world, filling in the gaps left behind by the quantitative analyses of the experiments and survey data.

Together, the experimental, survey, and case study data paint a picture suggesting that socially transmitted information can increase political engagement. Beyond the effects of social pressure, the *information* communicated socially can drive political participation. Moreover, these results demonstrate a largely ignored artifact of the two-step flow. Studies on the two-step flow have almost exclusively focused on cognitive consequences, such as learning and polarization. In addition to these consequences, which I examined in chapters 5 and 6, I show here that the two-step flow can increase political engagement when information flows between copartisans, even without the important social dynamics of face-to-face, personal interactions.

Ultimately, this chapter shows one of the potentially positive outcomes of socially transmitted information. The casually informed can become more likely to engage in politics—at least by contacting legislators and donating to campaigns—after receiving information from someone who was actively informed. Contacting legislators and donating to campaigns are important ways in which people can express their voices. These are important, generally reasonable, normatively appealing ways to participate in politics. Yet I conclude this chapter with a discussion about how socially transmitted information could also facilitate the spread of political violence, leaving the ultimate conclusion about the impact of socially transmitted information on political engagement normatively debatable.

Does Socially Transmitted Information Increase Political Engagement?

As described above, social influence has long been theorized to be a factor contributing to political engagement. While this work comes from dozens of rigorous studies with convincing evidence that social networks, broadly, and political discussions, specifically, can cause people to become more engaged in politics, there is not yet strong evidence that socially transmitted *information* is responsible for this outcome.

Information is viewed as central to political participation. The more information people have, the more interested in and knowledgeable about politics they will be and the more likely they will be to vote (Möller et al. 2014; Prior 2005; Bartels and Rahn 2000). While information is at the start of a long sequence of events that ultimately leads to participation, the mass media and political discussions could both, theoretically, increase political participation through information provision.

But information exchanged in political discussions has to come from somewhere. For many, information originates with the media and then spreads through conversations. Cramer Walsh's (2004) ethnographic study impressively demonstrates how people use political discussion to filter what they learn from the news. Complementing this ethnographic work, I have presented quantitative evidence that information *changes* in this process of flowing from the news to the actively informed to the casually informed. Bound by different incentives, the media and the actively informed provide different flavors of information, with the actively informed providing information that is more mobilizing.

Socially transmitted information provides content that could increase political knowledge (especially when that information comes from a more knowledgeable copartisan) and in turn political participation. In the best case, as identified in chapter 5, socially transmitted information can lead to as much learning as reading a news article would. In this case, we would not expect to observe much of a difference in political participation between socially transmitted information from a more knowledgeable copartisan and the media. However, socially transmitted information does something more. In addition to providing (some) information, it contains the mobilizing calls to action that could inspire people to engage in ways that information from the media simply does not. This could happen as a result of explicit calls to action, as I showed in chapter 4. It could also happen less directly, as a consequence of socially transmitted information containing more emotional language that could in turn be mobilizing (Berger 2014).

I expect that when people are exposed to socially transmitted information, they will be more likely to engage in politics than when they are exposed to no information or information from the media. However, I expect this effect to be limited to information from copartisans. When information is exchanged between copartisans, it is more likely to carry the mobilizing calls to action described in chapter 4, as well as to be more persuasive to the casually informed person who receives that information.

Approach: Experiments, Surveys, and Examples

Examining treatment effects on political engagement is challenging. There are many different forms of engagement, ranging from contacting legislators to turning out to vote to participating in a protest. Some of these activities, such as voting, are directly observable in public records, but others are not. Political engagement is also motivated by a wide range of factors, making it difficult to isolate the effect of a single treatment. Because of these challenges, I investigate the relationship between socially transmitted information and political engagement with three complementary approaches. First, I return to the experiments presented in chapter 6 to estimate the causal effect of exposure to socially transmitted information on self-reported political engagement. Second, I relax the causal identification and use cross-sectional survey data to examine more generalizable patterns. Third, I discuss a number of real-world examples of socially transmitted information affecting political participation. Each approach has strengths and weaknesses, but together the results suggest that socially transmitted information can contribute to political engagement.

In all three approaches, I examine different types of political engagement that are important in the political system but less studied than voting. Although voting is perhaps the most studied and among the most important forms of political engagement, there are many important factors that contribute to turnout, making it difficult to isolate the effect of socially transmitted information. For example, in the context of a simple survey experiment, it is unlikely that exposure to one piece of information would be enough to shift something as difficult to influence as voter turnout. I decided to focus on political behaviors that might be less common overall than turning out to vote, still play an important role in politics, and are directly tied to the content of the information in the news, which would allow me to better approximate the consequences of the two-step flow. In the quantitative analyses, I examine the likelihood that people contact legislators to express concerns, donate to political causes, or sign up to receive emails from political groups. It is important to note that these analyses only capture *self-reported* political engagement, which may or may not predict actual engagement. Some respondents might feel pressure to overreport political engagement, so this self-reported behavior needs to be interpreted carefully. In the experiments, the tendency to overreport political engagement should be evenly distributed between the treatment groups due to random assignment, meaning that the treatment effects can still be interpreted causally.

In my qualitative discussion of real-world examples, I focus on some of the most extreme forms of political engagement. I examine instances of political violence and protest that have garnered significant attention by scholars, journalists, and the public in recent years. This form of political engagement is rare overall, but tracing the social roots of these examples helps to illustrate the importance of socially transmitted information in these uncommon, but sometimes troubling expressions of political participation.

EXPERIMENTAL DATA

Testing the causal effect of socially transmitted information on political engagement requires isolating the effect of *information* from the effect of the social networks in which that information is exchanged. The experiments conducted in chapter 6 are nicely suited to meet this challenge because they strip away the social context to focus on the effect of the information itself. The first experiment focused on immigration policy, and the second focused on environmental policy. In summary, I first recruited a sample of actively informed survey respondents who read a news article about the topic in their study and then wrote a message to another person telling them about what they just read. I then recruited a sample of casually informed survey respondents who were randomly assigned to read either one of these messages written by an actively informed respondent (i.e., socially transmitted information), the original news article on which these messages were based, or no information at all.

In chapter 6, I analyzed their policy preferences, but in this chapter I focus on measures of political engagement. In the Immigration Policy Experiment, I examined whether respondents reported that they would contact their legislator about immigration policy. In the Environmental Policy Experiment, I examined whether respondents would contact their legislator about environmental policy, whether they would donate money to an organization that supported or opposed drilling for oil, and whether they would sign up to receive emails from such organizations. Each response was measured on a four-point scale ranging from 0 (very unlikely) to 3 (very likely).

Overall, I find general support for my expectation that socially transmitted information from copartisans causes people to become more engaged. Although political engagement remains relatively low overall, it was generally more common when the casually informed received information from a copartisan.

Figure 7.1 shows the average likelihood of contacting a legislator about immigration policy. The results reveal that when participants received

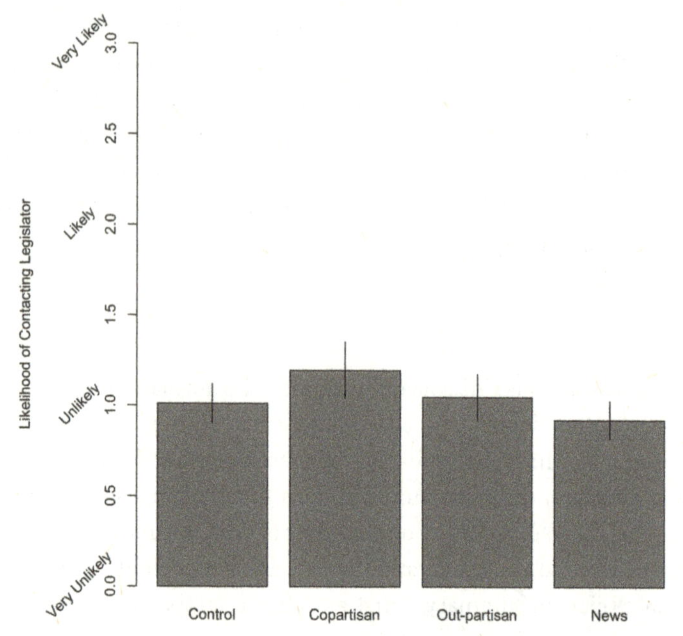

FIGURE 7.1. Average self-reported likelihood of contacting a legislator about immigration policy. Data are from the Immigration Policy Experiment. Vertical lines represent 95% confidence intervals.

information from a copartisan, they were significantly more likely to report that they would contact their legislator about immigration policy than did participants who received information from the news or no information at all. Even participants who received information from a copartisan were still unlikely to contact their legislator, but they were *more likely* than those who received information from other sources. Specifically, 12 percent of respondents who received information from a copartisan said that they would be "very likely" to contact a legislator, compared to 9 percent of respondents who received no information. On the other side, 27 percent of people who received information from a copartisan said they would be "very unlikely" to contact their legislator, compared to 39 percent of those who received information from the news and 35 percent of people who received no information at all. Although this pattern is consistent with my theoretical expectations, I did not find the same pattern in the Environmental Policy Experiment.

In the Environmental Policy Experiment, I examined additional political engagement variables that I did not measure in the Immigration Policy Experiment. Figure 7.2 shows the results for the self-reported likelihood that respondents would donate money to (left) and sign up to receive emails from (right) organizations that supported drilling for oil. The results show that respondents who received information from copartisans were more likely to report that they would donate ($p < .05$) and sign up to receive emails from these organizations. This pattern unfolds regardless of partisanship and underlying beliefs about drilling.

To contextualize these results further, I found that 13 percent of respondents who received information from a copartisan reported being "very likely" to donate to pro-drilling organizations, compared to only 8 percent of respondents who received information from the news and 7 percent of respondents who received no information at all. Respondents were thus 6 percentage points more likely to report that they would donate to a pro-drilling organization when they received information from a copartisan than if they received no information at all. This is similar to the relationship between pretreatment (baseline) attitudes toward drilling and likelihood of donating. Respondents who were supportive of drilling at baseline were 8 percentage points more likely to report that they would be "very likely" to donate to a pro-drilling organization than were people whose baseline attitudes were against drilling.

The patterns are very similar for signing up to receive pro-drilling emails. I found that about 15 percent of respondents who received information from a copartisan were "very likely" to sign up for emails from pro-drilling organizations, compared to only 6 percent of people who received information from the news and 8 percent of people who received no information at all. Respondents who received information from a copartisan were therefore about 7 percentage points more likely to report being "very likely" to sign up for

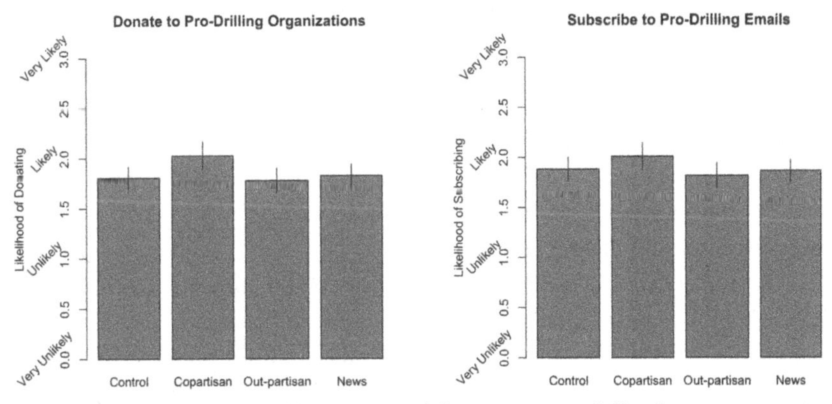

FIGURE 7.2. Average likelihood of donating to pro-drilling organizations (left) and signing up to receive emails from pro-drilling organizations (right). Data are from the Environmental Policy Experiment. Vertical lines represent 95% confidence intervals.

emails than people who received no information at all. This effect is similar to the relationship between pretreatment attitudes toward drilling: respondents who were in favor of drilling at baseline were 9 percentage points more likely to report being "very likely" to sign up to receive pro-drilling emails than were respondents who were against drilling at baseline.

Together, these results suggest that socially transmitted information from copartisans can make people more likely to contact legislators about immigration, donate money to interest groups, and sign up to receive additional information from interest groups. Importantly, the effect of these small, subtle informational treatments is comparable to the relationship between attitudes toward drilling and political engagement. This suggests that at scale, political conversations could have a profound impact on political engagement.

Like any study, these experiments have limitations. The impact of socially transmitted information on contacting a legislator was only statistically significant in the Immigration Policy Experiment. Though it is hard to untangle the mechanism using the data that I have, it is interesting to consider why socially transmitted information from copartisans increased the likelihood someone would contact a legislator about immigration but not environmental policy. It could be that participants were more interested in immigration policy or thought that contacting their legislator would have a more tangible impact on immigration policy than on environmental policy. However, the average likelihood of contacting a legislator in the control group (absent any information) was statistically indistinguishable between the two studies. This perhaps suggests that people were not fundamentally more likely to contact a legislator about immigration than environmental policy.

It could also be the case that people had weaker prior beliefs about environmental policy than on immigration policy. With immigration policy, any informational treatment might have done more to activate strong feelings which could in turn inspire people to contact their legislators. But feelings about environmental policy might not be as strong, leading to little effect of the information treatments on contacting legislators. These results could suggest that socially transmitted information from copartisans can mobilize people around salient, partisan, polarizing issues like immigration but perhaps less for issues that are less salient.

The normative implications of this distinction are important. On the one hand, it could suggest that it is easier to mobilize people to take action on issues they already care about. Paired with the findings presented in chapter 6, socially transmitted information from a copartisan could push someone to have more sorted and extreme political attitudes at the same time that they are pushing them to contact a legislator about those preferences. On the other hand, it suggests that it might be harder for the actively informed to get their casually informed peers to take action on less salient but still polarizing issues. Although socially transmitted information from copartisans still caused people to develop more extreme political attitudes about environmental policy, they do not appear more likely to contact a legislator to express those extreme preferences. Together, this could point to part of the reason legislators have biased perceptions of their constituents' preferences as being more extreme (Broockman and Skovron 2018). If legislators are more likely to be contacted by people with more extreme preferences who want to discuss polarizing, salient issues, it makes sense that they would then pursue those policy priorities, which may not reflect what the median voter wants.

Finally, in the Environmental Policy Experiment, where more political engagement outcomes were measured, the information treatments affected political engagement but only for involvement with *pro*-drilling organizations. Given that donating to pro- or anti-drilling organizations is likely correlated with partisanship, I examined whether Democrats and Republicans were uniquely affected by the information treatments. In general, Democrats in this sample were significantly more likely to report that they would donate to both anti- and pro-drilling organizations, whereas Republicans were unlikely to report that they would donate money to organizations (and were equally unlikely to donate to pro- or anti-drilling organizations). Republicans were more likely to sign up to receive emails from pro-drilling organizations than anti-drilling organizations. On the other side, Democrats were more likely to sign up to receive emails from anti-drilling organizations than from pro-drilling organizations. However, there is no significant interaction between partisanship and informational treatment. It furthermore was not the case that receiving information from a Republican led people to be more likely to donate to pro-drilling organizations, while information from a Democrat led people to be more likely to donate to anti-drilling organizations.

Curiously, the Environmental Policy Experiment showed that socially transmitted information from copartisans led to increased involvement with pro-drilling organizations but not anti-drilling organizations. Beyond the scope of environmental policy, this finding raises questions about how socially transmitted information can lead to political engagement that favors one side over another. Investigating these dynamics more carefully in future work would help us think about the nature of the relationship between socially transmitted information and political engagement but also the implications it could have for practitioners aimed at mobilizing groups to action.

SURVEY DATA

The results from the survey experiments described previously are useful for identifying the causal effect of exposure to different types of information on political engagement. However, the results are nuanced and have limited generalizability, particularly because the experiments do not allow for communication within real social networks. In this section, I use additional survey data to address these concerns. The survey data lacks causal identification but presents similar patterns as the experiments.

I use data from a nationally representative survey conducted in February 2023. This survey was conducted by NORC from their AmeriSpeak panel, which includes a national probability sample. This was a cross-sectional survey, so I could not examine within-respondent variation in information consumption. Simply examining the correlation between being casually or actively informed and political engagement does not allow me to examine *change*. And in general the casually informed are less engaged politically than the actively informed, as discussed in chapter 2. The actively informed are sufficiently interested in politics that they seek out information from the news and are also more likely to be engaged than the casually informed who acquire that information socially.[2] The key is that *when* people are exposed to information about politics, they are more likely to engage when that information is delivered socially.

To evaluate this in survey data, I could not simply ask the same question about whether people are generally casually or actively informed. Instead, I needed to ask them about changes in the amount of information they acquired socially. Specifically, I asked, "Some people learn about politics and elections from the news, while others learn about it from their friends and family through conversations and on social media. Leading up to the November 2022 elections, would you say that you learned about politics from conversations with friends and family . . ." Respondents could report their change in information consumption on a seven-point scale ranging from "a lot more than usual" to "a lot less than usual." I examined whether this self-reported change in socially transmitted information consumption was associated with political behaviors that were directly relevant to the November 2022 electoral context. Specifically, I examined the likelihood of contacting a legislator with concerns about election integrity, attending a protest, and patrolling outside a polling station.

Using a simple weighted logistic regression, controlling for age, race, education, party identification, and gender, I found that the more people consumed socially transmitted information leading up to the election, the more

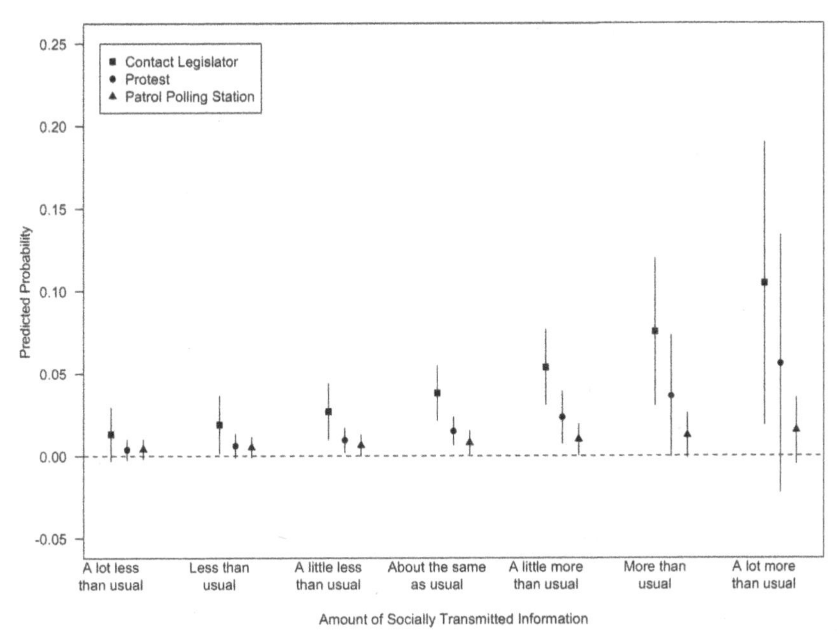

FIGURE 7.3. Predicted probability of engaging in political activities at different levels of socially transmitted information consumption. Data are from the February 2023 cross-sectional wave of TASS. Vertical lines represent 95% confidence intervals. Predicted probabilities were generated from a weighted logistic regression model, holding covariates at their means or modes.

likely they were to contact a legislator with concerns about election integrity ($p < .05$) and attend a protest ($p < .10$). To contextualize these results, figure 7.3 shows the predicted probability of engaging in the activity at different amounts of socially transmitted information.[3] People who reported learning a lot less than usual from conversations were extremely unlikely to contact a legislator with concerns about election integrity, with a predicted probability of .01. However, people who reported learning a lot more than usual from conversations were much more likely to report that they would contact a legislator to discuss election integrity concerns, with a predicted probability of .10. Similarly, the predicted probability that someone would attend a protest was .004 if they learned a lot less than usual from conversations and .06 if they learned a lot more than usual from conversations. In both cases, the predicted probability of contacting a legislator or attending a protest was very low, but it was much higher for those who learned a lot more from others than usual.

When it comes to the most extreme form of political participation examined, patrolling polling stations, it is hard to draw meaningful inferences. The relationship between information consumption and patrolling polling stations was not statistically significant, but only fourteen participants in the sample reported that they patrolled outside a polling station. However, twelve of the fourteen people who reported doing so also reported that they learned about politics from conversations about the same or *more* than usual, leaving only two people who reported learning less from conversations.

It is important to note that the results from the cross-sectional data do not allow for causal inference. That is, these data do not allow me to say that increased exposure to socially transmitted information *caused* people to be more likely to contact legislators about political issues or election integrity, run for office, or attend protests. These results are also limited to individuals' self-reported information consumption and political engagement, both of which could be subject to social desirability bias or errors in memory recall. However, when these findings are paired with the results from the experiment, which address some of these limitations, it is hard to ignore the likelihood that socially transmitted information pushes people to engage in politics.

REAL-WORLD EXAMPLES

Finally, it is important to consider types of political engagement beyond the mainstream. My experiments were not designed to investigate whether socially transmitted information would cause people to engage in political violence or protest. The cross-sectional survey data suggested that increased exposure to socially transmitted information was associated with a greater likelihood of participating in a protest. I round out the quantitative analyses presented previously by discussing some examples from the real world. Of course, these examples have been selected to illustrate the point that socially transmitted information can contribute to political engagement. These examples are rare, extreme cases. The overwhelming majority of Americans are *not* engaging in political violence or protest. The overwhelming majority of socially transmitted information is *not* causing political violence or protest. But there are a number of salient examples in recent memory that show direct relationships between exposure to socially transmitted information and instances of political violence as a result of a perfect blend of false information and calls to action.

One key example is the insurrection at the US Capitol on January 6, 2021. Hundreds of Americans stormed the Capitol in a last-ditch effort to stop the official certification of the November 2020 election. What began as a relatively peaceful protest against Joe Biden's victory quickly descended into mayhem and violence, due in part to perceptions of voter fraud. People around the world watched in awe, struggling to come to grips with what was happening and what it meant for the future of American democracy.

With the initial sting of the event fading, people soon started to try to understand what caused the insurrection to happen. Many pointed to a speech delivered by then-president Trump, suggesting that he directly encouraged people to violently storm the Capitol. Months later, however, people began pointing to Facebook as a lead actor in facilitating the spread of extreme conspiratorial content on its platform. In part motivated by internal Facebook documents leaked by a whistleblower, Frances Haugen, several current and former Facebook employees remarked that Facebook knew how its platform could radicalize users and watched the outcome of their passivity on January 6 (Timberg, Dwoskin, and Albergotti 2021).

Although Facebook itself may not be responsible for the actions taken by the protesters on January 6, the platform allows individual users to write and share content with others that could be politically mobilizing. Recall that in chapter 4 I demonstrated that socially transmitted information about the news on January 6 spread on another social media platform, Twitter, was more likely to contain explicit calls to action, including violence, than information communicated by the news. In the case of January 6, socially transmitted information spread on Facebook could have played a role in violent, extreme political engagement. Zuckerberg's 2019 description of his platform's important role in facilitating free expression to uphold democracy took a dark turn in 2021.

Examples of socially transmitted information contributing to political violence or extreme forms of political engagement need not be as intense or high profile as the insurrection at the Capitol. In summer 2020, social media posts circulating on Facebook and Twitter alleged that left-wing extremists who were part of Antifa were plotting a protest at Gettysburg National Cemetery.[4] Rumors that the group was going to desecrate monuments and burn flags spread widely, leading hundreds of right-wing counter-protesters to show up to defend the cemetery. Ultimately, no one was hurt in this instance, perhaps in part because there were no Antifa members to be found. Unlike the insurrection at the Capitol, this event only carried the potential for violence, but the broader point remains that false, socially transmitted information spread online and interpersonally can open the door to extreme political engagement.

More recently, the racially motivated Buffalo massacre has been linked directly to information shared on social media.[5] On May 14, 2022, an eighteen-year-old man drove two hundred miles from his home to attack a supermarket in a racially diverse neighborhood, killing ten people and injuring three. The suspect posted online a 180-page manifesto explaining his plans and ultimately livestreamed the massacre over the social media platform Twitch.

In the manifesto, the suspect explained that his actions were motivated by the Great Replacement Theory, which he learned about while surfing social media platforms like 4chan while he was bored during the COVID-19 pandemic. Platforms like 4chan with essentially no rules about what content can be posted can be safe havens for extreme political ideas to spread. In this case, an eighteen-year-old was exposed to socially transmitted information about a political theory that—in his words—ultimately led him to take ten lives.

Socially transmitted information can contribute to political violence and extremism on both sides of the ideological spectrum. In fall 2020, the Network Contagion Research Institute (NCRI) noted that left-wing extremist groups use social media in ways similar to groups on the right.[6] Such coordination online was linked to riots across the country in response to George Floyd's death. In their analysis, NCRI paid careful attention to the socially transmitted information posted by everyday users on online platforms such as Twitter, Facebook, and Reddit, noting increased use of antipolice rhetoric within left-wing networks on each platform. These posts sometimes called directly for violence. For example, a *Washington Post* article summarizing the NCRI report's findings stated, "One post from a left-wing group cited by the report called for the use of laser pointers to obstruct surveillance and the lighting of fires at police barricades. Another post urged people to use 3-D printers to make guns that can't be traced by authorities" (Timberg and Stanley-Becker 2020). This specific example might reflect more structured, coordinated information flows rather than the two-step flow processes I describe in this book. But the broader point is that left-wing extremist groups also engage in political violence, and some of this violence has been linked directly to activity on social media—a key context in which socially transmitted information spreads.

Answer: Socially Transmitted Information Can Increase Engagement

Across three empirical approaches, the results suggest that socially transmitted information *can* increase political engagement. The experiments, despite their limitations, demonstrated that exposure to socially transmitted information from a copartisan caused the casually informed to be more likely to report that they would contact a legislator, donate to interest groups, and sign up to receive information from interest groups. The survey data revealed that when people felt that they had increased their dose of socially transmitted information, they were more likely to engage in various political behaviors, including contacting legislators about election integrity concerns and attending a protest. Finally, several real-world cases point to social roots driving people to take action in ways that challenge democratic functioning. While none of these analyses definitively conclude that socially transmitted information increases political engagement, they at minimum demonstrate the possibility that it matters and merits additional consideration.

Conclusion

In this chapter, I demonstrated that socially transmitted information from like-minded people, absent the social pressure inherent in actual interpersonal interactions, can lead the casually informed to be more likely to contact their legislators about immigration policy, donate to pro-drilling interest groups, and sign up to receive emails from pro-drilling interest groups. Contacting legislators, donating to interest groups, and opting into additional information from interest groups are all mainstream forms of political engagement that allow individuals to express their voices in government. We could take these results—interpreted with caution—and conclude that socially transmitted information contributes to democracy without much distortion, because it facilitates these important forms of political engagement. Perhaps in this context, the distortion inherent in socially transmitted information helps democracy function better than it would if the casually informed had no information at all.

In concluding this chapter, I consider two key points that situate these results within my broader argument in this book and within American politics. The first point discusses the more optimistic view of these results, highlighting that mobilization can happen through everyday conversations even without intense efforts from campaigns and grassroots organizations. The results, therefore, have important implications for practitioners, as well as scholars interested in political participation. The second point considers the line in the sand separating political engagement that strengthens or weakens democracy.

INDIRECT MOBILIZATION BY TALKING ABOUT THE NEWS

The results in this chapter suggest that socially transmitted information about the news can have a mobilizing effect, even if the original news articles were not at all intended to mobilize. Practitioners and scholars alike can take these findings to think about new ways to increase political engagement without needing to focus exclusively on political campaigns. Given that some people are averse to the intensity of political competition in elections (e.g., Klar and Krupnikov 2016) and are inundated with campaign messaging during election cycles, perhaps approaches that foster discussions about current events more broadly could be an effective way to increase political engagement more subtly.

The results presented in this chapter suggest that political engagement can increase when information flows between copartisans. On the one hand, this is good news for practitioners because political discussion networks are largely (but not entirely) homogeneous (e.g., Mutz 2006; Huckfeldt, Johnson, and Sprague 2004). That is, most Americans tend to talk about politics with copartisans, though this is less true for Asian and Latino Americans than it is for white and Black Americans (Carlson, Abrajano, and García Bedolla 2020a, 2020b). On the other hand, this could run counter to many ongoing efforts to reduce partisan tension in the United States. Many organizations are dedicated to bringing Republicans and Democrats together to talk about important issues in an effort to reduce out-party animosity. Indeed, there is ample evidence that interacting with people from the other side has important benefits, such as increased tolerance (Mutz 2006; Gibson 1992; Rossiter 2020; Rossiter and Carlson 2023). But, these important heterogeneous interactions might come at the cost of decreased (or at least no improvement in) political engagement. This is consistent with previous work showing that people in more diverse political discussion networks are more likely to experience cross-pressure and are therefore less likely to turn out to vote (Mutz 2006).

Thus, one lesson for practitioners is that socially transmitted information can be mobilizing, even if it is simply about policy or the news. Information does not necessarily need to be focused on the task practitioners would like people to do (e.g., vote, contact a legislator, do more research, donate, register to vote) but could instead be focused on important issues. These policy-relevant conversations are more likely to be effective at increasing engagement if they are between copartisans, but this can also bring with it some challenges that practitioners would need to consider. Of course, future work is needed to unpack the scope of these implications. For example, future work could examine the types of issues socially transmitted information is most likely to mobilize around. But for now, there are at least some hints that simple conversations about the news between copartisans can be mobilizing, and this has important implications for voter engagement efforts.

THE LINE IN THE SAND

There are many ways in which people can express their voices in politics, and every type of political engagement can have a dark side. Contacting a legislator to politely, reasonably express one's opinion is different from yelling at, harassing, threatening, and doxing legislators, even if both behaviors are forms of political expression and engagement. Sharing information with others in our social networks to try to help them become better informed is another important and normatively good way to engage in politics. Yet sharing false and biased information with peers in a direct effort to mislead or persuade them is less desirable. Participating in peaceful protest is an important political action, especially for underrepresented, underresourced groups (Gause 2022), to achieve meaningful change. Violent protest and riots are not.

Where is the line? At what point do certain forms of political engagement weaken democracy rather than strengthen it? These are important questions with which scholars, politicians, and voters will continue to grapple. Considering the role that socially transmitted information can play in nudging people to engage in politics, particularly if it pushes them over the line, is fundamentally important. This is important for contextualizing whether to interpret the results of this book optimistically or pessimistically. It is also important for thinking more carefully about the information environment. As social media platforms take on an increasingly prominent role in the information environment, understanding the potential costs and benefits of socially transmitted information is vital.

The results in this chapter should lead us to think carefully about how the two-step flow can facilitate political engagement—for better and for worse. Pushing people to engage in extreme, violent political actions is probably something many would prefer to avoid. Pushing people to engage peacefully but based on false, misleading, or inaccurate information is also probably not a desirable outcome. But socially transmitted information about the news can also be a powerful tool to nudge people to express their voices in government. The two-step flow, therefore, can facilitate political engagement in line with more idealistic views of democracy. The challenge is to ensure that socially transmitted information stays within this positive form of political engagement without tipping into violence.

8

Distorted or Dysfunctional?

I opened this book by highlighting the similar criticism levied against the media by Thomas Jefferson and Donald Trump. While these former presidents served the American public in two very different time periods and in two very different information environments, both emphasized the importance of truth and questioned the media's ability to deliver that truth to the American public without bias.

Information and truth serve important roles at the heart of democracy. If people are to effectively participate in politics, their opinions and actions should ideally be based on truthful information. But what information actually reaches the American public? How does the infusion of political information in social interactions affect what people know, think, and do about politics?

In this book, I argued that to answer these questions, we need new attention to the oldest type of information: socially transmitted information. Although it can be generated and spread in different ways today, socially transmitted information about politics has been part of the information environment even before the time Thomas Jefferson cautioned that people who do not read the newspaper are better informed than those who do. But for one reason or another, our scholarship has largely failed to scrutinize socially transmitted information in the same way that we have scrutinized information from the mass media.

In returning the focus to socially transmitted information, I presented a theory of distorted democracy. I argued that information becomes distorted as it flows from the mass media to the actively informed people who consume the news directly to their casually informed peers. Socially transmitted information passed from the actively to the casually informed is sparse, more biased, less accurate, and more mobilizing than information communicated by mass media. These changes to the information environment matter. When the casually informed are exposed to this sparse, biased, less accurate, and mobilizing information, they are more misinformed and more polarized but more engaged.

The key expectations that stem from the theory of distorted democracy present a provocative image of American democracy, where seemingly simple conversations about the news can distort the information environment so badly that it can facilitate the spread of misinformation and amplify polarization, yet foster political engagement. However, the empirical evidence suggests that the story is complex. As I conclude this book, I begin by reviewing the key findings, with careful attention to the optimistic and pessimistic interpretations of the results. I review both the findings about how much the actively informed distort information from the media and the results about how these distortions affect the casually informed. Next, I consider the questions that remain and what the future of political communication research can bring. Finally, I consider whether the evidence presented in this book should lead us to conclude that American democracy is fundamentally dysfunctional or just distorted.

Socially Transmitted Information and Distorted Democracy

How does information change as it flows from the media to the actively informed to the casually informed? How do changes to the information itself affect political attitudes and behavior? In this section, I summarize the key results presented in this book that answer these questions. In summarizing the results, I carefully consider the ways in which we can interpret their broader implications.

SOCIAL TRANSMISSION DISTORTS INFORMATION

Through analyses of telephone game experiments and data from Twitter, I examined socially transmitted information across a range of topics. I showed that socially transmitted information, at minimum, looks *different* from information communicated by mass media. But the more interesting question is, different *how*? In short, information becomes sparse, more biased, less accurate, and more mobilizing.

In chapter 4 I showed that socially transmitted information is sparse compared to information from mass media. As the actively informed summarize the news for their peers, they leave out many details. On its face, this seems problematic. However, exposure to less information is not necessarily bad. Technological changes have facilitated the spread of information in short snippets (i.e., tweets, TikTok videos, article previews). Journalists and the public have adapted to this new, condensed form of storytelling, which may resemble the sparse nature of socially transmitted information. However, this new form of storytelling could come with important consequences when we consider *what* information is communicated and how it affects subsequent attitudes and behavior.

One way to consider what information is communicated is to evaluate the extent to which socially transmitted information is biased. As I demonstrated in chapter 4, socially transmitted information carries partisan bias and opinion added by the actively informed. Even when the actively informed consume nonpartisan news, they repackage that information to reflect their partisan biases when they pass it along to their peers.

If we are concerned about partisan media bias, we should be concerned about socially transmitted information. One reason we might even be more concerned about partisan bias in socially transmitted information, relative to partisan bias in the mass media, is that socially transmitted information can be sneaky. The casually informed might consider socially transmitted information less biased than the media—or fail to consider that their peers carry partisan bias.[1] While people can infer others' political views with reasonable accuracy (Carlson and Settle 2022, ch. 4; Carlson and Hill 2022; Hiaeshutter-Rice, Neuner, and Soroka 2023; Deichert 2019; Huckfeldt and Sprague 1987), this might not be enough to help people interpret socially transmitted information in light of their informant's biases, and it might not be possible if the socially transmitted information to which they are exposed comes from strangers online.

A step beyond bias, socially transmitted information is also less accurate than the original information from the news on which it was based. Across all of my experiments, about 4.8 percent of socially transmitted information contained at least one piece of false information. As I described in chapter 4, many of these inaccuracies could be perceived as trivial. Sometimes people slightly misreported a number (e.g., GDP rose by 1.7 percent instead of 1.4 percent). Sometimes people incorrectly reported whether the economy was growing or shrinking, suggested that some candidates were running for office when they were not, or implied that politicians were engaged in fraudulent behavior when there was no evidence at the time that they were. These latter examples could be more worrisome.

Without a good, normative benchmark against which to compare what we should expect the rate of false content in socially transmitted information to be, it is hard to evaluate whether the overall rate of inaccuracy in socially transmitted information is problematic. Moreover, just as news accuracy varies across topics (Soroka and Wlezien 2022), so too might the inaccuracy of socially transmitted information. What I can say about the accuracy of socially transmitted information is that when the actively informed read accurate news, the information they pass on has more false information than the news on which it is based. We can and, I hope, will continue to debate the *extent* to which socially transmitted information is inaccurate, but it is important that we consider the possibility that socially transmitted information at minimum *can* create and spread false information.

Finally, socially transmitted information is mobilizing. Where journalists typically refrain from making a direct call to action, everyday people are not so constrained. In chapter 4, I showed that socially transmitted information contains explicit calls to action. These requests vary greatly, with some simply being a plea to do additional research (though maybe this request is not so simple after all). Other actively informed participants directly encouraged people to vote, to vote for specific candidates or parties, and to get involved in politics broadly.

Just as with my discussion of the amount of false content in socially transmitted information, there is not a clear benchmark for the expected or optimal amount of mobilizing calls to action. Again, we need to consider the calls to action relative to the information on which they were based. The news articles participants read contained very few calls to action, which is consistent with professional norms for journalists that do not constrain the actively informed. One way to interpret this, then, is to suggest that any increase in mobilizing calls to action is a way in which socially transmitted information uniquely differs from information communicated by the mass media.

DISTORTED INFORMATION AFFECTS ATTITUDES AND BEHAVIOR

By focusing on the information exchanged in the second step of the two-step flow, I have shown some of the ways in which it is different from information communicated by the mass media. While these changes to the information environment are interesting in their own right, the key is to understand the extent to which they matter. To evaluate the consequences of exposure to socially transmitted information, I examined the ways in which socially transmitted information affected political learning, attitudes, and engagement relative to receiving no information at all and relative to receiving information from the mass media. Despite the limitations of the research designs employed to investigate each type of political behavior, the results suggest that socially transmitted information affects each of these outcomes in potentially important but not always negative ways.

First, I focused on what individuals are able to *learn* from socially transmitted information, both in terms of objective facts and in terms of explicit misinformation. I argued that the first ingredient of a distorted democracy is an underinformed electorate, meaning that people are both uninformed and misinformed. In chapter 5, I evaluated whether the casually informed seem to be underinformed. I showed that the casually informed learn less than their actively informed peers, unless they receive information from someone who is more knowledgeable and shares their partisanship. As long as these conditions are met, socially transmitted information, with all of its imperfections, seems to help the casually informed learn.

However, just as the actively informed can help the casually informed learn facts, they can also help them learn false information. In chapter 5, I showed that the casually informed, on average, are more likely to believe prominent political rumors and conspiracy theories than their actively informed counterparts. Additional survey evidence suggests that those who are misinformed recall learning the misinformation socially. Moreover, evidence from two experiments suggests that both in a standard telephone game experiment setup and in an experiment aimed at understanding dynamics on social media, exposure to socially transmitted information can cause people to become misinformed more than when they are exposed only to information from the mass media or no information at all.

Together, these results suggest that the actively informed have more responsibility than they may realize. On the one hand, they have the power to inform an otherwise inattentive part of the public to the point that in the right pairings, they can be just as knowledgeable as the actively informed themselves on a given topic. On the other hand, they have the power to misinform. Whether the actively informed intentionally try to misinform their peers or do so inadvertently is an open question. But the broader point remains that exposure to socially transmitted information can both inform and misinform.

Second, I considered whether exposure to socially transmitted information causes people to become more polarized. When it comes to attitudinal polarization, I found in chapter 6 that exposure to socially transmitted information from a copartisan caused the casually informed to develop more extreme policy preferences that were more sorted along partisan lines relative to receiving no information at all. Both on highly salient, deeply divisive issues like immigration and on less salient but polarized issues like environmental policy, exposure to socially transmitted information causes people to change their policy preferences to be more in line with their party.

But evaluating whether this is normatively good or bad requires engaging with two considerations. The first is that we need to consider what the appropriate comparison is. My results, presented in chapter 6, suggest that the key increase in partisan sorting comes from receiving socially transmitted information from a copartisan relative to receiving no information at all. However, socially transmitted information from a copartisan was no more polarizing than information from nonpartisan media. The implication here is that the casually informed would be less polarized if they were exposed to no information at all than if they received information from a copartisan, but the difference in polarization between receiving information from a copartisan or from nonpartisan media is immaterial. This introduces a complicated set of recommendations if the goal is to reduce polarization.

This raises the second consideration, which is that we must consider whether having sorted or extreme preferences is normatively bad. The answer to this question might look different if we think about polarization at the individual level as opposed to the societal level. Here, I consider the individual level and return to broader societal-level polarization at the end of the chapter.

While many may call for people to have more moderate views to facilitate compromise, sorting one's preferences along party lines could be viewed as a helpful way to facilitate representation. On the other hand, if people would have made different choices had they been exposed to more balanced information, for example, perhaps they would have updated their attitudes differently. If people develop such extreme preferences that there are no candidates espousing the same views, that could pose problems for representation.

Finally, I close this discussion of polarization by reminding readers that I found *no effects* of information on *affective* polarization. Attitudes toward the out-party did not change at all in response to information from a copartisan, an out-partisan, or the mass media. While political discussion with out-partisans has been shown to reduce affective polarization (Rossiter 2020; Rossiter and Carlson 2023; Levendusky and Stecula 2022; Levendusky 2023), and some theorize that interactions with copartisans could increase affective polarization, I find no evidence that information alone affects out-party animosity. While scholars disagree about the normative value of attitudinal polarization, most agree that affective polarization is not ideal, though some find that it is overestimated (Druckman et al. 2022). Together, these results suggest that at the individual level, socially transmitted information can increase attitudinal polarization but not affective polarization. Much like the finding in the analysis of (mis)information in chapter 5, socially transmitted information is likely not uniformly bad.

Even if we take the worst-case scenarios of being underinformed and polarized, one could argue that these features of the casually informed are irrelevant if they do not act politically. In chapter 7, I investigated the third consequence of socially transmitted information for distorted democracy: political engagement. With experiments, I looked at self-reported intentions to contact legislators, request more information about topics, and donate to relevant causes. I complemented these results with survey data and case studies that probed potentially concerning forms of engagement, such as contacting legislators about election integrity, patrolling polling stations, and engaging in political violence or protest. In general, socially transmitted information from a copartisan can cause people to be more likely to engage in these ways relative to receiving no information at all.

My findings suggest that socially transmitted information can nudge people toward political participation, both within and outside the system. Although the casually informed are generally less politically engaged than the actively informed, the actively informed can inspire the casually informed to take actions that they otherwise would not. The challenge is in thinking about which types of political participation support democratic functioning. This could be problematic if the casually informed are mobilized to action based on misinformation and extreme preferences, perhaps resulting in engagement counter to their interests or political violence. But in the best-case scenario, where socially transmitted information has led someone to learn more facts, have preferences on issues they otherwise had not considered, and then act on those preferences, socially transmitted information could be viewed as a key ingredient of participatory democracy.

The Future of Political Communication Research

Altogether, the evidence presented in this book underscores that political communication research needs to pay careful attention to socially transmitted information. I have shown that socially transmitted information is not a mere carbon copy of information from the mass media, and the ways in which it differs can lead the casually informed to be more misinformed, polarized, but engaged. The normative implications of these patterns are complex, but the bottom line is that socially transmitted information matters and needs to be considered more carefully in future scholarship. In this section, I consider paths forward in building on the work presented in this book. I start small, focusing on direct extensions of this book that would fill some of its theoretical and empirical gaps. I then zoom out to consider how socially transmitted information can be incorporated to better understand other features of political behavior.

DIRECT EXTENSIONS

This book begins to answer fundamental questions about socially transmitted information, but it also raises a number of new questions. While there are many possible extensions to the work presented here, and many methodological approaches that could be used, I focus on six extensions that would build directly on the theoretical and empirical contributions of this book.

The first direct extension of this book is to examine the ways in which socially transmitted information uniquely affects political behavior in online and face-to-face contexts. Research moving forward should apply the theoretical foundations outlined in this book to developing new theories about socially transmitted information specifically on social media, specifically in face-to-face contexts, and how the two contexts might differ. For example, future work might consider the role of anonymity, immediate access to additional information, and exposure to multimedia content, which might better characterize a social media context than a face-to-face context.

Second, new methodological tools should be applied (and developed) to account for a more complete picture of socially transmitted information. In chapter 3, I described the development of the telephone game experiment, which provided a novel approach to understanding socially transmitted information, and also discussed some of its limitations. Recent innovations in audio analysis (Knox and Lucas 2021; Dietrich, Hayes, and O'Brien 2019) and computer vision (Torres 2019) make it possible to analyze new features of conversation that could reveal more than what we can uncover from text alone (Damann, Knox, and Lucas n.d.). Future work could analyze audio recordings of political conversations to examine the emotional tenor that accompanies socially transmitted information. Computer vision technology could open new doors to examining the extent to which images, perhaps accompanying text, can further contribute to a broader understanding of socially transmitted information. For example, researchers could investigate how images included in the mass media and consumed by the actively informed affect the information that they transmit to their casually informed peers, who may or may not see the images themselves.

Third, future research should investigate the full complexities of conversation. As discussed in chapter 3, my methodological approach provides important advances over previous work, but it does not fully capture the complexities of real-world political discussion. For example, in other research, Jaime Settle and I point out the importance of considering what actually happens in conversations (Carlson and Settle 2022). One of the key methodological limitations in this book is that the communication is operationalized as purely unidirectional: information passes from the actively informed to the casually informed participant, without giving the casually informed person an opportunity to respond. This not only limits external validity because real-world conversations give people the opportunity to reply but also inhibits the ability of the casually informed to engage in deeper cognitive processing of the information they were presented. Conversations also take place in distinct physical spaces that also contribute to how we come to understand politics and participation (e.g., Makse, Minkoff, and Sokhey 2019; Enos 2017). With careful attention to the interplay between conversations and the spaces in which they occur, future work should analyze actual conversations between actively and casually informed participants, through transcripts of recorded in-person conversations (Levendusky 2023), transcripts of video chat conversations (e.g., Santoro and Broockman 2022; West 2022), and written online conversations using platforms like Chatter (Rossiter 2020).

Fourth, future work should consider the role of choice and selection in information consumption. Previous work has demonstrated the importance of selection in partisan media effects research (Arceneaux and Johnson 2013, 2015; de Benedictis-Kessner et al. 2019), but this has not been as carefully applied to the political discussion literature. Moreover, there are many points at which selection could be influential throughout the two-step flow that merit deeper study. Starting with the actively informed, their initial choice of which media to consume could affect the socially transmitted information to which their casually informed peers are exposed.

On the casually informed side, the choice of which person to turn to for socially transmitted information could be influential. More research is needed to unpack how they choose discussants, which could vary from one topic to another. The studies presented in this book force exposure to socially transmitted information from a stranger rather than allowing the casually informed to choose their active informants. One context in which this could be especially important to unpack is whether the casually informed choose a copartisan or out-partisan informant and one who is actually more knowledgeable. While these dynamics have been studied in the political discussion literature, the ways in which changes to information communicated occur in these various contexts has not been studied.

Fifth, future work could more carefully develop theories about how socially transmitted information contributes to more or less distorted democracy across different issue domains. Soroka and Wlezien (2022) forcefully demonstrate that accuracy in media (and its effects on public opinion and representation) varies across different issue areas. Similarly, some topics might lend themselves to more or less information distortion, perhaps based on factors like issue complexity, emotional valence, salience, and the extent to which it is linked to partisan identity. Moreover, it is possible that the casually informed have such strong opinions on some topics that even the most distorted socially transmitted information would not change their preferences or behavior, whereas opinions on other topics might be more malleable. Future work could develop theories about how distorted democracy varies across different topics.

The final opportunity for future research that I discuss here is to more precisely measure the behavioral implications of socially transmitted information. Although chapter 7 focused on political engagement, the results were based purely on self-reported likelihood of engaging in a few distinct types of political participation. Future work should examine directly observable political engagement, such as donation behavior, turnout, or signing petitions, or utilize web-tracking data to examine information-seeking and pathways to political engagement.

BROADER THEORETICAL IMPLICATIONS

In chapter 1, I noted that this book sets the agenda for future research in political communication. I have just described six ways in which future work could more narrowly build on the work presented in this book. In this section, however, I zoom out to consider how the broader substance of my argument and findings contribute to important topics in political behavior research.

Media Effects

Research on media effects needs to consider how they might propagate through social networks. I am not the first to make the argument that people are learning about politics socially. But this book suggests that socially transmitted information is not a replica of information from the media, which means that we need to consider its effects more carefully. If we want to understand how mass media affects political attitudes and behavior but fewer and fewer people consume mass media directly, we need to better understand the pathways through which they are exposed to information—and how that information might change along the way.

By way of example, consider the literature on partisan media and polarization. Druckman, Levendusky, and McLain (2018) demonstrate that people who had a conversation with someone exposed to partisan media had more polarized attitudes about the topic at hand, even if they were not directly exposed to partisan media themselves. Without analyzing the content of these conversations, we do not have a clear understanding of *why* this important pattern was uncovered. Did those who watched partisan media parrot the bias and frames to which they were exposed in their conversations with others?

Most of the studies analyzed in my book deliberately begin the two-step flow with a nonpartisan news story, which limits their ability to speak to this question directly. However, in October 2020, I fielded a small pilot study to tackle this very question. I conducted a telephone game experiment using partisan news articles that previous researchers had used to examine the effects of exposure to partisan media on persuasion and polarization (de Benedictis-Kessner et al. 2019). Participants in my study were randomly assigned to read either a Fox News article or an MSNBC article about marijuana legalization. Both articles used an economic frame to discuss the issue, but the Fox article suggested that legalization would hurt the economy and the MSNBC article suggested that it would help the economy. After reading the article, participants wrote messages to others, telling them about what they read. The messages were then coded for a number of attributes, just as in chapter 4, but specifically for whether they reported that the economy would improve as a result of marijuana legalization. I found that 97 percent of participants who read the MSNBC article wrote messages indicating that the economy would improve compared to only 36 percent of participants who read the Fox article. This stark pattern holds even after controlling for the respondent's ideology and whether they prefer to consume Fox or MSNBC in general.

The results from this study indicate that partisan media bias does not disappear through the two-step flow. So long as the two-step flow contributes to how at least some Americans learn about politics, political communication scholars need to consider what happens after the actively informed are initially exposed to media. More carefully considering socially transmitted information could help explain some of the mixed evidence on media effects, especially in an era in which direct exposure to media is limited.

Political Discussion Networks

While media scholars need to consider the second stage of the two-step flow, political discussion network scholars need to consider the first. Social networks scholars have long demonstrated the power of social influence to shape political attitudes and participation (Sinclair 2012; Huckfeldt and Sprague 1995; Mutz 2006; Ahn, Huckfeldt, and Ryan 2014; Minozzi et al. 2021; Baker et al. 2020). Although this work pushes back against the "atomistic" Michigan model of political behavior, it tends to isolate social networks from the mass media, often failing to account for the chain of influence characterized by the two-step flow. By ignoring the first step of the two-step flow, this scholarship misses an important opportunity to more fully characterize social network effects.

My book makes a broader contribution to the social networks literature that is worth highlighting here. The vast majority of research on political discussion and social networks focuses on the effects of exposure to disagreement on political outcomes, such as knowledge, engagement, and tolerance. Although disagreement is—and will continue to be—an important feature of political networks, my work here shows that even absent disagreement there can be pernicious consequences of political discussion. By looking under the hood at the information actually exchanged in both agreeable and disagreeable dyads, this book shows that the information exchanged within a conversation might be just as important as the mere presence or absence of disagreement. Moreover, the patterns of information distortion described in chapter 4 are largely consistent across agreeable and disagreeable dyads. By laying this foundation, future work on political networks can begin to take steps beyond disagreement to more fully understand the impact of political discussion on political behavior.

Political Influencers

Scholars are fundamentally interested in understanding who has influence in American politics. From Schattschneider's "heavenly chorus" to the opinion leaders of the Columbia School and Zaller, scholars across the discipline care about who has voice in American democracy. Studying political influence requires careful consideration of who the key actors are within any given theoretical framework. In this book, I investigate how the actively informed intentionally or unintentionally influence the casually informed through information transmission. Although the more obvious contribution of this book is unpacking the behavior and attitudes of the casually informed, the findings reveal that the actively informed are pivotal actors in American politics who merit more attention moving forward.

Most media effects research describes the behavior of people who are directly exposed to the media. Therefore, most of this research is actually describing the actively informed, without using the term. Although we know a lot about their behavior from this literature, I suggest that we need to more carefully consider the influence the actively informed have on their peers.

This group is similar to, though distinct from, opinion leaders, as initially conceptualized seventy years ago (see ch. 3). This group is similar to "prosumers" or "interest actors" on social media (Weeks, Ardèvol-Abreu, and Zúñiga 2017; Moses n.d.). While they are less focused on interpersonal influence, the actively informed share qualities with the deeply involved and political hobbyists (Krupnikov and Ryan 2022; Hersh 2020). While each of these actors are slightly different from one another conceptually, they share an investment in politics that leads them to consume more news and sometimes share that news with others. Previous work has shown the important, often outsized influence these actors can have on American politics broadly, and I show the impact that they can have on their peers more directly by determining the information to which they are exposed.

In some ways, the actively informed have likely always played an important role in American politics. They have served as information gatekeepers to their peers, likely affecting their preferences. Yet the expansion of social media has empowered the actively informed to influence more people with greater speed than ever before. The reach that the actively informed can have in both their offline and online networks merits closer scrutiny. Just as journalists have a responsibility to communicate accurate, objective information to the public, so too do the actively informed have a responsibility to communicate accurate, objective information to their peers. I hope that after reading this book, those who consider themselves actively informed think critically about the information they share with others.

Beyond American Politics

My argument and findings should speak beyond the borders of American politics. As briefly discussed in chapter 1, socially transmitted information is an important source of political news for many people around the world. My theoretical framework and empirical evidence focus more narrowly on the American political context, but the broad patterns uncovered here could be applied to other political and media contexts, perhaps with important theoretical implications (e.g., Larson and Lewis 2017, 2018; Arias et al. 2019).

One important cross-national consideration is access to media and the internet. In some contexts, particularly in developing countries with limited internet access, word of mouth might be the only practical way people learn about politics. We can also consider factors such as the number of news outlets available, literacy rates, language variation, and the presence of state-owned media as factors that might contribute to the dominance of socially transmitted information and its effects. Variation in trust in media and the presence of a free press are also likely to structure the extent to which people turn to each other for news, how they weigh their choice to be actively or casually informed, and how their chosen information affects their attitudes and behavior.

The implications of socially transmitted information for political behavior might be different across unique political contexts. The factors discussed above might contribute to variation in how important socially transmitted information is from one context to another, but its effects on the political environment should be considered more broadly. I have focused on features of political behavior that scholars have argued are important for democratic functioning in the United States. But in other contexts polarization might be a trivial consequence of socially transmitted information compared to, for example, violent protest, recruitment into radical extremist networks, or other expressions of political violence.

Beyond the News

There are other forms of political communication for which socially transmitted information is relevant, such as political campaigns. Researchers interested in campaign effects on political behavior might also consider how messages communicated by campaigns get distorted through social transmission. My broader theoretical argument and framework could reshape the way we think about campaign effects too.

As an illustration of why socially transmitted information is relevant to understanding campaign effects, I present results from a telephone game experiment I fielded on the 2018 CCES, which yields a nationally representative sample from YouGov. As in my other studies, participants were asked to read something and write a message telling someone else about what they read. Instead of reading a news article, however, participants were asked to view one of the GOTV postcards used in the seminal Gerber and Green (2000) field experiment. In the original experiment, individuals received postcards that encouraged them to turn out to vote using a civic duty frame, a close election frame, or a neighborhood solidarity frame. I kept the content of the postcards as identical to the original study as possible, simply updating the dates to reflect the 2018 election. I then worked with a team of research assistants to code the messages written by the study participants for the presence of each of these frames.

The results suggest that the frames used in the original experiment largely persisted through social transmission but were not equally resistant to getting lost in transmission. Figure 8.1 shows the percentage of respondents in each

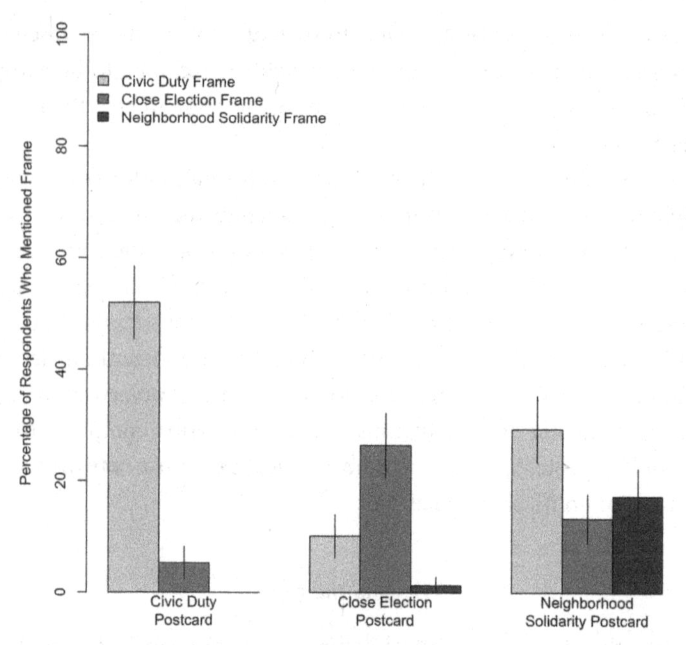

FIGURE 8.1. Frames transmitted from Get-Out-the-Vote postcards. Percentage of respondents in each postcard treatment who mentioned each frame: civic duty (light gray), close election (medium gray), and neighborhood solidarity (dark gray). Data are from the 2018 CCES. Vertical lines represent 95% confidence intervals. Blank and nonsense responses were removed from this analysis, but results are largely similar when they are included.

condition in my experiment (i.e., those who read each postcard) who mentioned civic duty, close elections, or neighborhood solidarity frames when they transmitted the information to another person. The results show that the civic duty condition was especially resistant to distortion: over half of respondents (52 percent) who read the civic duty postcard transmitted a message with a civic duty theme to their peers. The close election frame was also somewhat likely to be passed on to the next person, with about 26 percent of respondents who viewed this postcard passing along a theme about a close election. The neighborhood solidarity theme was not nearly as sticky. Only 17 percent of respondents who viewed this postcard passed along a message that used a neighborhood solidarity frame. People who viewed the neighborhood solidarity postcard were more likely to mention civic duty (29 percent) than neighborhood solidarity.

These results point to a general pattern of frames persisting through social transmission. However, there is clearly still a lot that gets lost. Even among those who viewed the civic duty postcard, which was the stickiest frame, nearly half of the respondents did *not* pass along the civic duty message to their peers. The loss is even greater in the close election and neighborhood solidarity conditions, where about 74 and 83 percent of respondents did not pass along the intended frame. This suggests that when frames *do* get passed along, they tend to be roughly consistent with the intended frame, but most frames simply get lost.

Altogether, this study reveals that much information gets lost from the initial GOTV message to the next person. GOTV messaging can cause spillover effects, and these results raise new questions about the extent to which the spillovers are driven by information. For practitioners, it is worth noting that some frames are more persistent than others, such as civic duty, but perhaps more complicated frames can lead to more direct downstream requests to vote. Still, very little specific information is passed along and the frame itself gets lost in the majority of cases.

I introduce these results to highlight that socially transmitted information matters beyond the news and beyond the contexts explored specifically in this book. While the applications of this book to political communication, media, and social network scholars might be more immediately apparent, my argument that social scientists should devote more attention to socially transmitted information, how it changes, and how it affects political behavior extends to other corners of the discipline.

Shaping Democratic Values

American democracy has suffered during my research for this book. Two presidential elections have passed, with one Republican and one Democrat taking office. Both elections were hotly contested. Donald Trump's election was met with widespread, worldwide protests; Joe Biden's election was met with claims of election fraud and the January 6 insurrection at the Capitol. There has thus been a surge in research on support for democratic values (Voelkel, Chu et al. 2023; Voelkel, Stagnaro et al. 2023). This literature largely grew after I developed my main theoretical argument, but I would be remiss not to examine the ways in which socially transmitted information might contribute to this ongoing conversation.

Can socially transmitted information affect support for democratic values? To shed some light on this possibility, I analyzed the relationship between socially transmitted information and perceptions of election integrity in a nationally representative panel survey fielded by NORC. The same respondents were interviewed before and after the 2020 US presidential election, allowing me to examine variation within individuals. On each survey wave, respondents were asked to report where they got most of their news about national and international issues, with a range of options, including in-person discussion. I used this question to measure whether each respondent *added* socially transmitted information to their news diets after the election. As one measure of perceptions of election integrity, I asked respondents whether they thought their "vote and the votes of other citizens were counted fairly in the November 2020 election." I used this question as the dependent variable in a weighted logistic regression, controlling for age, party identification, gender, education, and race. The results suggest that people who added socially transmitted information to their news diets after the election were less likely to believe that their votes were counted fairly. To contextualize this finding, the model suggests that the predicted probability that someone who added socially transmitted information to their news diet would think their vote was counted fairly was .67, which was about nine points lower than those who did not add socially transmitted information to their news diets. This 9-point gap is statistically significant and could be interpreted as large. However, it pales in comparison to the 76-point gap between strong Democrats and strong Republicans that the same model predicts. Partisan identity is much more strongly associated with perceptions of election integrity than information source. But information source is still relevant even after controlling for partisan identity, which suggests that it should not be ignored.

With these data, I cannot demonstrate that the relationship between socially transmitted information and perceptions of election integrity is causal. It is also worth noting that the majority of people, regardless of their information source, still thought that their votes were counted fairly. However, the association alone suggests that socially transmitted information could be an important pathway through which people come to doubt the validity of American elections. Thus, if we are to understand the consequences of socially transmitted information, we ought to consider democratic values. And if we are to understand support for democracy, we should consider the role that socially transmitted information could play.

Conclusion: Distorted or Dysfunctional?

Does socially transmitted information make American democracy distorted or entirely dysfunctional? Some of the consequences of socially transmitted information highlighted in this book certainly do not paint a portrait of an ideally functioning democracy, as many political scientists and theorists envisioned. But maybe these distortions from an "ideal" democracy are not so bad. Readers may come away from the findings in this book feeling more or less comfortable with the state of American democracy. I want to close with some points to help readers conclude for themselves whether American democracy is distorted or dysfunctional.

One of the central arguments of this book is that we need to pay more attention to the socially transmitted information component of the two-step flow. It is important to keep in mind that this unique type of information is *social*. It is exchanged between people, the people who structure American politics. The beautiful thing about democracy is that it is a system of self-governance. However, self-governance is not always easy.

Many scholars before me have wrestled with the challenges of participatory democracy, particularly in the context of political discussion. For example, in *Hearing the Other Side: Deliberative versus Participatory Democracy*, Diana Mutz (2006, 16) writes, "Theories of participatory democracy are in important ways inconsistent with theories of deliberative democracy. The best possible social environment for purposes of either one of these two goals would naturally undermine the other." In *Talking about Politics: Informal Groups and Social Identity in American Life*, Katherine Cramer Walsh (2004, 170) writes, "Although [public discussion] can foster trust, it can also clarify social identities and reinforce exclusion, challenging claims that more discussion and interaction are the answers to the decline of civic life." Both scholars point to tensions between what is expected in participatory democracy and the realities of how political discussion operates within it.

My central argument highlights similar tensions arising from the role that socially transmitted information and the two-step flow play in participatory democracy. At first glance, it might seem that socially transmitted information can render democracy dysfunctional. If one-third of the public is dependent on information that has been distorted by their peers and as a consequence becomes more likely to be misinformed, polarized, and engaged, this seems problematic. We have seen what a misinformed, polarized, and engaged minority of the public can do. At the same time, it is worth taking a step back to think about the extent to which misinformation, polarization, and engagement are necessarily bad at the aggregate level.

First, misinformation has bad connotations, but most survey data suggest that belief in misinformation among the public is relatively low overall. Misbeliefs might vary by topic, and we might be more concerned about misbeliefs about some topics (e.g., public health) than others (e.g., celebrity gossip), but on average most Americans are not misinformed about most topics for which we have data. Although socially transmitted information can increase belief in misinformation, *most* people—whether casually or actively informed—still get it right. Again, a world without any misinformation would probably be better than a world with some. But misinformation, gossip, and rumors have existed since humans could communicate socially. Perhaps having a misinformed portion of the electorate is inevitable, and perhaps democracy can function just fine with some misinformation.

On the other hand, even if large events like the January 6 insurrection are rare, they can be powerful, dangerous, and decrease trust in political institutions. Moreover, if misinformation pushes people to elect candidates who ultimately prove to be otherwise bad representatives of their constituents, then we could argue that misinformation, even in small doses, is a problem. If socially transmitted information contributes to any amount of the spread of misinformation, it could be viewed as inherently nudging American democracy toward dysfunction.

Second, when it comes to polarization at the mass level, I want to remind readers that political science, as a field, once begged for more polarization in American politics. The infamous 1950 APSA report suggested that increased polarization was necessary to help improve democratic accountability. When the parties are polarized and well sorted, it is easier for voters to choose which candidate best represents their preferences. If socially transmitted information can nudge the casually informed to have more sorted preferences, this could be viewed as normatively desirable. Moreover, affective polarization, the type that most agree is normatively bad, does not seem to be affected by socially transmitted information. In fact, other work suggests that political discussion can help reduce affective polarization (Levendusky 2023; Rossiter and Carlson 2023; Levendusky and Stecula 2021; Rossiter 2020; Santoro and Broockman 2022).

Third, engagement is usually viewed as normatively good. Of course, there are dark sides of all forms of political engagement. My argument can speak to large-scale protest events that could be bad forms of participation, but my evidence so far does not directly point to it. Rather, it suggests that socially transmitted information can lead to small nudges toward requesting additional information, donating to particular causes, and contacting legislators. These behaviors are generally not viewed as normatively bad, perhaps even if they are based on questionable information.

The impact of socially transmitted information on American politics is nuanced. By overlooking *information* in the two-step flow, how it changes and why it matters, we have missed these important complexities to understanding whether the two-step flow and political discussion more broadly help or hurt American democracy. Ultimately, I argue that the socially transmitted information exchanged in the second step of the two-step flow leads to *distorted* democracy, not dysfunctional democracy.

Socially transmitted information is but one part of the American political system. Sometimes it contributes to imperfections in democratic functioning. Sometimes it helps inform and mobilize those less attentive to politics. The net effect of socially transmitted information on democratic functioning is normatively ambiguous, but perhaps this tells us that we need to rethink our normative stance entirely. Socially transmitted information has always been part of American politics, and it likely always will be. Because socially transmitted information is not going away—and could become more dominant with the growth of social media—perhaps we need to revise our expectations for what an ideal democracy looks like in light of this reality.

As Americans learn about politics through the grapevine, we, as a field and as a society, need to consider what that means for the state of American politics. I have shown how the grapevine can distort information and how that distorted information can affect political attitudes and behavior. These attitudinal and behavioral outcomes might change how we view the American public. If humans are prone to imperfection, socially transmitted information is also going to be imperfect. Socially transmitted information contributes to some of the imperfections in American democracy. To some, its distortions from reality make it meaningful and something to hold on to; to others, its distortions are unpleasant and alarming. Perhaps it is through the grapevine that we can come to appreciate and understand American politics.

Acknowledgments

My grandparents' living room is one of the first places I remember observing and participating in political discussions. My family shared what they had seen on the news, I shared what I had learned in school, and we all recalled personal experiences. Sometimes these discussions got heated, particularly when arguing over facts. When we had had enough, someone would shout, "Get the *Britannica*!" My grandparents' 1979 World Book encyclopedia set would settle the debate once and for all. I have fond memories of these conversations, and in some ways they serve as the inspiration for parts of this book. I learned a lot about candidates and policy by listening to these conversations, without directly seeking information from the news (or an encyclopedia) on my own. I was casually informed. Much of what I understood about politics came from my family's retelling of what they heard on the news. Some of this included what we call "Bud Facts," which are facts my grandfather would share that were sometimes true, sometimes stretched a bit, and sometimes forgotten.

As I continued to develop an interest in politics and eventually political science, these conversations have always been in the back of my mind. I thought more carefully about where we learn about politics and how day-to-day political conversations can shape the way we come to understand and engage in politics. I am indebted to these conversations with my family, particularly my grandparents, for providing much of the inspiration for this book.

I have had the unique opportunity to use my social science training to better understand Bud Facts and the political conversations that shaped my interest in politics. I am grateful to the training I received at the College of William & Mary, particularly from Jaime Settle and Ron Rapoport, and the University of California, San Diego. Much of the research for this book stems from my dissertation, and I am grateful to Seth Hill, James Fowler, Marisa Abrajano, Molly Roberts, Cheryl Boudreau, and Craig McKenzie for feedback and encouragement. Washington University in St. Louis provided me with time, resources, and helpful colleagues to conduct this research.

I am fortunate to have so many wonderful colleagues who generously spent time reading and commenting on this book. With support from the political science department at Washington University, I hosted a virtual book conference with Jamie Druckman, Matt Pietryka, Jaime Settle, Betsy Sinclair, Anand Sokhey, and Stuart Soroka. I am grateful for their time and careful comments. They pushed me to more carefully consider the normative implications and tone of the book. Betsy encouraged me to "plant [my] flag on the moon," and Anand persuaded me it was okay to "tap dance" on previous scholars to push the field forward. Stuart and Jamie reminded me to consider the more optimistic interpretation of the results. Matt helped me anchor my argument in conversation with giants in the political discussion literature. Jaime helped me clarify some central theoretical points about what it means to be actively and casually informed. More importantly, she encouraged me to write the book that *I* wanted to write. Jaime was also there, cheering me on at each stage of the process, including last-minute gut reactions to many sleep-deprived ideas I had. The feedback from this conference was transformative for the book.

I am also indebted to the informal book club that helped me finish the book. Inspired by advice from Ana Bracic, Eunji Kim and I formed a book club in which we tracked words written per day on a Google sheet for social pressure and accountability and exchanged feedback on chapter drafts at biweekly meetings. The greatest outcome of this book club was our friendship, but the feedback was second to none. Eunji's honest feedback helped me write a stronger book with more confidence. She was bold enough to tell me when my writing was unclear or an example was silly (and she was usually right). She helped me write accessibly and think about the bigger picture and was always there to tell me my book mattered in ways I couldn't always see. Later, Nicole Yadon joined the book club, which only made the group better. I am grateful for Nicole's careful eye, especially on things that might not be so obvious to people outside of political communication. Nicole helped me clarify and broaden the contributions of the book, communicate and contextualize the findings, and reorganize some chapters to provide a better structure; I am grateful to have her as a friend and colleague.

I am grateful to the team at the University of Chicago Press. First and foremost, Adam Berinsky has been incredibly supportive of the project since the beginning. I will never forget the first emails we had about transforming an article into a book. Adam's advice on book publishing and writing shaped the way I approached the book. I am grateful to him for all the time he spent working with me on the proposal, honing the argument ("not a happy story here—embrace it!"), and commenting on the final manuscript. I am also grateful for his patience as it took me far longer than I anticipated to complete the book. I thank Sara Doskow for her support of the project. I am also grateful to the anonymous reviewers for reading the initial manuscript so carefully and providing feedback that pushed me to make the book better, both empirically and theoretically.

I am grateful for feedback from colleagues and seminar participants at Harvard, Utah Valley University, Dartmouth College, Vanderbilt, Texas A&M, University of Nevada Reno, Appalachian State University, University of Colorado, and the College of William & Mary. At Washington University, I thank the best junior colleagues I could ask for. The junior group chat is one of the highlights of my professional life thus far, and the junior faculty workshop is just as helpful. This book would not have been possible without feedback and support from Carly Wayne, Mike Olson, Lucia Motolinia, Christopher Lucas, and Ted Enamorado. I am also grateful to Keith Schnakenberg for helping me think about the differences between attitudes and preferences and to Andrew Reeves for reading early drafts of the book proposal.

It took a small army of research assistants to conduct the research for this book. I thank undergraduate students at UCSD and Washington University for hand-coding messages from the experiments: Tal, Lindsey, Halle, Natalyn, Lea, Oliver, Maggie, Taylor, and Orli. I am especially grateful to Orli Sheffey for her hard work, keen eye, and incredible spirit. I miss her and hope that she knows how important she was to this project and to me as an educator. Tremendous Washington University graduate students also helped with this project. Erin Rossiter and Dominique Lockett scraped, cleaned, and analyzed the data from Twitter for the Replies dataset. I am grateful for their expertise and patience. I am equally grateful to Cecilia Sui, who collected and helped analyze the data for the Quote Tweets dataset. Peter Bachman replicated every analysis in the book and helped create and polish the figures. I am grateful for his time and attention to detail, especially when sifting through ancient code and outdated packages. Benjamin Noble helped develop the coding for the panel data analysis in chapter 8. Zhaozhi Li helped with several last-minute tasks to get the manuscript over the finish line. Without the hard work of all these students, this book would not be possible.

This book was also made possible by significant financial support from the University of California, San Diego; Washington University in St. Louis; the Weidenbaum Center on the Economy, Government, and Public Policy;

the National Science Foundation (1423788); and the Social Science Research Council (SSRC). The SSRC funded two experiments and the development of the Replies dataset. The Weidenbaum Center funded the American Social Survey, from which I collected extensive data for this book, as well as an Impact Grant that funded the development of the Quote Tweets dataset. The National Science Foundation funded an experiment. Resources from the political science department at Washington University helped fund remaining experiments and research assistants. UCSD provided support through the research apprenticeship program and a dissertation grant that funded an experiment.

Finally and most importantly, I am grateful to my family. Eric helped me brainstorm everything from titles to terms for the actively and casually informed and distorted democracy. He helped me find examples and read parts of the manuscript to help ensure I was balanced and clear. He held down the fort while I powered through to hit deadlines and kept me balanced with immature (but also objectively hilarious) pranks. Daniel and Madeline each made their debut while I worked on this book, which gave it new meaning and purpose. I am grateful for their patience while I worked more than I should have. Words will never be able to sufficiently capture the gratitude I have for my mom. She has always encouraged me to be the best me I can be. She leads by example, balancing an incredible career against being an incredible mom. I hope that one day my kids can look at me the way I look at her. Thank you, Mom, for giving me the strength, encouragement, and drive to set goals and achieve them. Without you as my role model, I would not have developed the skills needed to write this book.

Notes

Chapter One

1. https://twitter.com/realdonaldtrump/status/1039107129880272896.

2. https://twitter.com/USATODAY/status/1265964037336113153.

Chapter Two

1. This literature typically uses the term "social information" to refer to the information that flows between people in a network, which is what I call socially transmitted information. Other lines of research consider "social information" information about other people. For consistency with my argument, I use the term "socially transmitted information" even when referring to earlier research that calls it "social information."

2. I occasionally use "preferences" and "attitudes" interchangeably due to inconsistencies in these terms throughout the literature.

Chapter Four

1. https://twitter.com/PortlandPolice/status/1303544462136586243.

2. https://www.facebook.com/DouglasCoSO/photos/a.102713029813203/3294082244009583/?type=3.

3. See, e.g., Society of Professional Journalists Ethics Committee Position Papers on Political Involvement, https://www.spj.org/ethics-papers-politics.asp; Pulitzer Center Ethics and Standards Policies, https://pulitzercenter.org/about/ethics-and-standards-policies; or individual news publications' ethical standards.

4. It is important to consider the features of Twitter during the time of data collection because platforms change quickly, which can affect the way we think about temporal validity (Munger 2022).

5. The Replies dataset was created using Twitter's API. The dataset includes the text of the tweets, the URLs to any external links or news articles, emojis, and available metadata about the tweets and replies, such as the date, time, number of retweets, etc. The replies represent the

socially transmitted information, or the second step of the two-step flow. The list of news outlets for the original tweets was obtained from a Pew Research Center analysis of media use, which has been used by previous researchers (e.g., Guess et al. 2021). The list includes ABC News, BBC, Bloomberg, Breitbart, CBS News, CNN, *Late Show with Stephen Colbert*, *Daily Kos*, Fox News Channel, Glenn Beck, *Huffington Post*, *Mother Jones*, MSNBC, NBC News, Drudge Report, *New Yorker*, *New York Times*, NPR, PBS, *Politico*, Rush Limbaugh, Sean Hannity, *Slate*, *Blaze*, *Daily Show*, *Economist*, *Guardian*, *Rachel Maddow Show*, *Think Progress*, *USA Today*, *Washington Post*, *Wall Street Journal*, and Yahoo! News.

6. In 2017, Twitter switched from a 140-character limit to a 280-character limit.

7. Our models obtained 89.2 percent accuracy in identifying partisan quote tweets.

8. This acronym stands for, "Where we go one, we go all," which is a phrase commonly used by QAnon supporters.

9. Our models obtained 96.4 percent accuracy in identifying conspiratorial quote tweets.

10. Our models reached 97.6 percent accuracy for identifying quote tweets as mobilizing and 99.7 percent accuracy for identifying calls to violent action.

Chapter Five

1. https://www.youtube.com/watch?v=sx2scvIFGjE.

2. Note that most of these citations refer to research conducted many years ago. Researchers have continued to explore political knowledge in the United States, but with a much stronger focus on examining the causes and consequences of political knowledge (e.g., Jerit et al. 2006), political knowledge measurement (Mondak and Anderson 2004; Pietryka and MacIntosh 2022), and the gaps (or lack thereof) in political knowledge along the lines of gender (e.g., Dolan 2011; Dolan and Hansen 2021; Kraft and Dolan 2023; Jerit and Barabas 2017) and race and ethnicity (e.g., Abrajano 2015; Pérez 2015; Cohen and Luttig 2021).

3. https://www.annenbergpublicpolicycenter.org/americans-civics-knowledge-increases-2019-survey/.

4. https://www.annenbergpublicpolicycenter.org/americans-civics-knowledge-increases-2019-survey/.

5. https://www.washingtonpost.com/news/answer-sheet/wp/2016/09/27/many-americans-know-nothing-about-their-government-heres-a-bold-way-schools-can-fix-that/.

6. https://www.cnn.com/2017/09/13/politics/poll-constitution/index.html.

7. https://www.loyola.edu/academics/emerging-media/blog/2016/viral-misinformation-political-engagement.

8. https://ballotpedia.org/Jeff_Boss.

9. https://www.factcheck.org/2021/03/false-claims-cited-in-bogus-theory-that-biden-isnt-president/.

10. https://www.politifact.com/factchecks/2019/dec/18/nancy-pelosi/nancy-pelosi-claims-200k-will-be-prohibited-voting/.

11. *USA Today*, USA Today Poll, September 2015, Question 34, USSUFF.100115.R38; Suffolk University Political Research Center (Cornell University, Roper Center for Public Opinion Research, 2015).

12. Survey Center on American Life, American Perspectives Survey, September 2020, Question 7, 31118231.00006, Ipsos (Cornell University, Roper Center for Public Opinion Research, 2020).

13. Survey Center on American Life, American Perspectives Survey, September 2020, Question 11, 31118231.00010, Ipsos (Cornell University, Roper Center for Public Opinion Research, 2020).

14. Survey Center on American Life, American Perspectives Survey, September 2020, Question 13, 31118231.00012, Ipsos (Cornell University, Roper Center for Public Opinion Research, 2020).

15. Survey Center on American Life, American Perspectives Survey, September 2020, Question 8, 31118231.00007, Ipsos (Cornell University, Roper Center for Public Opinion Research, 2020).

16. Participants were not given a "don't know" option.

17. If "don't know" responses are excluded from the analysis, rather than being coded as correctly informed, most results are similar, but estimates of belief in misinformation are much higher. For example, when "don't knows" are removed, about 60 percent of the casually informed believed that Nancy Pelosi diverted Social Security funds to the impeachment proceedings, compared to only about 17.9 percent when "don't knows" are included in the analysis as being correctly informed. Detailed analyses of all results including and excluding "don't know" responses are available in the appendix, but I summarize the key differences here. In the 2020 TASS data, when "don't knows" are excluded, the casually informed were significantly more likely to believe that Obama is Muslim, that Pelosi diverted Social Security funds, and that McConnell's donor was a Russian oligarch. In the 2017 Original Survey, the difference between the actively and casually informed in believing Obama was born outside the United States is no longer statistically significant ($p = .11$) if "don't knows" are excluded. In the 2016 CCAP, the difference between the casually and actively informed in believing Obama is Muslim is statistically significant when "don't knows" are excluded. The results presented in the book are therefore more conservative in the rates of misinformation and in supporting my key argument.

18. In the 2020 TASS survey, being casually informed is measured as "bumping into the news and information as I do other things or hear about it from other people," as described in chapter 3. In the 2016 CCAP survey, being casually informed is defined as people reporting that they get most or all of their information directly from other people, which comprises only 7 percent of the full sample. In the 2017 Original Survey, fielded with SSI, the casually informed are defined as reporting that they receive at least 50 percent of their information about politics, candidates, and elections from conversations with other people.

19. Matching performed using the quickmatch package in R (Savje, Sekhon, and Higgins 2018).

20. Logistic regressions and simulations performed using the clarify package in R (Greifer et al. 2023).

21. E.g., if a participant reported that the statement, "Obama was not born in the United States," is true, I followed up by asking, "Where do you recall learning that the statement 'Barack Obama was not born in the United States' is TRUE?"

22. To account for acquiescence bias (Hill and Roberts 2022), participants were randomly assigned to one of two question wordings when asked to report whether the statement was true or false: Oil and gas [do not] account for the largest portion of human-caused fossil fuel emissions from federal lands.

23. Approximately 15.2 percent of Democrats in the control group were misinformed, while 26.8 percent of Democrats who received socially transmitted information from a copartisan

were misinformed ($p < .05$). Among Republicans, the difference between control (28.3 percent) and copartisan socially transmitted information (32 percent) was not statistically significant.

Chapter Six

1. https://www.cnn.com/2021/09/11/politics/transcript-george-w-bush-speech-09-11-2021/index.html.

2. https://obamawhitehouse.archives.gov/the-press-office/2016/01/12/remarks-president-barack-obama-%E2%80%93-prepared-delivery-state-union-address.

3. https://www.pewresearch.org/politics/2021/05/03/most-americans-are-critical-of-governments-handling-of-situation-at-u-s-mexico-border/.

Chapter Seven

1. https://www.washingtonpost.com/technology/2019/10/17/zuckerberg-standing-voice-free-expression/.

2. Cross-sectional survey data reveal that the casually informed are less politically engaged than the actively informed. Data from surveys collected in key primary states in 2022 (n = 10,156) show that the casually informed are less likely to vote in primaries, contact legislators, volunteer with or work for campaigns, attend local meetings, and donate to political candidates or causes. Cross-sectional data from a nationally representative YouGov survey, including an oversample of Fox News viewers, fielded in April 2022 (n = 1,564) shows that the casually informed are less likely to persuade someone to support their party, publicly express support for their party by wearing a campaign sticker, t-shirt, or displaying a yard sign or bumper sticker, and privately express support for their party, compared to the actively informed.

3. Predicted probabilities were estimated using the margins package in R (Leeper 2021). See the appendix for a replication of figure 7.3 using simulations from the clarify package in R (Greifer et al. 2023). The direction and statistical significance of the results are the same, but uncertainty is estimated differently and slightly different predicted probabilities are generated.

4. https://www.fox43.com/article/news/community/armed-counter-protesters-in-gettysburg-but-no-antifa-protest/521-f52c2293-8065-4f30-b8d7-75a7603785da.

5. https://www.cnn.com/2022/05/16/tech/4chan-buffalo-shooting/index.html.

6. https://www.washingtonpost.com/technology/2020/09/14/violent-antipolice-memes-surge/.

Chapter Eight

1. On the 2016 CCAP, participants reported *why* they preferred to get information from other people or from the news directly. Trust emerged as the number one reason both groups chose their preferred source, followed by the presumption that the opposite was biased.

References

Aarøe, Lene, and Michael Bang Petersen. 2020. "Cognitive Biases and Communication Strength in Social Networks: The Case of Episodic Frames." *British Journal of Political Science* 50, no. 4: 1561–81.

Abrajano, Marisa. 2015. "Reexamining the 'Racial Gap' in Political Knowledge." *Journal of Politics* 77, no. 1: 44–54.

Abramowitz, Alan I., and Kyle L. Saunders. 2008. "Is Polarization a Myth?" *Journal of Politics* 70, no. 2: 542–55.

Adamic, Lada A., and Natalie Glance. 2005. "The Political Blogosphere and the 2004 US Election: Divided They Blog." In *Proceedings of the 3rd International Workshop on Link Discovery* (August), 36–43. https://doi.org/10.1145/1134271.1134277.

Ahn, T. K., Robert Huckfeldt, and John Barry Ryan. 2014. *Experts, Activists, and Democratic Politics: Are Electorates Self-Educating?* New York: Cambridge University Press.

Allcott, Hunt, Levi Boxell, Jacob Conway, Matthew Gentzkow, Michael Thaler, and David Yang. 2020. "Polarization and Public Health: Partisan Differences in Social Distancing during the Coronavirus Pandemic." *Journal of Public Economics* 191: 104254.

Allport, Gordon W., and Leo Postman. 1947. *The Psychology of Rumor*. Oxford: Henry Holt.

Angelucci, Charles, and Andrea Prat. 2023. "Is Journalistic Truth Dead? Measuring How Informed Voters Are about Political News." April 8. https://ssrn.com/abstract=3593002 or http://dx.doi.org/10.2139/ssrn.3593002.

Annenberg Public Policy Center. 2019. "Americans' Civics Knowledge Increases But Still Has a Long Way to Go." Annenberg Public Policy Center, University of Pennsylvania, September 12. https://www.annenbergpublicpolicycenter.org/americans-civics-knowledge-increases-2019-survey/.

Anspach, Nicolas M., and Taylor N. Carlson. 2020. "What to Believe? Social Media Commentary and Belief in Misinformation." *Political Behavior* 42, no. 3: 697–718.

———. 2022. "Not Who You Think? Exposure and Vulnerability to Misinformation." *New Media & Society*: 14614448221130422. https://doi.org/10.1177/14614448221130422.

Anspach, Nicolas M., Jay T. Jennings, and Kevin Arceneaux. 2019. "A Little Bit of Knowledge: Facebook's News Feed and Self-Perceptions of Knowledge." *Research & Politics* 6, no. 1: 2053168018816189.

Arceneaux, Kevin, and Martin Johnson. 2013. *Changing Minds or Changing Channels? Partisan News in an Age of Choice*. Chicago: University of Chicago Press.

———. 2015. "How Does Media Choice Affect Hostile Media Perceptions? Evidence from Participant Preference Experiments." *Journal of Experimental Political Science* 2, no. 1: 12–25.

———. 2019. "Selective Avoidance and Exposure." In *Oxford Research Encyclopedia of Communication*.

Arceneaux, Kevin, Martin Johnson, René Lindstädt, and Ryan J. Vander Wielen. 2016. "The Influence of News Media on Political Elites: Investigating Strategic Responsiveness in Congress." *American Journal of Political Science* 60, no. 1: 5–29.

Arechar, Antonio A., Jennifer Allen, Adam J. Berinsky, Rocky Cole, Ziv Epstein, Kiran Garimella, and Andrew Gully et al. 2023. "Understanding and Combatting Misinformation across 16 Countries on Six Continents." *Nature Human Behaviour*: 1–12.

Arias, Eric, Pablo Balán, Horacio Larreguy, John Marshall, and Pablo Querubín. 2019. "Information Provision, Voter Coordination, and Electoral Accountability: Evidence from Mexican Social Networks." *American Political Science Review* 113, no. 2: 475–98.

Ash, Elliott, Sergio Galletta, Matteo Pinna, and Christopher Warshaw. 2022. "The Effect of Fox News Channel on US Elections: 2000–2020." SSRN 3837457.

Avelar, Daniel. 2019. "WhatsApp Fake News during Brazil Election 'Favoured Bolsonaro.'" *The Guardian*, October 30. https://www.theguardian.com/world/2019/oct/30/whatsapp-fake-news-brazil-election-favoured-jair-bolsonaro-analysis-suggests.

Baek, Young Min, Magdalena Wojcieszak, and Michael X. Delli Carpini. 2012. "Online versus Face-to-Face Deliberation: Who? Why? What? With What Effects?" *New Media & Society* 14, no. 3: 363–83.

Bail, Christopher A., Lisa P. Argyle, Taylor W. Brown, John P. Bumpus, Haohan Chen, M. B. Fallin Hunzaker, Jaemin Lee, Marcus Mann, Friedolin Merhout, and Alexander Volfovsky. 2018. "Exposure to Opposing Views on Social Media Can Increase Political Polarization." *Proceedings of the National Academy of Sciences* 115, no. 37: 9216–21.

Baker, Andy, Barry Ames, and Lucio R. Renno. 2006. "Social Context and Campaign Volatility in New Democracies: Networks and Neighborhoods in Brazil's 2002 Elections." *American Journal of Political Science* 50, no. 2: 382–99.

Bakshy, Eytan, Solomon Messing, and Lada A. Adamic. 2015. "Exposure to Ideologically Diverse News and Opinion on Facebook." *Science* 348, no. 6239: 1130–32.

Barberá, Pablo. 2015. "Birds of the Same Feather Tweet Together: Bayesian Ideal Point Estimation Using Twitter Data." *Political Analysis* 23, no. 1: 76–91.

———. 2020. "Social Media, Echo Chambers, and Political Polarization." In *Social Media and Democracy: The State of the Field, Prospects for Reform*, edited by Nathaniel Persily and Joshua A. Tucker, 34–55. Cambridge: Cambridge University Press.

Barberá, Pablo, John T. Jost, Jonathan Nagler, Joshua A. Tucker, and Richard Bonneau. 2015. "Tweeting from Left to Right: Is Online Political Communication More Than an Echo Chamber?" *Psychological Science* 26, no. 10: 1531–42.

Barnidge, Matthew. 2017. "Exposure to Political Disagreement in Social Media versus Face-to-Face and Anonymous Online Settings." *Political Communication* 34, no. 2: 302–21.

Bartels, Larry M. 1996. "Uninformed Votes: Information Effects in Presidential Elections." *American Journal of Political Science* 40, no. 1: 194–230.

———. 2002. "Beyond the Running Tally: Partisan Bias in Political Perceptions." *Political Behavior* 24, no. 2: 117–50.

Bartels, Larry M., and Wendy M. Rahn. 2000. "Political Attitudes in the Post-Network Era." Paper presented at the Annual Meeting of American Political Science Association, Washington, DC. https://citeseerx.ist.psu.edu/document?repid=rep1&type=pdf&doi=af68d8c6af2e5fc71418177213b0eefd9c7bf21e.

Bartlett, Frederic Charles. 1932. *Remembering: A Study in Experimental and Social Psychology.* Cambridge: Cambridge University Press.

Baum, Matthew A. 2002. "Sex, Lies, and War: How Soft News Brings Foreign Policy to the Inattentive Public." *American Political Science Review* 96, no. 1: 91–109.

———. 2003. "Soft News and Political Knowledge: Evidence of Absence or Absence of Evidence?." *Political Communication* 20, no. 2: 173–90.

Baum, Matthew A., and Angela S. Jamison. 2006. "The Oprah Effect: How Soft News Helps Inattentive Citizens Vote Consistently." *Journal of Politics* 68, no. 4: 946–59.

Baumeister, Roy F., Ellen Bratslavsky, Catrin Finkenauer, and Kathleen D. Vohs. 2001. "Bad Is Stronger Than Good." *Review of General Psychology* 5, no. 4: 323–70.

Bebbington, Keely, Colin MacLeod, T. Mark Ellison, and Nicolas Fay. 2017. "The Sky Is Falling: Evidence of a Negativity Bias in the Social Transmission of Information." *Evolution and Human Behavior* 38, no. 1: 92–101.

Beck, Paul Allen, Russell J. Dalton, Steven Greene, and Robert Huckfeldt. 2002. "The Social Calculus of Voting: Interpersonal, Media, and Organizational Influences on Presidential Choices." *American Political Science Review* 96, no. 1: 57–73.

Berelson, Bernard R., Paul F. Lazarsfeld, and William N. McPhee. 1954. *Voting: A Study of Opinion Formation in a Presidential Campaign.* Chicago: University of Chicago Press.

Berger, Jonah. 2014. "Word of Mouth and Interpersonal Communication: A Review and Directions for Future Research." *Journal of Consumer Psychology* 24, no. 4: 586–607.

Bode, Leticia. 2016. "Political News in the News Feed: Learning Politics from Social Media." *Mass Communication and Society* 19, no. 1: 24–48.

Bode, Leticia, Ceren Budak, Jonathan M. Ladd, Frank Newport, Josh Pasek, Lisa O. Singh, Stuart N. Soroka, and Michael W. Traugott. 2020. *Words That Matter: How the News and Social Media Shaped the 2016 Presidential Campaign.* Washington, DC: Brookings Institution Press.

Bøggild, Troels, Lene Aarøe, and Michael Bang Petersen. 2021. "Citizens as Complicits: Distrust in Politicians and Biased Social Dissemination of Political Information." *American Political Science Review* 115, no. 1: 269–85.

Bond, Robert M., Christopher J. Fariss, Jason J. Jones, Adam D. I. Kramer, Cameron Marlow, Jaime E. Settle, and James H. Fowler. 2012. "A 61-Million-Person Experiment in Social Influence and Political Mobilization." *Nature* 489, no. 7415: 295–98.

Boxell, Levi, Matthew Gentzkow, and Jesse M. Shapiro. 2017. "Greater Internet Use Is Not Associated with Faster Growth in Political Polarization among US Demographic Groups." *Proceedings of the National Academy of Sciences* 114, no. 40: 10612–17.

Brenan, Megan. 2022. "Americans' Trust in Media Remains Near Record Low." Gallup, October 18. Accessed May 27, 2023. https://news.gallup.com/poll/403166/americans-trust-media-remains-near-record-low.aspx.

Brewer, Marilynn B. 2007. "The Importance of Being We: Human Nature and Intergroup Relations." *American Psychologist* 62, no. 8: 728.

Broockman, David E., and Joshua L. Kalla. 2023. "Consuming Cross-Cutting Media Causes Learning and Moderates Attitudes: A Field Experiment with Fox News Viewers." *OSF Preprints*, April 14. doi:10.31219/osf.io/jrw26.

Broockman, David E., and Christopher Skovron. 2018. "Bias in Perceptions of Public Opinion among Political Elites." *American Political Science Review* 112, no. 3: 542–63.

Budak, Ceren, Sharad Goel, and Justin M. Rao. 2016. "Fair and Balanced? Quantifying Media Bias through Crowdsourced Content Analysis." *Public Opinion Quarterly* 80, no. S1: 250–71.

Bullock, John G. 2009. "Partisan Bias and the Bayesian Ideal in the Study of Public Opinion." *Journal of Politics* 71, no. 3: 1109–24.

Burrus, Jeremy, Justin Kruger, and Amber Jurgens. 2006. "The Truth Never Stands in the Way of a Good Story: The Distortion of Stories in the Service of Entertainment." SSRN 946212.

Busby, Ethan C., Adam J. Howat, Jacob E. Rothschild, and Richard M. Shafranek. 2021. *The Partisan Next Door: Stereotypes of Party Supporters and Consequences for Polarization in America*. New York: Cambridge University Press.

Byler, David, and Kate Woodsome. 2021. "Opinion: False, Toxic Sept. 11 Conspiracy Theories Are Still Widespread Today." *Washington Post*, September 10. https://www.washingtonpost.com/opinions/2021/09/10/false-toxic-sept-11-conspiracy-theories-are-still-widespread-today/.

Campbell, Angus, Philip E. Converse, Warren E. Miller, and Donald E. Stokes. 1960. *The American Voter*. Chicago: University of Chicago Press.

Carlson, Taylor N. 2018. "Modeling Political Information Transmission as a Game of Telephone." *Journal of Politics* 80, no. 1: 348–52.

———. 2019. "Through the Grapevine: Informational Consequences of Interpersonal Political Communication." *American Political Science Review* 113, no. 2: 325–39.

Carlson, Taylor N., Marisa Abrajano, and Lisa García Bedolla. 2020a. "Political Discussion Networks and Political Engagement among Voters of Color." *Political Research Quarterly* 73, no. 1: 79–95.

———. 2020b. *Talking Politics: Political Discussion Networks and the New American Electorate*. New York: Oxford University Press.

Carlson, Taylor N., and Seth J. Hill. 2022. "Experimental Measurement of Misperception in Political Beliefs." *Journal of Experimental Political Science* 9, no. 2: 241–54.

Carlson, Taylor N., and Jaime E. Settle. 2016. "Political Chameleons: An Exploration of Conformity in Political Discussions." *Political Behavior* 38, no. 4: 817–59.

———. 2022. *What Goes without Saying: Navigating Political Discussion in America*. New York: Cambridge University Press.

Charman, Steve D., Melissa Kavetski, and Dana Hirn Mueller. 2017. "Cognitive Bias in the Legal System: Police Officers Evaluate Ambiguous Evidence in a Belief-Consistent Manner." *Journal of Applied Research in Memory and Cognition* 6, no. 2: 193–202.

Chung, Cindy M. Y., and Peter R. Darke. 2006. "The Consumer as Advocate: Self-Relevance, Culture, and Word-of-Mouth." *Marketing Letters* 17: 269–79.

Cillizza, Chris. 2017. "Americans Know Literally Nothing about the Constitution." *The Point with Chris Cillizza*, CNN, September 13. https://www.cnn.com/2017/09/13/politics/poll-constitution/index.html.

Clinton, Joshua D., and Ted Enamorado. 2014. "The National News Media's Effect on Congress: How Fox News Affected Elites in Congress." *Journal of Politics* 76, no. 4: 928–43.

Cohen, Cathy J., and Matthew D. Luttig. 2020. "Reconceptualizing Political Knowledge: Race, Ethnicity, and Carceral Violence." *Perspectives on Politics* 18, no. 3: 805–18.

Connors, Elizabeth C., Matthew T. Pietryka, and John Barry Ryan. 2022. *Examining Motivations in Interpersonal Communication Experiments*. Elements in Experimental Political Science. New York: Cambridge University Press.

Converse, Philip E. 1964. "The Nature of Belief Systems in Mass Publics." In *Ideology and Discontent*, edited by David E. Apter. New York: Free Press.

Coppock, Alexander. 2022. *Persuasion in Parallel.* Chicago Studies in American Politics. Chicago: University of Chicago Press.

Cowan, Nelson. 2001. "The Magical Number 4 in Short-Term Memory: A Reconsideration of Mental Storage Capacity." *Behavioral and Brain Sciences* 24, no. 1: 87–114.

Cramer Walsh, Katherine. 2004. *Talking about Politics: Informal Groups and Social Identity in American Life.* Chicago: University of Chicago Press.

Dale, Dennis. 2021. "Anatomy of a Lie: How the Myth That Antifa Stormed the Capitol Became a Widespread Belief among Republicans." CNN, March 2. Accessed June 13, 2023. https://www.cnn.com/2021/03/02/politics/fact-check-antifa-capitol-lie-republicans-polls/index.html.

Damann, Taylor, Dean Knox, and Christopher Lucas. n.d. "More Than Words: How Political Rhetoric Shapes Voters' Affect and Evaluation." Working Paper. http://christopherlucas.org/files/PDFs/more_than_words.pdf.

Darr, Joshua P., Matthew P. Hitt, and Johanna L. Dunaway. 2018. "Newspaper Closures Polarize Voting Behavior." *Journal of Communication* 68, no. 6: 1007–28.

Davidson, Richard J. 1993. "Parsing Affective Space: Perspectives from Neuropsychology and Psychophysiology." *Neuropsychology* 7, no. 4: 464.

de Benedictis-Kessner, Justin, Matthew A. Baum, Adam J. Berinsky, and Teppei Yamamoto. 2019. "Persuading the Enemy: Estimating the Persuasive Effects of Partisan Media with the Preference-Incorporating Choice and Assignment Design." *American Political Science Review* 113, no. 4: 902–16.

Deichert, Maggie. 2019. "Partisan Cultural Stereotypes: The Effect of Everyday Partisan Associations on Social Life in the United States." PhD diss., Vanderbilt University.

DellaVigna, Stefano, and Ethan Kaplan. 2007. "The Fox News Effect: Media Bias and Voting." *Quarterly Journal of Economics* 122 (3): 1187–1234.

Delli Carpini, Michael X., and Scott Keeter. 1996. *What Americans Know about Politics and Why It Matters.* New Haven, CT: Yale University Press.

Deutschmann, Paul J., and Wayne A. Danielson. 1960. "Diffusion of Knowledge of the Major News Story." *Journalism Quarterly* 37: 345–55.

Dietrich, Bryce J., Matthew Hayes, and Diana Z. O'Brien. 2019. "Pitch Perfect: Vocal Pitch and the Emotional Intensity of Congressional Speech." *American Political Science Review* 113, no. 4: 941–62.

Ditto, Peter H., Brittany S. Liu, Cory J. Clark, Sean P. Wojcik, Eric E. Chen, Rebecca H. Grady, Jared B. Celniker, and Joanne F. Zinger. 2019. "At Least Bias Is Bipartisan: A Meta-Analytic Comparison of Partisan Bias in Liberals and Conservatives." *Perspectives on Psychological Science* 14, no. 2: 273–91.

Djupe, Paul, Scott McClurg, and Anand Edward Sokhey. 2018. "The Political Consequences of Gender in Social Networks." *British Journal of Political Science* 48, no. 3: 637–58.

Doherty, Carroll, Jocelyn Kiley, Nida Asheer, and Calvin Jordan. 2021. "Biden Begins Presidency with Positive Ratings; Trump Departs with Lowest-Ever Job Mark." Pew Research Center, January 15. Accessed June 13, 2023. https://www.pewresearch.org/politics/2021/01/15/voters-reflections-on-the-2020-election/.

Dolan, Kathleen. 2011. "Do Women and Men Know Different Things? Measuring Gender Differences in Political Knowledge." *Journal of Politics* 73, no. 1: 97–107.

Dolan, Kathleen, and Michael A. Hansen. 2020. "The Variable Nature of the Gender Gap in Political Knowledge." *Journal of Women, Politics & Policy* 41, no. 2: 127–43.

Downs, Anthony. 1957. *An Economic Theory of Democracy*. New York: Harper.

Druckman, James N., Samara Klar, Yanna Krupnikov, Matthew Levendusky, and John Barry Ryan. 2022. "(Mis)Estimating Affective Polarization." *Journal of Politics* 84, no. 2: 1106–17.

Druckman, James N., and Matthew S. Levendusky. 2019. "What Do We Measure When We Measure Affective Polarization?" *Public Opinion Quarterly* 83, no. 1: 114–22.

Druckman, James N., Matthew S. Levendusky, and Audrey McLain. 2018. "No Need to Watch: How the Effects of Partisan Media Can Spread via Interpersonal Discussions." *American Journal of Political Science* 62, no. 1: 99–112.

Druckman, James N., Erik Peterson, and Rune Slothuus. 2013. "How Elite Partisan Polarization Affects Public Opinion Formation." *American Political Science Review* 107, no. 1: 57–79.

Duggan, Maeve, and Aaron Smith. 2016. "The Political Environment on Social Media." Pew Research Center, October 25. https://www.pewresearch.org/internet/2016/10/25/the-political-environment-on-social-media/.

Easton, Matthew J., and John B. Holbein. 2021. "The Democracy of Dating: How Political Affiliations Shape Relationship Formation." *Journal of Experimental Political Science* 8, no. 3: 260–72.

Enos, Ryan D. 2017. *The Space Between Us: Social Geography and Politics*. New York: Cambridge University Press.

Eveland, William P., Jr., and Myiah Hutchens Hively. 2009. "Political Discussion Frequency, Network Size, and 'Heterogeneity' of Discussion as Predictors of Political Knowledge and Participation." *Journal of Communication* 59, no. 2: 205–24.

Eveland, William P., Jr., Hyunjin Song, Myiah J. Hutchens, and Lindsey Clark Levitan. 2019. "Not Being Accurate Is Not Quite the Same as Being Inaccurate: Variations in Reported (In)Accuracy of Perceptions of Political Views of Network Members due to Uncertainty." *Communication Methods and Measures* 13, no. 4: 305–11.

Feezell, Jessica T., and Brittany Ortiz. 2021. "'I saw it on Facebook': An Experimental Analysis of Political Learning through Social Media." *Information, Communication & Society* 24, no. 9: 1283–1302.

Fichera, Angelo. 2021. "False Claims Cited in Bogus Theory That Biden Isn't President." FactCheck.org., March 2. https://www.factcheck.org/2021/03/false-claims-cited-in-bogus-theory-that-biden-isnt-president/.

Findahl, Olle, and Brigitta Höijer. 1985. "Some Characteristics of News Memory and Comprehension." *Journal of Broadcasting & Electronic Media* 29, no. 4: 379–96.

Fiorina, Morris P., Samuel A. Abrams, and Jeremy C. Pope. 2008. "Polarization in the American Public: Misconceptions and Misreadings." *Journal of Politics* 70, no. 2: 556–60.

Flaccus, Gillian. 2020. "Portland's Grim Reality: 100 Days of Protests, Many Violent." Associated Press. September 4. https://apnews.com/article/virus-outbreak-ap-top-news-race-and-ethnicity-id-state-wire-or-state-wire-b57315d97dd2146c4a89b4636faa7b70.

Flynn, D. J., Brendan Nyhan, and Jason Reifler. 2017. "The Nature and Origins of Misperceptions: Understanding False and Unsupported Beliefs about Politics." *Political Psychology* 38: 127–50.

Ford, Andrew. 2016. "Viral Misinformation and Political Engagement." *Emerging Media 360*. Loyola University, MD. https://www.loyola.edu/academics/emerging-media/blog/2016/viral-misinformation-political-engagement.

Fowler, James H. 2005. "Turnout in a Small World." In *The Social Logic of Politics: Personal Networks as Contexts for Political Behavior*, edited by Alan S. Zuckerman, 269–87. Philadelphia: Temple University Press.

Fowler, James H., Michael T. Heaney, David W. Nickerson, John F. Padgett, and Betsy Sinclair. 2011. "Causality in Political Networks." *American Politics Research* 39, no. 2: 437–80.

Gaines, Brian J., James H. Kuklinski, Paul J. Quirk, Buddy Peyton, and Jay Verkuilen. 2007. "Same Facts, Different Interpretations: Partisan Motivation and Opinion on Iraq." *Journal of Politics* 69, no. 4: 957–74.

Ganske, Kathryn H., and Michelle R. Hebl. 2001. "Once upon a Time There Was a Math Contest: Gender Stereotyping and Memory." *Teaching of Psychology* 28, no. 4: 266–68.

Garrett, R. Kelly, Brian E. Weeks, and Rachel L. Neo. 2016. "Driving a Wedge between Evidence and Beliefs: How Online Ideological News Exposure Promotes Political Misperceptions." *Journal of Computer-Mediated Communication* 21, no. 5: 331–48.

Gause, LaGina. 2022. *The Advantage of Disadvantage*. New York: Cambridge University Press.

Gerber, Alan S., and Donald P. Green. 2000. "The Effects of Canvassing, Telephone Calls, and Direct Mail on Voter Turnout: A Field Experiment." *American Political Science Review* 94, no. 3: 653–63.

Gerber, Alan S., Donald P. Green, and Christopher W. Larimer. 2008. "Social Pressure and Voter Turnout: Evidence from a Large Scale Field Experiment." *American Political Science Review* 102, no. 1: 33–48.

Gibson, James L. 1992. "The Political Consequences of Intolerance: Cultural Conformity and Political Freedom." *American Political Science Review* 86, no. 2: 338–56.

Green, Donald, Bradley Palmquist, and Eric Schickler. 2002. *Partisan Hearts and Minds*. New Haven, CT: Yale University Press.

Greifer, Noah, Steven Worthington, Stefano Iacus, and Gary King. 2023. "Clarify: Simulation-Based Inference for Regression Models." Version 0.1.3, May 4. https://cran.r-project.org/web/packages/clarify/index.html.

Guess, Andrew M. 2021. "(Almost) Everything in Moderation: New Evidence on Americans' Online Media Diets." *American Journal of Political Science* 65, no. 4: 1007–22.

Guess, Andrew M., and Kevin Munger. 2023. "Digital Literacy and Online Political Behavior." *Political Science Research and Methods* 11, no. 1: 110–28.

Habermas, Jürgen. 1984. "Habermas: Questions and Counterquestions." *Praxis International* 4, no. 3: 229–49.

Hall, Andrew B. 2015. "What Happens When Extremists Win Primaries?" *American Political Science Review* 109, no. 1: 18–42.

Harari, Yuval Noah. 2014. *Sapiens: A Brief History of Humankind*. New York: HarperCollins.

Hayes, Danny, and Jennifer L. Lawless. 2015. "As Local News Goes, So Goes Citizen Engagement: Media, Knowledge, and Participation in US House Elections." *Journal of Politics* 77, no. 2: 447–62.

Heath, Chip, Chris Bell, and Emily Sternberg. 2001. "Emotional Selection in Memes: The Case of Urban Legends." *Journal of Personality and Social Psychology* 81, no. 6: 1028.

Hersh, Eitan. 2020. *Politics Is for Power: How to Move beyond Political Hobbyism, Take Action, and Make Real Change*. New York: Simon and Schuster.

Hetherington, Marc J. 2001. "Resurgent Mass Partisanship: The Role of Elite Polarization." *American Political Science Review* 95, no. 3: 619–31.

Hiaeshutter-Rice, Dan, Fabian G. Neuner, and Stuart Soroka. 2023. "Cued by Culture: Political Imagery and Partisan Evaluations." *Political Behavior* 45, no. 2: 741–59.

Hochschild, Jennifer L., and Katherine Levine Einstein. 2015. *Do Facts Matter? Information and Misinformation in American Politics*. Norman: University of Oklahoma Press.

Hovland, Carl I. 1954. "Communication and Persuasion." *Journal of Consulting Psychology* 18, no. 2: 152.

Huber, Gregory A., and Neil Malhotra. 2017. "Political Homophily in Social Relationships: Evidence from Online Dating Behavior." *Journal of Politics* 79, no. 1: 269–83.

Huckfeldt, Robert, Paul Allen Beck, Russell J. Dalton, Jeffrey Levine, and William Morgan. 1998. "Ambiguity, Distorted Messages, and Nested Environmental Effects on Political Communication." *Journal of Politics* 60, no. 4: 996–1030.

Huckfeldt, Robert, Paul E. Johnson, and John Sprague. 2004. *Political Disagreement: The Survival of Diverse Opinions within Communication Networks*. Cambridge University Press.

Huckfeldt, Robert, Jeanette Morehouse Mendez, and Tracy Osborn. 2004. "Disagreement, ambivalence, and engagement: The political consequences of heterogeneous networks." *Political Psychology* 25, no. 1: 65–95.

Huckfeldt, Robert, and John Sprague. 1987. "Networks in Context: The Social Flow of Political Information." *American Political Science Review* 81, no. 4: 1197–1216.

———. 1995. *Citizens, Politics and Social Communication: Information and Influence in an Election Campaign*. New York: Cambridge University Press.

Hutchens, Myiah J., Jay D. Hmielowski, and Michael A. Beam. 2019. "Reinforcing Spirals of Political Discussion and Affective Polarization." *Communication Monographs* 86, no. 3: 357–76.

Iyengar, Shanto, Yphtach Lelkes, Matthew Levendusky, Neil Malhotra, and Sean J. Westwood. 2019. "The Origins and Consequences of Affective Polarization in the United States." *Annual Review of Political Science* 22: 129–46.

Iyengar, Shanto, Gaurav Sood, and Yphtach Lelkes. 2012. "Affect, not Ideology: A Social Identity Perspective on Polarization." *Public Opinion Quarterly* 76, no. 3: 405–31.

Jefferson, Thomas. 1789. Letter from Thomas Jefferson to Richard Price. January 8. Manuscript letter. Manuscript Division (60). https://www.loc.gov/exhibits/jefferson/60.html.

Jerit, Jennifer, and Jason Barabas. 2012. "Partisan Perceptual Bias and the Information Environment." *Journal of Politics* 74, no. 3: 672–84.

———. 2017. "Revisiting the Gender Gap in Political Knowledge." *Political Behavior* 39, no. 4: 817–38.

Jerit, Jennifer, and Yangzi Zhao. 2020. "Political Misinformation." *Annual Review of Political Science* 23: 77–94.

Jimmy Kimmel Live. 2013. "Six of One – Obamacare vs. the Affordable Care Act." October 1. https://www.youtube.com/watch?v=sx2scvIFGjE.

Kalmoe, Nathan P., and Lilliana Mason. 2022. *Radical American Partisanship: Mapping Violent Hostility, Its Causes, and the Consequences for Democracy*. Chicago: University of Chicago Press.

Karpowitz, Christopher F., and Tali Mendelberg. 2014. *The Silent Sex*. Princeton, NJ: Princeton University Press.

Katz, Elihu. 1957. "The Two-Step Flow of Communication: An Up-to-Date Report on an Hypothesis." *Public Opinion Quarterly* 21, no. 1: 61–78.

Katz, Elihu, and Paul F. Lazarsfeld. 1955. *Personal Influence: The Part Played by People in the Flow of Mass Communication*. New York: Free Press.

Kaufman, Aaron R. 2014. Estimating the Partisan Bias in Survey Questions (0.1.3) [Application Software]. https://arkaufman.shinyapps.io/textbias/.

Kenny, Christopher. 1992. "Political Participation and Effects from the Social Environment." *American Journal of Political Science* 36, no. 1: 259–67.

Kim, Eunji. 2023. "Entertaining Beliefs in Economic Mobility." *American Journal of Political Science* 67, no. 1: 39–54.

Kim, Jin Woo, Andrew Guess, Brendan Nyhan, and Jason Reifler. 2021. "The Distorting Prism of Social Media: How Self-Selection and Exposure to Incivility Fuel Online Comment Toxicity." *Journal of Communication* 71, no. 6: 922–46.

Kim, Jin Woo, and Eunji Kim. 2021. "Temporal Selective Exposure: How Partisans Choose When to Follow Politics." *Political Behavior* 43, no. 4: 1663–83.

King, Charles W., and John O. Summers. 1970. "Overlap of Opinion Leadership across Consumer Product Categories." *Journal of Marketing Research* 7, no. 1: 43–50.

Klar, Samara. 2014. "Partisanship in a Social Setting." *American Journal of Political Science* 58, no. 3: 687–704.

Klar, Samara, and Yanna Krupnikov. 2016. *Independent Politics*. New York: Cambridge University Press.

Klofstad, Casey A., Scott D. McClurg, and Meredith Rolfe. 2009. "Measurement of Political Discussion Networks: A Comparison of Two 'Name Generator' Procedures." *Public Opinion Quarterly* 73, no. 3: 462–83.

Klofstad, Casey A., Anand Edward Sokhey, and Scott D. McClurg. 2013. "Disagreeing about Disagreement: How Conflict in Social Networks Affects Political Behavior." *American Journal of Political Science* 57, no. 1: 120–34.

Knopf, Terry Ann. 1975. "Beating the Rumors: An Evaluation of Rumor Control Centers." *Policy Analysis* 1, no. 4: 599–612.

Knox, Dean, and Christopher Lucas. 2021. "A Dynamic Model of Speech for the Social Sciences." *American Political Science Review* 115, no. 2: 649–66.

Kraft, Patrick W., and Kathleen Dolan. 2023. "Asking the Right Questions: A Framework for Developing Gender-Balanced Political Knowledge Batteries." *Political Research Quarterly* 76, no. 1: 393–406.

Kraft, Patrick W., Yanna Krupnikov, Kerri Milita, John Barry Ryan, and Stuart Soroka. 2020. "Social Media and the Changing Information Environment: Sentiment Differences in Read versus Recirculated News Content." *Public Opinion Quarterly* 84, no. S1: 195–215.

Krosnick, Jon A. 1990. "Government Policy and Citizen Passion: A Study of Issue Publics in Contemporary America." *Political Behavior* 12: 59–92.

Krupnikov, Yanna, Kerri Milita, John Barry Ryan, and Elizabeth C. Connors. 2020. "How Gender Affects the Efficacy of Discussion as an Information Shortcut." *Political Science Research and Methods* 8, no. 2: 268–84.

Krupnikov, Yanna, and John Barry Ryan. 2022. *The Other Divide: Polarization and Disengagement in American Politics*. Cambridge: Cambridge University Press.

Kuklinski, James H., Paul J. Quirk, Jennifer Jerit, David Schwieder, and Robert F. Rich. 2000. "Misinformation and the Currency of Democratic Citizenship." *Journal of Politics* 62, no. 3: 790–816.

Kunda, Ziva. 1990. "The Case for Motivated Reasoning." *Psychological Bulletin* 108, no. 3: 480–98.

Larson, Jennifer M., and Janet I. Lewis. 2017. "Ethnic Networks." *American Journal of Political Science* 61, no. 2: 350–64.

———. 2018. "Rumors, Kinship Networks, and Rebel Group Formation." *International Organization* 72, no. 4: 871–903.

Lau, Richard R. 2013. "Correct Voting in the 2008 US Presidential Nominating Elections." *Political Behavior* 35: 331–55.

Lau, Richard R., and David P. Redlawsk. 1997. "Voting Correctly." *American Political Science Review* 91, no. 3: 585–98.

Lazarsfeld, Paul F., Bernard Berelson, and Hazel Gaudet. [1944] 2021. *The People's Choice: How the Voter Makes Up His Mind in a Presidential Campaign*. New York: Columbia University Press.

Lee, Jae Kook, Jihyang Choi, Cheonsoo Kim, and Yonghwan Kim. 2014. "Social Media, Network Heterogeneity, and Opinion Polarization." *Journal of Communication* 64, no. 4: 702–22.

Leigh, Harri. 2020. "Armed Counter-Protesters in Gettysburg, but No Antifa Protest." Fox 43, July 4. https://www.fox43.com/article/news/community/armed-counter-protesters-in-gettysburg-but-no-antifa-protest/521-f52c2293-8065-4f30-b8d7-75a7603785da.

Leonhardt, David. 2022. "A Functional Congress? Yes." *New York Times*, August 16. Accessed June 7, 2023. https://www.nytimes.com/2022/08/16/briefing/congress-productive-democrats-republicans.html.

Levendusky, Matthew. 2009. *The Partisan Sort: How Liberals Became Democrats and Conservatives Became Republicans*. Chicago Studies in American Politics Series. Chicago: University of Chicago Press.

———. 2013. *How Partisan Media Polarize America*. Chicago: University of Chicago Press.

———. 2023. *Our Common Bonds: Using What Americans Share to Help Bridge the Partisan Divide*. Chicago: University of Chicago Press.

Levendusky, Matthew, and Dominik A. Stecula. 2021. *We Need to Talk: How Cross-Party Dialogue Reduces Affective Polarization*. Cambridge Elements in Experimental Political Science. New York: Cambridge University Press.

Levitan, Lindsey C., and Brad Verhulst. 2016. "Conformity in Groups: The Effects of Others' Views on Expressed Attitudes and Attitude Change." *Political Behavior* 38, no. 2: 277–315.

Lipset, Seymour Martin. 1960. "Party Systems and the Representation of Social Groups." *European Journal of Sociology/Archives Européennes de Sociologie* 1, no. 1: 50–85.

Lodge, Milton, and Ruth Hamill. 1986. "A Partisan Schema For Political Information Processing." *American Political Science Review* 80, no. 2: 505–19.

Lodge, Milton, and Charles S. Taber. 2013. *The Rationalizing Voter*. New York: Cambridge University Press.

Luca, Mario, Kevin Munger, Jonathan Nagler, and Joshua A. Tucker. 2022. "You Won't Believe Our Results! But They Might: Heterogeneity in Beliefs about the Accuracy of Online Media." *Journal of Experimental Political Science* 9, no. 2: 267–77.

Lupia, Arthur. 1994. "Shortcuts versus Encyclopedias: Information and Voting Behavior in California Insurance Reform Elections." *American Political Science Review* 88, no. 1: 63–76.

Lupia, Arthur, and Mathew D. McCubbins. 1998. *The Democratic Dilemma: Can Citizens Learn What They Need to Know?* Cambridge: Cambridge University Press.

Lyons, Jeffrey, and Anand E. Sokhey. 2017. "Discussion Networks, Issues, and Perceptions of Polarization in the American Electorate." *Political Behavior* 39: 967–88.

Makse, Todd, Scott Minkoff, and Anand Sokhey. 2019. *Politics on Display: Yard Signs and the Politicization of Social Spaces*. New York: Oxford University Press.

Mallen, Michael J., Susan X. Day, and Melinda A. Green. 2003. "Online versus Face-to-Face Conversation: An Examination of Relational and Discourse Variables." *Psychotherapy: Theory, Research, Practice, Training* 40, no. 1–2: 155–63.

Martin, Gregory J., and Ali Yurukoglu. 2017. "Bias in Cable News: Persuasion and Polarization." *American Economic Review* 107, no. 9: 2565–99.

Mason, Lilliana. 2015. "'I disrespectfully agree': The Differential Effects of Partisan Sorting on Social and Issue Polarization." *American Journal of Political Science* 59, no. 1: 128–45.

———. 2018. *Uncivil Agreement: How Politics Became Our Identity*. Chicago: University of Chicago Press.

McCarty, Nolan, Keith T. Poole, and Howard Rosenthal. 2016. *Polarized America: The Dance of Ideology and Unequal Riches*. Cambridge, MA: MIT Press.

McClurg, Scott D. 2003. "Social Networks and Political Participation: The Role of Social Interaction in Explaining Political Participation." *Political Research Quarterly* 56, no. 4: 449–64.

McGraw, Meridith. 2018. "Top White House Economist Says Trump's GDP and Unemployment Claim Was Wrong." *ABC News*, September 10. Accessed June 10, 2023. https://abcnews.go.com/Politics/top-white-house-economist-trumps-gdp-unemployment-claim/story?id=57731637.

Miller, George A. 1956. "The Magical Number Seven, Plus or Minus Two: Some Limits on Our Capacity for Processing Information." *Psychological Review* 63, no. 2: 81–97.

Miller, Joanne M., Kyle L. Saunders, and Christina E. Farhart. 2016. "Conspiracy Endorsement as Motivated Reasoning: The Moderating Roles of Political Knowledge and Trust." *American Journal of Political Science* 60, no. 4: 824–44.

Min, Seong-Jae. 2007. "Online vs. Face-to-Face Deliberation: Effects on Civic Engagement." *Journal of Computer-Mediated Communication* 12, no. 4: 1369–87.

Minozzi, William, Hyunjin Song, David M. J. Lazer, Michael A. Neblo, and Katherine Ognyanova. 2020. "The Incidental Pundit: Who Talks Politics with Whom, and Why?" *American Journal of Political Science* 64, no. 1: 135–51.

Mitchell, Amy, Mark Jurkowitz, J. Baxter Oliphant, and Elisa Shearer. 2020. "Americans Who Mainly Get Their News on Social Media Are Less Engaged, Less Knowledgeable." Pew Research Center, July 30. https://www.pewresearch.org/journalism/2020/07/30/americans-who-mainly-get-their-news-on-social-media-are-less-engaged-less-knowledgeable/.

Mitchell, Amy, Elisa Shearer, and Galen Stocking. 2021. "News on Twitter: Consumed by Most Users and Trusted by Many." Pew Research Center, November 15. https://www.pewresearch.org/journalism/2021/11/15/news-on-twitter-consumed-by-most-users-and-trusted-by-many/.

Moeller, Judith, Claes De Vreese, Frank Esser, and Ruth Kunz. 2014. "Pathway to Political Participation: The Influence of Online and Offline News Media on Internal Efficacy and Turnout of First-Time Voters." *American Behavioral Scientist* 58, no. 5: 689–700.

Molay, Autumn, and Ian Essling. 2020. "Media Consumption during the Coronavirus Pandemic." Comscore, March 17. Accessed June 7, 2023. https://www.comscore.com/fre/Perspectives/Blog/Media-Consumption-during-the-Coronavirus-Pandemic.

Mondak, Jeffery J., and Mary R. Anderson. 2004. "The Knowledge Gap: A Reexamination of Gender-Based Differences in Political Knowledge." *Journal of Politics* 66, no. 2: 492–512.

Moore, Cortney. 2021. "91-Year-Old Grandpa Sends Lovingly Hilarious Texts to His Single Granddaughter: Video." Fox News, July 22. https://www.foxnews.com/lifestyle/91-year-old-grandpa-hilarious-texts-single-granddaughter-tiktok.

Moses, Laura. n.d. "Conceptualizing and Identifying 'Interest Actors.'" Working Paper. https://lmmoses.github.io/research.html.

Moussaïd, Mehdi, Henry Brighton, and Wolfgang Gaissmaier. 2015. "The Amplification of Risk in Experimental Diffusion Chains." *Proceedings of the National Academy of Sciences* 112, no. 18: 5631–36.

Munger, Kevin. 2020. "All the News That's Fit to Click: The Economics of Clickbait Media." *Political Communication* 37, no. 3: 376–97.

———. 2023. "Temporal Validity as Meta-Science." Working Paper. https://kmunger.github.io/pdfs/tv.pdf.

Mutz, Diana C. 2002. "The Consequences of Cross-Cutting Networks for Political Participation." *American Journal of Political Science* 46, no. 4: 838–55.

———. 2006. *Hearing the Other Side: Deliberative versus Participatory Democracy*. New York: Cambridge University Press.

Neuman, W. Russell. 1976. "Patterns of Recall among Television News Viewers." *Public Opinion Quarterly* 40, no. 1: 115–23.

Nickerson, David. 2008. "Is Voting Contagious? Evidence from Two Field Experiments." *American Political Science Review* 102 (February): 49–57.

Noelle-Neumann, E. 1983. *Spiegel Dokumentation: Personlichkeitsstarke*. Hamburg: Spiegel Verlag.

Nyhan, Brendan. 2020. "Facts and Myths about Misperceptions." *Journal of Economic Perspectives* 34, no. 3: 220–36.

Nyhan, Brendan, Ethan Porter, Jason Reifler, and Thomas J. Wood. 2020. "Taking Fact-Checks Literally but Not Seriously? The Effects of Journalistic Fact-Checking on Factual Beliefs and Candidate Favorability." *Political Behavior* 42: 939–60.

Orr, Lilla V., and Gregory A. Huber. 2020. "The Policy Basis of Measured Partisan Animosity in the United States." *American Journal of Political Science* 64, no. 3: 569–86.

O'Sullivan, Donie. 2022. "Buffalo Massacre Puts Spotlight on Hate-Filled Website." CNN Business, May 16. https://www.cnn.com/2022/05/16/tech/4chan-buffalo-shooting/index.html.

Ovide, Shira. 2020. "False Rumors Often Start at the Top." *New York Times*, October 8. Updated October 13, 2020. Accessed June 3, 2023. https://www.nytimes.com/2020/10/08/technology/misinformation-communication.html.

Pariser, Eli. 2012. *The Filter Bubble: How the New Personalized Web Is Changing What We Read and How We Think*. New York: Penguin.

Patt, Anthony, and Richard Zeckhauser. 2000. "Action Bias and Environmental Decisions." *Journal of Risk and Uncertainty* 21: 45–72.

Pedersen, Jenna, and Taylor N. Carlson. 2022. "Let's Talk About It: How Election Outcomes Affect Media Choice." Paper presented at the Annual Meeting of the Midwest Political Science Association, April 7. [Virtual meeting.]

Pennycook, Gordon, and David G. Rand. 2019. "Fighting Misinformation on Social Media Using Crowdsourced Judgments of News Source Quality." *Proceedings of the National Academy of Sciences* 116, no. 7: 2521–26.

Pereira, Gabriel, Iago Bueno Bojczuk Camargo, and Lisa Parks. 2022. "WhatsApp Disruptions in Brazil: A Content Analysis of User and News Media Responses, 2015–2018." *Global Media and Communication* 18, no. 1: 113–48.

Pérez, Efrén O. 2015. "Mind the Gap: Why Large Group Deficits in Political Knowledge Emerge—and What to Do about Them." *Political Behavior* 37, no. 4: 933–54.

Phoenix, Davin L. 2019. *The Anger Gap: How Race Shapes Emotion in Politics*. Cambridge: Cambridge University Press.

Pickett, Cynthia L., and Marilynn B. Brewer. 2001. "Assimilation and Differentiation Needs as Motivational Determinants of Perceived In-Group and Out-Group Homogeneity." *Journal of Experimental Social Psychology* 37, no. 4: 341–48.

Pietryka, Matthew T. 2016. "Accuracy Motivations, Predispositions, and Social Information in Political Discussion Networks." *Political Psychology* 37, no. 3: 367–86.

Pietryka, Matthew T., and Randall C. MacIntosh. 2022. "ANES Scales Often Do Not Measure What You Think They Measure." *Journal of Politics* 84, no. 2: 1074–90.

Popkin, Samuel L. 1991. *The Reasoning Voter: Communication and Persuasion in Presidential Campaigns*. Chicago: University of Chicago Press.

Prior, Markus. 2005. "News vs. Entertainment: How Increasing Media Choice Widens Gaps in Political Knowledge and Turnout." *American Journal of Political Science* 49, no. 3: 577–92.

———. 2009. "The Immensely Inflated News Audience: Assessing Bias in Self-Reported News Exposure." *Public Opinion Quarterly* 73, no. 1: 130–43.

———. 2013. "Media and Political Polarization." *Annual Review of Political Science* 16: 101–27.

Rahn, Wendy M. 1993. "The Role of Partisan Stereotypes in Information Processing about Political Candidates." *American Journal of Political Science* 37, no. 2: 472–96.

Redlawsk, David P. 2002. "Hot Cognition or Cool Consideration? Testing the Effects of Motivated Reasoning on Political Decision Making." *Journal of Politics* 64, no. 4: 1021–44.

———. 2006. "Motivated Reasoning, Affect, and the Role of Memory in Voter Decision Making." In *Feeling Politics*, edited by David P. Redlawsk, 87–107. New York: Palgrave Macmillan.

Robinson, John P. 1976. "Interpersonal Influence in Election Campaigns: Two Step-Flow Hypotheses." *Public Opinion Quarterly* 40, no. 3: 304–19.

Rogowski, Jon C., and Betsy Sinclair. 2012. "Estimating the Causal Effects of Social Interaction with Endogenous Networks." *Political Analysis* 20, no. 3: 316–28.

Romm, Tony. 2019. "Zuckerberg: Standing for Voice and Free Expression." *Washington Post*, October 17. https://www.washingtonpost.com/technology/2019/10/17/zuckerberg-standing-voice-free-expression/.

Rossiter, Erin L. 2020. "The Consequences of Interparty Conversation on Outparty Affect and Stereotypes." Working Paper. http://erossiter.com/files/conversations.pdf.

Rossiter, Erin L., and Taylor N. Carlson. 2023. "Cross-Partisan Conversation Reduced Affective Polarization for Republicans and Democrats Even after the Contentious 2020 Election." *Journal of Politics*, forthcoming. http://erossiter.com/files/rossiter_carlson_threat_contact_letter.pdf.

Rothschild, Jacob E., Adam J. Howat, Richard M. Shafranek, and Ethan C. Busby. 2019. "Pigeonholing Partisans: Stereotypes of Party Supporters and Partisan Polarization." *Political Behavior* 41, no. 2: 423–43.

Ryan, John Barry. 2011. "Accuracy and Bias in Perceptions of Political Knowledge." *Political Behavior* 33, no. 2: 335–56.

Santoro, Erik, and David E. Broockman. 2022. "The Promise and Pitfalls of Cross-Partisan Conversations for Reducing Affective Polarization: Evidence from Randomized Experiments." *Science Advances* 8, no. 25: eabn5515.

Savje, Fredrik, Jasjeet Sekhon, and Michael Higgins. 2018. "quickmatch: Quick Generalized Full Matching." Version 0.2.1, August 24. https://cran.r-project.org/web/packages/quickmatch/index.html.

Settle, Jaime E. 2018. *Frenemies: How Social Media Polarizes America*. New York: Cambridge University Press.

Shearer, Elisa, and Amy Mitchell. 2021. "How Americans Tweet about the News." Pew Research Center, December 14. https://www.pewresearch.org/fact-tank/2021/12/14/how-americans-tweet-about-the-news/.

Shoemaker, Pamela. 1991. *Gatekeeping*. Thousand Oaks, CA: Sage.

Sieff, Kevin, and Maya Averbuch. 2018. "What Happened to the Caravan after the Midterm Elections?" *Washington Post*, November 8. https://www.washingtonpost.com/world/2018/11/08/what-happened-caravan-after-midterm-elections/.

Sinclair, Betsy. 2012. *The Social Citizen: Peer Networks and Political Behavior*. Chicago: University of Chicago Press.

Sinclair, Betsy, Margaret McConnell, and Donald P. Green. 2012. "Detecting Spillover Effects: Design and Analysis of Multilevel Experiments." *American Journal of Political Science* 56, no. 4: 1055–69.

Sinclair, Betsy, Margaret McConnell, and Melissa R. Michelson. 2013. "Local Canvassing: The Efficacy of Grassroots Voter Mobilization." *Political Communication* 30, no. 1: 42–57.

Sokhey, Anand E., and Paul A. Djupe. 2011. "Interpersonal Networks and Democratic Politics." *PS: Political Science & Politics* 44, no. 1: 55–59.

———. 2014. "Name Generation in Interpersonal Political Network Data: Results from a Series of Experiments." *Social Networks* 36: 147–61.

Soroka, Stuart N. 2012. "The Gatekeeping Function: Distributions of Information in Media and the Real World." *Journal of Politics* 74, no. 2: 514–28.

Soroka, Stuart N., and Christopher Wlezien. 2022. *Information and Democracy*. New York: Cambridge University Press.

Standage, Tom. 2013. *Writing on the Wall: Social Media—the First 2,000 Years*. New York: Bloomsbury Publishing.

Stromer-Galley, J., L. Bryant, and B. Bimber. 2020. "Context and Medium Matter: Expressing Disagreements Online and Face-to-Face in Political Deliberations." *Journal of Deliberative Democracy* 11, no. 1: 1–22. https://doi.org/10.16997/jdd.218.

Stubbersfield, Joseph M., Lewis G. Dean, Sana Sheikh, Kevin N. Laland, and Catharine P. Cross. 2019. "Social Transmission Favours the 'Morally Good' over the 'Merely Arousing.'" *Palgrave Communications* 5, no. 1: 1–11.

Sunstein, Cass R. 2018. *#Republic*. Princeton, NJ: Princeton University Press.

Taber, Charles S., and Milton Lodge. 2006. "Motivated Skepticism in the Evaluation of Political Beliefs." *American Journal of Political Science* 50, no. 3: 755–69.

Tajfel, Henri and John C. Turner. 1979. "An Integrative Theory of Intergroup Conflict." In *The Social Psychology of Intergroup Relations*, edited by W. G. Austin and S. Worchel, 33–47. Monterey, CA: Brooks/Cole.

Thompson, Stuart A. 2023. "These Activists Distrust Voting Machines. Just Don't Call Them Election Deniers." *New York Times*, June 4. https://www.nytimes.com/2023/06/04/technology/voting-machines-election-deniers.html.

Timberg, Craig, Elizabeth Dwoskin, and Reed Albergotti. 2021. "Inside Facebook, Jan. 6 Violence Fueled Anger, Regret over Missed Warning Signs." *Washington Post*, October 22. https://www.washingtonpost.com/technology/2021/10/22/jan-6-capitol-riot-facebook/.

Timberg, Craig, and Isaac Stanley-Becker. 2020. "Violent Memes and Messages Surging on Far-Left Social Media, a New Report Finds." *Washington Post*, September 17. https://www.washingtonpost.com/technology/2020/09/14/violent-antipolice-memes-surge/.

Torres Pacheco, Silvia Michelle. 2019. "A Visual Political World: Determinants and Effects of Visual Content." PhD diss., Washington University in St. Louis.

Troldahl, Verling C. 1966. "A Field Test of a Modified 'Two-Step Flow of Communication' Model." *Public Opinion Quarterly* 30, no. 4: 609–23.

Tversky, Amos, and Daniel Kahneman. 1991. "Loss Aversion in Riskless Choice: A Reference-Dependent Model." *Quarterly Journal of Economics* 106, no. 4: 1039–61.

———. 1992. "Advances in Prospect Theory: Cumulative Representation of Uncertainty." *Journal of Risk and Uncertainty* 5: 297–323.

US Census Bureau. 2021. "2020 Presidential Election Voting and Registration Tables Now Available." Press Release Number CB21-TPS.49. April 29. Accessed June 7, 2023. https://www.census.gov/newsroom/press-releases/2021/2020-presidential-election-voting-and-registration-tables-now-available.html.

Valentino, Nicholas A., Ted Brader, Eric W. Groenendyk, Krysha Gregorowicz, and Vincent L. Hutchings. 2011. "Election Night's Alright for Fighting: The Role of Emotions in Political Participation." *Journal of Politics* 73, no. 1: 156–70.

Voelkel, Jan G., James Chu, Michael N. Stagnaro, Joseph S. Mernyk, Chrystal Redekopp, Sophia L. Pink, James N. Druckman, David G. Rand, and Robb Willer. 2023. "Interventions Reducing Affective Polarization Do Not Necessarily Improve Anti-Democratic Attitudes." *Nature Human Behaviour* 7, no. 1: 55–64.

Voelkel, Jan G., Michael Stagnaro, James Chu, Sophia Pink, Joseph Mernyk, Chrystal Redekopp, Isaias Ghezae et al. 2023. "Megastudy Identifying Effective Interventions to Strengthen Americans' Democratic Attitudes." https://osf.io/y79u5/download.

Wason, Peter. 1960. "On the Failure to Eliminate Hypotheses in a Conceptual Task." *Quarterly Journal of Experimental Psychology* 12, no. 3: 129–40.

Webster, Steven W., Elizabeth C. Connors, and Betsy Sinclair. 2022. "The Social Consequences of Political Anger." *Journal of Politics* 84, no. 3: 1292–1305.

Weeks, Brian E. 2018. "Media and Political Misperceptions." In *Misinformation and Mass Audiences*, edited by Brian G. Southwell, Emily A. Thorson, and Laura Sheble, 140–56. Austin: University of Texas Press.

Weeks, Brian E., Alberto Ardèvol-Abreu, and Homero Gil de Zúñiga. 2017. "Online Influence? Social Media Use, Opinion Leadership, and Political Persuasion." *International Journal of Public Opinion Research* 29, no. 2: 214–39.

Weeks, Brian E., Ericka Menchen-Trevino, Christopher Calabrese, Andreu Casas, and Magdalena Wojcieszak. 2021. "Partisan Media, Untrustworthy News Sites, and Political Misperceptions." *New Media & Society* 25, no. 10: 2644–62.

Weimann, Gabriel. 1982. "On the Importance of Marginality: One More Step into the Two-Step Flow of Communication." *American Sociological Review* 47, no. 6: 764–73.

Weimann, Gabriel, Deon Harold Tustin, Daan Van Vuuren, and J. P. R. Joubert. 2007. "Looking for Opinion Leaders: Traditional vs. Modern Measures in Traditional Societies." *International Journal of Public Opinion Research* 19, no. 2: 173–90.

West, Emily A. 2022. "The Effect of Political Discussion on Whites' Racial Attitudes and Positions." Working Paper. Draft, September 27. https://www.dropbox.com/s/l395x3m4zp9uavi/West_ZoomExp_DiscussionAffectsRR.pdf?dl=0.

Wojcieszak, Magdalena, Sjifra de Leeuw, Ericka Menchen-Trevino, Seungsu Lee, Ke M. Huang-Isherwood, and Brian Weeks. 2023. "No Polarization from Partisan News: Over-Time Evidence from Trace Data." *International Journal of Press/Politics* 28, no. 3: 601–26.

Wojcieszak, Magdalena E., and Diana C. Mutz. 2009. "Online Groups and Political Discourse: Do Online Discussion Spaces Facilitate Exposure to Political Disagreement?" *Journal of Communication* 59, no. 1: 40–56.

Yong, Ed. 2021. "America Is Getting Unvaccinated People All Wrong." *The Atlantic*, July 22. https://www.theatlantic.com/health/archive/2021/07/unvaccinated-different-anti-vax/619523/.

Young, Lori, and Stuart Soroka. 2012. "Affective News: The Automated Coding of Sentiment in Political Texts." *Political Communication* 29, no. 2: 205–31.

Zaller, John R. 1992. *The Nature and Origins of Mass Opinion*. Cambridge: Cambridge University Press.

Zuckerman, Miron. 1979. "Attribution of Success and Failure Revisited, or: The Motivational Bias Is Alive and Well in Attribution Theory." *Journal of Personality* 47, no. 2: 245–87.

Index

Chicago Studies in American Politics

A series edited by Susan Herbst, Lawrence R. Jacobs, Adam J. Berinsky, and Frances Lee; Benjamin I. Page, editor emeritus

Series titles, continued from front matter

A Troubled Birth: The 1930s and American Public Opinion
by Susan Herbst

Power Shifts: Congress and Presidential Representation
by John A. Dearborn

Prisms of the People: Power and Organizing in Twenty-First-Century America
by Hahrie Han, Elizabeth McKenna, and Michelle Oyakawa

Democracy Declined: The Failed Politics of Consumer Financial Protection
by Mallory E. SoRelle

Race to the Bottom: How Racial Appeals Work in American Politics
by LaFleur Stephens-Dougan

The Limits of Party: Congress and Lawmaking in a Polarized Era
by James M. Curry and Frances E. Lee

America's Inequality Trap
by Nathan J. Kelly

Good Enough for Government Work: The Public Reputation Crisis in America (And What We Can Do to Fix It)
by Amy E. Lerman

Who Wants to Run? How the Devaluing of Political Office Drives Polarization
by Andrew B. Hall

From Politics to the Pews: How Partisanship and the Political Environment Shape Religious Identity
by Michele F. Margolis

The Increasingly United States: How and Why American Political Behavior Nationalized
by Daniel J. Hopkins

Legacies of Losing in American Politics
by Jeffrey K. Tulis and Nicole Mellow

Legislative Style
by William Bernhard and Tracy Sulkin

Why Parties Matter: Political Competition and Democracy in the American South
by John H. Aldrich and John D. Griffin

Neither Liberal nor Conservative: Ideological Innocence in the American Public
by Donald R. Kinder and Nathan P. Kalmoe

Strategic Party Government: Why Winning Trumps Ideology
by Gregory Koger and Matthew J. Lebo

Post-Racial or Most-Racial? Race and Politics in the Obama Era
by Michael Tesler

The Politics of Resentment: Rural Consciousness in Wisconsin and the Rise of Scott Walker
by Katherine J. Cramer

Legislating in the Dark: Information and Power in the House of Representatives
by James M. Curry

Why Washington Won't Work: Polarization, Political Trust, and the Governing Crisis
by Marc J. Hetherington and Thomas J. Rudolph

Who Governs? Presidents, Public Opinion, and Manipulation
by James N. Druckman and Lawrence R. Jacobs

Trapped in America's Safety Net: One Family's Struggle
by Andrea Louise Campbell

Arresting Citizenship: The Democratic Consequences of American Crime Control
by Amy E. Lerman and Vesla M. Weaver

How the States Shaped the Nation: American Electoral Institutions and Voter Turnout, 1920–2000
by Melanie Jean Springer

White-Collar Government: The Hidden Role of Class in Economic Policy Making
by Nicholas Carnes

How Partisan Media Polarize America
by Matthew Levendusky

Changing Minds or Changing Channels? Partisan News in an Age of Choice
by Kevin Arceneaux and Martin Johnson

The Politics of Belonging: Race, Public Opinion, and Immigration
by Natalie Masuoka and Jane Junn

Trading Democracy for Justice: Criminal Convictions and the Decline of Neighborhood Political Participation
by Traci Burch

Political Tone: How Leaders Talk and Why
by Roderick P. Hart, Jay P. Childers, and Colene J. Lind

Learning While Governing: Expertise and Accountability in the Executive Branch
by Sean Gailmard and John W. Patty

The Social Citizen: Peer Networks and Political Behavior
by Betsy Sinclair

Follow the Leader? How Voters Respond to Politicians' Policies and Performance
by Gabriel S. Lenz

The Timeline of Presidential Elections: How Campaigns Do (and Do Not) Matter
by Robert S, Erikson and Christopher Wlezien

Electing Judges: The Surprising Effects of Campaigning on Judicial Legitimacy
by James L. Gibson

Disciplining the Poor: Neoliberal Paternalism and the Persistent Power of Race
by Joe Soss, Richard C. Fording, and Sanford F. Schram

The Submerged State: How Invisible Government Policies Undermine American Democracy
by Suzanne Mettler

Selling Fear: Counterterrorism, the Media, and Public Opinion
by Brigitte L. Nacos, Yaeli Bloch-Elkon, and Robert Y. Shapiro

Why Parties? A Second Look
by John H. Aldrich

Obama's Race: The 2008 Election and the Dream of a Post-Racial America
by Michael Tesler and David O. Sears

News That Matters: Television and American Opinion, Updated Edition
by Shanto Iyengar and Donald R. Kinder

Filibustering: A Political History of Obstruction in the House and Senate
by Gregory Koger

Us Against Them: Ethnocentric Foundations of American Opinion
by Donald R. Kinder and Cindy D. Kam

The Partisan Sort: How Liberals Became Democrats and Conservatives Became Republicans
by Matthew Levendusky

Democracy at Risk: How Terrorist Threats Affect the Public
by Jennifer L. Merolla and Elizabeth J. Zechmeister

In Time of War: Understanding American Public Opinion from World War II to Iraq
by Adam J. Berinsky

Agendas and Instability in American Politics, Second Edition
by Frank R. Baumgartner and Bryan D. Jones

The Party Decides: Presidential Nominations Before and After Reform
by Marty Cohen, David Karol, Hans Noel, and John Zaller

The Private Abuse of the Public Interest: Market Myths and Policy Muddles
by Lawrence D. Brown and Lawrence R. Jacobs

Same Sex, Different Politics: Success and Failure in the Struggles over Gay Rights
by Gary Mucciaroni